Bonnie Dundee

Behave yourselves, therefore, like true Scotchmen: and let us, by this action, redeem the credit of this nation, that is laid low by the treacheries and cowardice of some of our countrymen . . .

Viscount Dundee's speech to his troops before the Battle of Killiecrankie, 27 July 1689

Bonnie Dundee

John Graham of Claverhouse

Andrew Murray Scott

JOHN DONALD PUBLISHERS
EDINBURGH

In memory of
Charles Cameron Scott (1920–73)

This revised edition published in 2000 by
John Donald Publishers
an imprint of Birlinn Ltd
8 Canongate Venture
5 New Street
Edinburgh EH8 8BH

© Andrew Murray Scott 1989 and 2000

Originally published in 1989 by
John Donald Publishers Ltd

ISBN 0 85976 532 6

British Library Cataloguing-in-Publication Data
A catalogue record for this book is available from the
British Library

Typeset in Sabon by Brinnoven, Livingston
Printed and bound by Creative Print and Design Wales, Ebbw Vale

Contents

Acknowledgements

The author would like to record his thanks to Hugh Andrew of Birlinn for allowing me the satisfaction of revising what was, in 1989, my first published book. I would like to thank the many readers who commended *Bonnie Dundee* and wrote to me making helpful suggestions.

The advice of Professor Michael Lynch, Dr Julian Goodare and the late Thomas I. Rae of the Scottish History Society proved invaluable in the compilation, in 1990, of the collected Letters of John Graham of Claverhouse which assisted me so greatly in this new edition.

Acknowledgements are due to Mr Robert N. Smart, Keeper of the Muniments at St Andrews University; the late Mrs Joan Auld, Dundee University Archivist; Mr Ian Hill and staff at the Historical Search Room, Scottish Record Office; the staff of the National Library of Scotland; Mr Ian MacIntosh, formerly Chief Architect at Dundee District Council; Mr D. M. Walker, Principal Inspector of Historic Buildings, Scottish Development Department; Miss Barbara Smythe of Methven; Mrs Silvie Taylor; Mr Martin Horan; Colonel T. D. Lloyd-Jones, Administrator, and Mr David Duncan, Assistant Administrator of Glamis Castle; Mr James Halliday, who read an early draft of the manuscript; and Mr John Tuckwell who assisted it through the editing process.

I would also like to thank my former history tutors at Dundee University: Professor Chris Whatley, Chris Davey, Chris Storrs and Dr Bob Harris, for the new insights and encouragement they provided during my course.

Introduction

Scottish history has produced many heroes and heroines, but few have been characterised – or mythologised – in such starkly contrasting terms as John Graham of Claverhouse, 1st Viscount Dundee. To some, he was a demon who had bargained with the devil for immortality, and was despatched finally with a silver bullet. To others, he was a charming, cultured cavalier – a Scottish Prince Rupert of the Palatine, a new Montrose risen from the ashes like a phoenix – and there are some superficial similarities with that other great Graham, although his military career was far less glorious. Despite undoubted qualities of leadership, Claverhouse commanded troops in pitched battle only twice: defeated on the first occasion, he was killed on the second. Another school of opinion regards him as an unimaginative soldier obsessed with discipline, unthinking obedience and duty; a devoted creature of the Stuart Kings, believing absolutely in their Divine Right to rule. To the Highlanders – and in the second half of the seventeenth century at least half the population of the country were Gaelic-speaking Highlanders – he was their beloved 'Dark John of the Battles'. To Dean Swift he was simply 'the best man in Scotland'. Dryden penned him a famous elegy. Jacobite sentiment was expressed in a short pamphlet written by 'an officer of the army' in 1711, but for nearly two centuries after that his name was blackened by lowland Presbyterians and writers such as Hogg, Galt and

Macauley. The nickname they gave him – 'Bluidy Clavers' – stood as a byword for dispassionate and unfeeling cruelty. Even Sir Walter Scott, who coined the epithet of 'Bonnie Dundee', altering the words of an older song about the town, was deeply ambivalent about him (see Further Reading, p. 252).

An increasing list of biographies have attempted to sort the man from the myth and sift the evidence from the propaganda. Most of these biographies presented Claverhouse in an epic, heroic light, but it is my contention that his story has to be read as a tragedy. Like his great kinsman Montrose, half a century earlier, and many others, Claverhouse was betrayed by a monarch – and his leading adviser – who was unworthy of him. As an effective leader, an able military tactician, perhaps the ablest man of his generation, he upheld the deserted cause of James VII and II and refused, publicly at least, to acknowledge the fact of his betrayal. Privately, he must have felt deeply hurt by it – and that all his efforts had been in vain. In his pocket at the Battle of Killiecrankie was the final despatch he was to receive from Melfort, King James' odious adviser, which served notice that Catholicism was to be forcibly re-imposed as soon as the King was back in power. All his appeals for moderation and all his careful advice had been ignored. And yet, in that very letter an amnesty and pardon was announced for those who were in arms against him, those soon to be responsible for his death.

Surveying his paltry Highland army – and some had come rather unwillingly – and the 300 indisciplined and inexperienced Irish soldiers he had finally been sent from the Royal army – he must have wondered whether James was even aware of the predicament of his faithful officer. He had failed, despite months of campaigning, to rally enough support to ensure even the faint possibility of success. The situation looked hopeless. He had less than twenty pounds of gunpowder. Thus his fall at Killiecrankie, rather than a tragic accident in the midst of glorious victory, can be viewed as the final, almost premeditated act of a desperate and bitterly disillusioned soldier, trying to over-compensate for his lack of resources by sheer bravado. Claverhouse was simply another in the long line of able men to be sacrificed in the unfortunate cause of the Stuarts; another faithful soldier dying bravely, needlessly, for a King, and a dynasty who did not deserve such devotion.

This book has been compiled from the original source documents and papers, in an attempt to review the evidence more rigorously. I have attempted to locate 'Bonnie Dundee' in context within the politics of his time, and have relied heavily on his own inimitable letters and those of contemporaries to build up a picture of the man and assess his lasting importance to Jacobitism and his role in seventeenth-century Scotland.

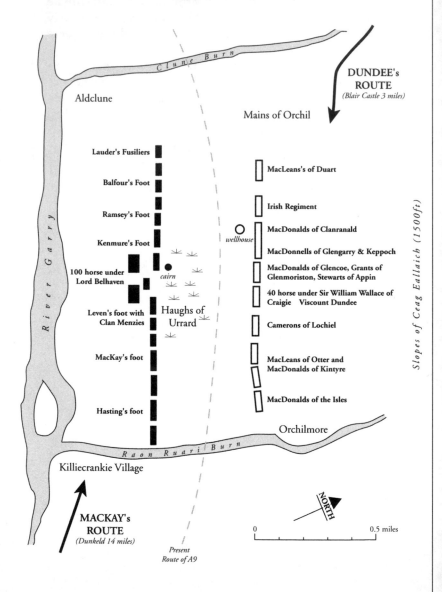

The Battle of Killiecrankie 27th July 1689
diagram by A.M. Scott

Clune Burn

DUNDEE's ROUTE
(Blair Castle 3 miles)

Aldclune

Mains of Orchil

Lauder's Fusiliers

MacLeans's of Duart

Balfour's Foot

Irish Regiment

Ramsey's Foot

MacDonalds of Clanranald

wellhouse

Kenmure's Foot

MacDonnells of Glengarry & Keppoch

100 horse under Lord Belhaven

cairn

MacDonalds of Glencoe, Grants of Glenmoriston, Stewarts of Appin

40 horse under Sir William Wallace of Craigie Viscount Dundee

Leven's foot with Clan Menzies

Haughs of Urrard

Camerons of Lochiel

MacKay's foot

MacLeans of Otter and MacDonalds of Kintyre

Hasting's foot

MacDonalds of the Isles

Orchilmore

Slopes of Ceag Eallaich (1500ft)

River Garry

Raon Ruari Burn

Killiecrankie Village

NORTH

0   0.5 miles

MACKAY's ROUTE
(Dunkeld 14 miles)

Present Route of A9

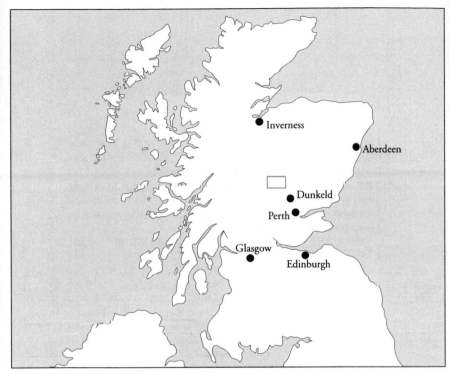

Map of Scotland, showing the location of the Battle of Killiecrankie

Edinburgh Castle, 28th July 1689

Daybreak, and the capital city bathed in an eerie half-light. The early sun hardly penetrated the barred, unglazed window of the cold chamber in Edinburgh Castle where Colin Lindsay, the Earl of Balcarres, lay in bed. Rivulets of water trickled continuously down the rough stone walls to disappear miraculously through the floor. The Earl, who lay under a few ragged blankets, coughed, but continued to drowse. Gradually he became aware that he was not alone.

He opened one eye, then the other, then sat up abruptly, a look of amazement on his face.

Standing looking at him, one hand holding aside the curtain, was his friend and comrade, Claverhouse, Viscount Dundee, dressed for battle. Beneath his steel breastplate he wore a buff cavalry jacket with a green silk scarf, thigh-length leather boots covered his lower half, and he carried in his other hand a white-plumed chapeau. His dark ringed hair hung down to his chest, and his face bore a serious expression. Balcarres' mind was so full of questions that he could not speak. At last he stuttered:

'Clavers! How came you here? How? . . . '

His comrade made no reply but stepped over to the mantelpiece and leaned heavily against it. He looked tired to the point of exhaustion. It was only then that Balcarres noticed the dark stain beneath the breastplate on his left side. He gasped:

'Clavers, man! Ye're wounded? . . .'

By the time the middle-aged Earl scrambled out of bed, Dundee was gone as mysteriously as he had come. Shaking with fear and apprehension, Balcarres called out twice, his tremulous words ringing in a room as cold – and empty – as it had always been:

'Clavers! Clavers . . .'[1]

1

Young Graham

Clavers haunts the pages of history with the ghostly presence of a man betrayed; a man who died needlessly in a political tragedy. For several months in the summer of 1689, this relatively minor Scotsman – virtually unknown on the national stage – held in his hand the fate of the Kingdom of Scotland, England and Ireland; the destiny of the Stuart monarchy itself. With all the odds heavily stacked against him, he yet came within striking distance of achieving the unachievable: restoring a King who would not be restored; turning back the pages of history. Then, in a few seconds he charged almost casually into the annals of glory as if a heroic death was the only achievement that remained within his reach.

His was a life recklessly thrown away and with it tumbled the chances of restoration of the Stuart Kings. No other Jacobite leader was to come so close to ultimate victory. The calamity of 1689 was followed by bungling military ineptitude and gross failure in 1715, 1719, 1745. After the death of Claverhouse it could be said that Scotland began to lose its separate political identity, for the passage to Union of the Parliaments was expedited, and led to political and economic domination by the English. So, in those few glorious months in that distant summer, John Graham of Claverhouse staked his claim to greatness as the first Jacobite leader, an extraordinary man in an extraordinary period of British history. The task of historians is to assess his character and the nature of his role. Was he a romantic hero, intent on making his name by foolhardy bravado, or an unswervingly diligent servant of the Stuarts doomed by the corruption and intrigue of royal advisers? Or was he a more calculating political figure who imagined great rewards from a Stuart victory? And what of that death in victory? Was it unfortunate accident – or did a sense of betrayal, and abandonment by his monarch condition an over-reckless attitude to his own safety? His life and his role are capable of many interpretations: What is the evidence of his personality?

He was born into an eventful, turbulent period. In the year he was born the sons of Charles I had fled to France, and before he was a year old, the 'Rump' Parliament had tried and executed the King. A year later, the great Marquis of Montrose stood beneath the scaffold and would not blame the King who had left him to his fate. But Cromwell was dead, the army of Occupation withdrew from Scotland, and their leader, General Monck, invited back the King's eldest son, who duly became Charles II. There was a new spirit of optimism in the air. The Scottish Parliament was meeting again in Edinburgh; the nine-year forcible Union of the English and Scottish Parliaments had been dissolved.

Scotland in the second half of the seventeenth century was, by all accounts, a harsh and spartan place. While the English had prospered in relative peace for years, most Scots remembered only too well the indignities of Cromwell's Invasion, Argyll's Rising and the campaigns of Montrose. As well as these recent memories of Civil War, there were continuing feuds and barbarities occurring beyond the Highland Line – which at this time meant all land 'benorth Tay'. All classes of society lived in conditions of relative poverty, and even the nobility in their fortified tower-houses existed on a lower level of luxury than would have been tolerated by their English counterparts. The country was frequently ravaged by hostile weather and mysterious 'murrains' or blights affected livestock and the sparse crops. The culture encompassed 'hellfire and brimstone' beliefs which commanded cruel atrocities in the name of a stern God, and even harsher punishments for these atrocities in the name of the same God. It was a country of bizarre superstitions, harsh morality and astonishing cruelty – judged by our standards of today. But the events of the seventeenth century must be judged by its own standards, and personalities can be considered only in relative terms. Few emerge as saints – or as wholly justified. Life, perhaps more than now, was hard and unfair – even for the wealthiest.

The Grahams of Claverhouse were neither a rich nor important branch of the family, although the Graham name itself was an illustrious one. Sir William Graham of Kincardine, ancestor of the Montrose branch, had married into royalty – Princess Mary Stewart, daughter of King Robert III. One son of that marriage had become the first Archbishop of St Andrews, another married into the family of the Scrimgeours – hereditary Earls of Dundee. Sir William, Claverhouse's grandfather, was tutor to the legendary Marquis of Montrose, Sir James Graham. There were numerous other cadet branches, such as the Grahams of Fintry, of Morphie, of Inchbrakie, of Duntrune, Graham of Braco, of Scotstown and of Menteith.

There were three principal holdings in the Claverhouse branch of the family at this time: a mansion and tower-house at Mill of Mains, the Castle of Claypotts, which was practically uninhabitable due to its neglect by Claverhouse's grandfather, and another building in Glen Ogilvie in the Sidlaw Hills near Glamis, which had been purchased with its estate in 1640 by Claverhouse's great-grandfather, Sir William. This was grander and more spacious than the others, of two storeys and surrounded by farm steadings and outbuildings. There is no trace of the property, which stood on a small knoll in what is now a cultivated field belonging to the farm of Hatton of Ogilvie. It was described as 'a toure, fortalice and maner-place', whereas Claypotts was only 'a fortalice and maner-place'. The field is still known locally as the 'castle park'.

In this country seat hung portraits of Sir John de Graham,

a friend of William Wallace, Sir David de Graham, one of the hostages for the ransom of King David II, and Lady Magdalen Graham, Claverhouse's mother – by all accounts a beauty. The artist was George Jameson 'The Scottish Van Dyke', who had earlier painted the greatest Graham of all: the 1st Marquis of Montrose.

There is reputedly a beautiful wrought-iron key for the door of the building at Glen Ogilvie still in existence, although the building itself is no more. Claypotts Castle is in the care of Historic Scotland, and has been restored, but is at the time of writing unfurnished. It is one of the earliest and best examples of a Z-plan tower-house in Scotland. Probably no other flaunts its strength as aggressively.

The Castle of Mains has also undergone restoration. Studded doors and an outer wall have been added, and wrought-iron gates. The Castle, which has rounded parapets and wide-mouthed gun-ports, is an early example of the pre-Cromwellian fortified house. It has been leased and now operates as a licensed restaurant, having been 'de-scheduled' in 1985. The historical plaque has been resited on the tower wall inside the courtyard.

Claverhouse's father, William Graham, married Lady Magdalen Carnegie, fifth daughter of the 1st Earl of Southesk, in February 1645 in the Parish Church of Kinnaird near Brechin. The Marriage Papers were written in close script on parchments which, if taped together, would form a roll approximately ten feet long! The Laird of Claverhouse was active in local matters. He was named in a list of civic officials warranted in June 1642 to collect a levy for the repair of Monifieth Bridge. He was an elder of the Church of Scotland, and attended meetings of the Commission of the General Assembly held in Dundee in 1651,[2] although he was to die shortly after, leaving his widow to bring up the four children.

There are no documents giving the precise date of birth of John Graham, and biographers have proposed dates as far apart as 1643 and 1649. The first is obviously wrong because of the marriage date. He had two sisters, Anne and

Magdalen, Magdalen several years older than him, and a younger brother David; thus his date of birth could hardly be earlier than 1647, and can be fixed more accurately.

The family spent their early life playing around the farmstead and barns of Glen Ogilvie. The glen has two meanings in Gaelic – 'yellow-haired youth' and 'glen of the yellow wood' – and was, according to legend, the home of the 'Nine Maidens' – lovely but melancholy daughters of Pictish King Donaldevus, a contemporary of Fergus. The Laird of Claverhouse died between 17th June 1652 and 19th January 1653 as two legal documents among the Papers of Sir John James Graham of Fintry make clear, and could not have been as important an influence on four-year-old John or his brother and sisters as their Highland nanny with her Celtic legends of Fionn and Ossian and modern tales of their kinsman, the great Montrose who had died on the scaffold.

Although most of the branches of the Grahams had supported the great Marquis, Claverhouse's father had managed to avoid supporting his military campaign without losing face in the family. He had also managed the tricky task of avoiding reprisals once the conflict was over. This ambivalence between loyalty and prudence may have taken root in the son, for in later life Claverhouse was to make little mention of his famous forebear, even when, in 1689, the comparisons of history were forced upon him.

It is probable that John learned something of the Gaelic language from their nanny, and certain that he learned of the fierce pride and love of honour of the Highlanders – which would stand him in good stead later.

In the Papers of Graham of Fintry there is also a discharge dated 10th December 1656, of a debt due to the Laird by an Edinburgh merchant. There are three signatories: David Graham of Fintry, Walter Graham and J. Fotheringham, described as 'tutors testamentary' of John Graham of Claverhouse. One reason for the cancellation of the debt was that the merchant had made 'certain assignations to the Earl of Rothes to the behoof of their pupil'. Whether these gentlemen were actual tutors, or simply legal guardians is not known.[3]

At an early age, as was customary, John and his brother David were sent off to St Andrews University along with the sons of the gentry and the minor nobility. Those were the days when matriculation was necessary purely for the purposes of voting in the Rectorial elections, but a 'Johannes Grahamus' matriculates from third year into final year at St Salvator's College on 27th February 1660, and a David Graham matriculates on the 10th. There is also, however, a Graham signature on the list of graduates for 27th July 1659, and both a John and, several names further down, a David Graham on the list of entrants of St Leonard's College for 13th February 1665.[4] A little detective work is now required.

The Grahams matriculating in 1660 duly graduated Master of Arts on 27th July 1661, and the fact that these names are signed consecutively must imply that these were indeed the brothers, whereas the Graham of 1665 does not appear to have completed his course. There is also the evidence of social status from the Faculty Quaestor's Book, which is kept among the Muniments of the University Archive. Claverhouse's father was not a Lord and Claverhouse would have been a 'secundar' rather than a 'primur'. The graduate of 1665 was the son of a Lord, whereas the Grahams of 1661 were secundars.

It is fascinating to speculate on these scanty facts, but what is certain is that John Graham made good use of his time as a student and was well known to the Archbishop, Dr James Sharp, and his Secretary, George Martine of Clermont, both of whom regarded him as the ideal student. According to a contemporary historian, 'he was admired for his parts and respects to Churchmen, which made him dear to the Archbishop of that See, who ever after honour'd and lov'd him'. Another informs us he had 'inflamed his mind . . . by the perusal of the ancient poets, historians and orators; with the love of the great actions they paint and describe'.[5,6]

University life at that time was disciplined and rather monastic. Daily prayers were conducted by the Principal and there were long regular sessions of catechism. Students caught speaking in other than Latin were fined, gowns had to be worn at all times, and every student was expected to have his own copy of Aristotle in Greek. The brothers would have spent their 'bajan' or first year studying Greek grammar, Hebrew and Arithmetic. Logic, Dialectic, Rhetoric and Oration were tackled in the second year, Geometry, Aristotle's Ethics and Metaphysics in the third, and Astronomy, Geography and Anatomy in the final year. While golf and archery were considered suitable recreations for students, fines were imposed on those caught playing cards or 'dicing', and hawking and attendance at Cupar Races were frowned on, unless of course, you were an important 'primur'.

John and David Graham were made Burgesses of Dundee and Brothers of the Guild 'on their father's privilege' in 1660. William Graham's name does not appear, however, on the Burgess Roll, although their uncle, George Graham, had held this office since 1620, and it was probably done at his behest. About this time, too, the first portrait was painted of him, at the approximate age of eleven or twelve.[7]

The brothers came under the wardship of their other uncle, David, Lord Lour, who became the 2nd Earl of Northesk in 1662. This implies that they had left St Andrews by this time, and tends to confirm the graduation date of July 1661. It is probable that John Graham, the eldest son, inherited his father's title as Laird of Claverhouse in 1667 when he would have been eighteen or nineteen. A petition in February of that year to the Privy Council by the Master of Dundee Hospital claims exemption from rent payments for ground that 'formerly pertained to John Graham of Claverhouse'. It is unlikely he would have attained the title much before this date. Lord Lour's influence was almost certainly the key factor in the obtaining of a post for him as Commissioner of Excise and justice of the Peace for Forfarshire. He received his Commission on 11th February 1669:

> The Lords of his Majesties Privy Council, considering that sundry of the Commissioners of Excyse and Justices of the Peace within the shyre of Forfar are deceased, and leist his Majesties service might be retarded throw the want of fitt persons to supply their places, they doe nominat and appoynt

the Earl of Southesk . . . Grahame of Claverhouse . . . to be
commissioners of excyse and justices of the peace on the said
shyre in the place of those deceased, and ordaines them to
be receaved in the usuall forme; with power to them to site,
vote and act as freely as any other commissioners of excyse
and justices of the peace in the said shyre.[8]

On 24th June, however, his commission was withdrawn on
the grounds that he was still a minor. The commission was
restored on 2nd September. Assuming that twenty-one was
then, as now, the age of majority, this lends credence to the
belief that John Graham was born between late June and
early September 1648.

Young Claverhouse must have found the duties humdrum,
or perhaps the years at St Andrews had widened his horizons,
for he now set his mind on travel and adventure in Europe.
Many young Scots of birth and breeding had been lured to the
battlefields of the Continent in search of excitement, settling
for careers as mercenaries alongside the kings, princes and
great leaders of Europe, although they were generally younger
sons, not eldest sons and heirs like Claverhouse. However, on
25th July 1672, at the age of twenty-three or twenty-four, he
received a long-awaited commission as a Junior Lieutenant
in Sir William Lockhart's Scots Regiment which was serving
under the general command of the Duke of Monmouth in
the French army of Marshall Turenne.

It was Claverhouse's first trip abroad and he quickly settled
to the discipline of military life, rapidly earning a reputation
among the English and Scottish officers for his diligence. It is
not known whether he saw action in this campaign, for early
the next year Charles II withdrew his forces from Holland,
and Monmouth, the King's favourite, returned to England.
Claverhouse may have spent some time travelling in Europe
but soon drifted into the service of the opposition, William,
Prince of Orange, where he became a Cornet in the Princes'
own troop of guards.

He was certainly present at the Battle of Senneffe, near
Mons, on 14th August 1674, as described by the anonymous
poet of 'The Muses New Yeares Gift And Hansell':

I saw a man who at St Neffe did sie
His conduct, prowess, martial gallantrie.
He wore a white plumash that day, not one

Of Belgians wore a white but him alone.
And though that day was fatal, yet he fought
And for his part fair triumphs with him brought.[9]

At this battle William, two years younger than Claverhouse, was commanding his forces from the front and rather risking his own safety, though it is a matter of dispute whether he was ever in direct danger. His motley army of Flemish, Dutch and Spanish soldiers were sent into retreat by the Prince of Condé's French army. His horse foundered in the marshes – but dashing in to the rescue was young Cornet Graham. Whatever the precise details of the event, it was celebrated in a poem written many years after the occasion:

Did not I, when thou fleddest on wearied steed
Through Belgic marsh from the conquering troops of
    lily-bearing France
Did I not myself snatch thee from the enemy,
And mount thee on the back of my fresh steed
And restore thee safe to the camp?[10]

It was said that the Prince gratefully promoted Claverhouse to the rank of Captain of Horse, and promised him the first Colonel's post that fell vacant. The promotion is not recorded however until November 1676, nearly two years later, which deepens the enigma.

After the siege of Grave in October 1674, many other Scottish and English officers joined the service of the United Netherlands, and among them was Hugh Mackay of Scourie in Sutherland. Mackay, who was already in his forties, had left the place of his birth as soon as conveniently possible and had not revisited. Instead he had married a Dutch wife, Clara de Bie and, after switching armies, enthusiastically adopted Dutch customs and manners: 'he was speedily united to . . . the object of his affection, whose country he appears, from this date, to have adopted as his own'.[11] It is certain that the two officers would have met, but Claverhouse's mother, Lady

Magdalen, died in October, and Claverhouse, the dutiful
son, returned to Scotland where he remained for six months
sorting out the affairs of his family. He had a well-developed
sense of family loyalty, and did not, like Mackay, feel any
sense of shame at his lowly heritage.

He sailed to Holland in April 1676, and participated in
the unsuccessful Siege of Maastricht. Shortly afterwards,
his Captain's commission was ratified. In the annals of *The
Scots Brigade in Holland,* after a report on the casualties at
Maastricht, there is the terse statement:

> Cornet Grahame is named in a list of officers quitting the
> service.[12]

Not even *Captain* Graham. And no reason is given for this
sudden decision. The Peace of Nijmegen was not signed until
August 1678, but Claverhouse had left the service of William
of Orange by 1677. Some historians, principally Drummond
of Balhaldie, describe a quarrel between Claverhouse and
Alexander Collier (or Colyear), the future Earl of Portmore,
after the latter was appointed Colonel of the Scottish Regiment of Foot (from 1st January 1675):

> Captain Grahame . . . chancing to meet Mr Collier in the
> Palace Court, expostulated the matter in very harsh terms,
> and gave him some blows with his cane . . .[13]

Others have claimed, less believably, that it was Hugh Mackay
of Scourie who was appointed Colonel.[14] At any event, Claverhouse felt that William had broken a promise and he threw
up his career – though not immediately – and returned to Scotland. It is just possible of course that the 'Cornet Grahame' in
the annals was not Claverhouse – the Scots Brigade contained
many Grahams of all ranks – yet it has never been explained
satisfactorily why Claverhouse should quit the service after
a quarrel with Collier, who was, after all, appointed two
years before. Indeed, Collier was recommended for bravery
at the same siege of Maastricht, and was at that time not
only Colonel but also Adjutant-General. For a junior officer,
and one as disciplined as Claverhouse, to strike a senior

officer of Collier's rank seems rather far-fetched. Strict military discipline was enforced with severe punishments for insubordination – and it seems that, under the circumstances, Claverhouse may have escaped lightly – if indeed the quarrel took place at all – which is, at the least, questionable.

Balhaldie relates the story of an angry Prince of Orange offering Claverhouse something more valuable than a regiment. This 'something' was his liberty from punishment. Claverhouse is supposed to have replied haughtily that if his Highness 'had the goodness to give him his liberty, he would employ himself elsewhere rather than serve a Prince who has broke his word'.

As Claverhouse packed to return to Scotland, a messenger arrived from the Prince bearing 200 guineas payment for the horse on which his life had been saved. This was many times the horse's worth; clearly a conciliatory gesture. It reveals the Prince's esteem for Claverhouse's qualities. Others have asserted that William's homosexual leanings tended to over-rule his commonsense where young and handsome officers were concerned.

Claverhouse, apparently a man of unbending principle, did send the horse, but distributed the Prince's money among the grooms of the Royal stables. Another colourful and dubious tale.

Even this – if it occurred – seems not to have prejudiced the Prince from writing to his uncle James, Duke of York, commending Claverhouse's ability. William had recently married James' daughter Mary, and James was now his father-in-law. The Duke of York contacted the Marquis of Montrose through a kinsman of the Grahams, the Laird of Monorgan. Montrose had been authorised to raise a regiment of horseguards to quell the disturbances in the West of Scotland.

Claverhouse had not as yet resigned himself to remaining in Scotland, and was considering further service abroad. In the Privy Council Register for 1678 there is a cryptic entry for 27th February:

> Licence granted to the Laird of Claverhouse and Majour Windrahame to goe aff the kingdom.[15]

We have no way of knowing whether in fact he did go abroad again at this time. He may have changed his mind when he was named as a lieutenant in the Marquis of Montrose's troop of horse. Montrose was keen to persuade him to accept the offer, entreating him to ignore the lowly rank because 'only gentlemen shall ride with him'.

Shortly afterwards, Claverhouse's mind was made up for him when he was offered the rank of Captain and command of a troop of horse commissioned to police the South-Western shires. He decided to make his career in Scotland.

2

The Good Policeman

As reported in the State Papers of Charles II, large numbers of people attended illegal open-air prayer-meetings or Conventicles held by the preachers of the Solemn League and Covenant. This, which had followed the earlier National Covenant, sought to overthrow the Episcopalian Bishops and establish Presbyterianism. Since the King had renounced his signing, in 1650 under duress, of the Covenant, and insisted upon a return to Episcopacy, the supporters of the Covenant, the Conventiclers, had become more extreme than the moderates. One Conventicle described in the papers numbers the congregation at 10,000. The preaching was often followed by 'drilling and exercising themselves in feats of arms'.[16] Many 'outrages' were perpetrated against the 'non-covenanted' churches and ministers, while hundreds of ministers abandoned their pulpits rather than support the new forms of worship. The Scottish Convention of Estates met on 26th June 1678 expressly to find ways of dealing with the threat to law and order. *That was one version of events.* Another was that the King was conspiring to enforce a return to mass Catholicism and the Bishops had persuaded him to send the militia, the so-called 'Highland Host' to the troubled shires in the hope that this would so provoke the Presbyterians that they would take up arms – to be denounced as traitors – and cruelly suppressed. Whichever version of events you prefer to believe, a military force was being assembled to police the Western Shires where the 'disorders' were worst.

In an undated letter to the Duke of Lauderdale, Charles writes: 'You and we are all much obliged to Claverhouse, who is our generous friend'. What could have caused the King to write so warmly of him? It is possible that he was simply acting on the instruction of his younger brother, the Duke of York, who must have been informed of the talents of the junior officer by William of Orange, but the terms of this letter seem to exceed the conventions of civility. Claverhouse's appointment as one of three captains of the newly-formed troops of horse cavalry clearly show the sign of early royal favour. The captains of the other troops were the 5th Earl of Home and the 2nd Earl of Airlie, both distinguished soldiers, and of noble birth. Airlie, indeed, had been a friend of the Great Montrose and had escaped from prison on the very day appointed by Parliament for his execution. While Airlie and Home's troops were officered by gentlemen of noble breeding, Claverhouse appointed Andrew Bruce of Earlshall, a Fife laird, as his lieutenant and two of his kinsmen, Robert and James Graham as his cornet and quartermaster. Later, Claverhouse's brother, David, was to become quartermaster on the death of James, and when Robert was killed at Drumclog a year later, the place was taken by William Graham of Balquhaple. The other ranks consisted of three corporals, two trumpeters and sixty cavalrymen. It was to become a tight-knit troop, well-organised, led by trusted officers, and would remain, almost to a man, loyal to Claverhouse until after Killiecrankie.[17]

Claverhouse's importance in quelling rebellions and disruptions in the South-West has been inflated. He was merely one of a number of officers with similar commissions. Previous biographers devoted considerable time to raking the embers of long-refuted slanders and myths that formerly attached to his name. This period of his career does not, frankly, deserve such attention except as it might elucidate his character. He was a soldier who did his duty and effectively and rigorously applied the law but there is evidence, as we shall see, that he acted scrupulously and sometimes also sympathetically. The best source of information on his activities are his own meticulous and lengthy reports written on the day of the incidents described, which can hardly be considered to be anything other than accurate accounts.

Resplendent in a new red uniform coat, and at the head of his new command, thirty-year-old Captain John Graham arrived in Moffat late in the evening of 27th December 1678, and settled in to his lodgings. Next day he wrote his first report to his Commander-in-Chief, the Earl of Linlithgow, advising him that he planned to move on to Dumfries to establish a base.

> I am informed since I came, that this contry has been very loose . . . ther wer grate field conventikles just by here, with great contempt of the regular clergy, who complain extreamly . . .[18]

Claverhouse had been brought up an Episcopalian, and, as we have seen, had always behaved with great courtesy towards the clergy. Thus he would have been a sympathetic audience for their complaints. His main problem was that he had been given jurisdiction for Dumfries and Annandale only – and many of the Conventicles promptly crossed the River Nith to Galloway. His letter complains:

> they may hold conventicles at our nose, we not dare to disspat them, seeing our orders confines us to Dumfriche and Anandell . . . I am unwilling to exceed orders . . .

He was at this time empowered only to take the names of those attending the assemblies, though his powers were soon increased. He promises to send reports twice a week – and he does – at great length and in meticulous detail. The elderly Earl of Linlithgow, it must be said, was not greatly interested in the detail, but they provide a fascinating diary of a scrupulous and effective soldier striving to introduce order and the rule of law to the South-West. His letters are informative and well-written and I have relied heavily on them in the present work; Claverhouse is best able to tell his own story, and thus in the extracts I have quoted I have not altered the orthography.

In his second letter he reports two unfortunate incidents.

A soldier firing out indiscriminately from a guard hall has killed a horse in the street: 'An ogly business; for beseids the wrong the poor man has got in loosing his horse, it is extreamly against military disciplin to fyr out of a gaird.' He investigates the incident, and discovers the bullet which killed the horse is indeed army issue. He arrests the sentry pending further investigation. The second incident involves the shooting by the dragoons of a man carrying baggage for Claverhouse's officers, although this incident is not further elucidated. Possibly the man was a thief. Further letters relate the problems he has in obtaining fodder and 'quartering' for his men and the horses.

But by early 1679 his thoughts were turning in quite another direction – towards the idea of marriage. He was now thirty years old, and keenly felt the need of a permanent home and a family. Marriage was also an opportunity to improve his social standing. The numerous portraits of Claverhouse reveal a man who was certainly attractive. His intelligent face has an almost androgynous beauty, with a dreamy, wistful expression, characteristic of a romantic, an idealist – the kind of face in fact that was guaranteed to appeal to the spirit of romance in every woman. Yet he was curiously modest in his dealings with women. Even one of his most vehement detractors, Patrick Walker, author of *Six Saints of The Covenant*, admits that 'the hell wicked-witted, bloodthirsty Graham of Claverhouse hated to spend his time with wine and women'. No-one, in fact, has ever accused him of sins of immorality or decadence.[19]

His friend, the young Marquis of Montrose, the foppish grandson of the great Montrose, had written to him about a lady who might, in his opinion, be suitable for matrimony. The woman he had in mind was a Court beauty, Helen Graham, the only child of Sir James and Isabella Graham, and also heiress of the 8th Earl of Menteith. A fascinating correspondence soon developed between Claverhouse and the wily Menteith.[20]

The first of these letters, undated, but probably written in January or February 1679, reminds the Earl that:

> Julius Caesar had no need to regrait the want of issue, having
> adopted Augustus, for he kneu certenly that he had secured
> to himself a thankfull and usefull friend, as well as a wyse
> successor, neither of which he could have promised himself
> by having childring; for nobody knous whether they begit
> wyse men or fooles . . .

Menteith had considered many unscrupulous ways of raising
money to pay off the huge debts his family had accumulated.
He had considered defrauding his legal heirs by obtaining
the right from the King to nominate his own successor. He
planned, in effect, to sell his title to Sir John Dalrymple,
Master of Stair, but Sir James Graham managed to prevent
him.

Claverhouse certainly regarded the matter of the marriage
as a business deal. This was not unusual for the times; for
him it was a deal that would 'continue your family in the right
lyne'. Claverhouse laid great store by the family name, the
honour of the Grahams, and he was concerned that the Menteith title might revert to the Crown. There was little other
advantage in the deal as he would have to pay off the debts
of the estate in the hope that the King could be persuaded to
transfer the title to himself, as Helen's husband.

Montrose, aided by another friend, Sir George Mackenzie
of Rosehaugh, helped him pursue his suit. Mackenzie, who
was about twelve years older, and also a St Andrews graduate, was to become one of the most eminent advocates and
intellectuals of his day – and a lifelong friend of Claverhouse.
He was the founder of the Advocates' Library in Edinburgh –
now the National Library of Scotland – and is commemorated
there in a stained-glass window.

The Privy Council Register records on 24th July: 'The
Laird of Claverhouse having desyred a forloff for some tyme
to goe about his necessar affairs, the samen is granted for
two moneths.'[21] And at first the affair looked to be successful.
Menteith wrote to Sir James and Lady Isabella that he would
'never consent to the marriage unless it be Claverhouse'. But it
soon became obvious that all was not well, and in November,
Menteith announced to Sir James that he was proposing

another match for his cousin with a 'very noble and eminent person' whom he finally named in a letter dated 4th December 1679:

> Be pleased to know of the most intimate and sincere friend-
> ship which that noble and honourable young Lord my Lord
> Marquess of Montrose . . .

Later in the letter he boldly denies any understanding with Claverhouse:

> Such I never in all my life before this writ or said the like
> condition to none living . . .

It has been suggested that the motive for Montrose's change of heart – and his devious behaviour – was his desire to head off what he may have viewed as Claverhouse's challenge to his position as titular head of the Grahams. Claverhouse was certainly zealous for the fortunes of the family, which was, after all, the main aim of his courtship of Lady Helen. Shortly after this letter, Montrose managed to persuade Menteith to grant him his estates on the promise of marriage to Helen Graham at a later date, although he was at this time already secretly married to the daughter and heiress of the Lord Chancellor of Scotland. He had persuaded this girl to keep the marriage secret, and it was not announced until 1681. In the meantime he began to use Menteith's signature at the Council. Menteith wrote no fewer than eighteen letters to Montrose without reply, and, in desperation, on 5th December 1681 wrote again to Claverhouse. The tone of this letter is decid-edly conciliatory, as if nothing untoward has happened in the interim, and Claverhouse, in his eager reply, six days later, is already making arrangements for Sir James and Lady Isabella to come to Scotland. He concludes his letter: 'I am perswaded that we may bring it yet to a hapie close, if your lordship doe your pairt, of which I shall not doubt' and he ends in jovial mood by hoping that 'we will be all merry about the hall fyr'.

Early in 1682, however, Helen Graham married Captain Arthur Rawdon, heir-apparent to the Earl of Conway in

Ireland, and that was an end of the matter. The whole affair left Claverhouse looking foolish and revealed the deviousness of Montrose and Menteith. Claverhouse did not suffer the pangs of unrequited love, for he had, after all, barely met the girl. No doubt he muttered to himself darkly that if marriage was so complicated he would have none of it, though in two years time he would be a married man.

He was encountering great difficulties in Dumfries and Annandale. Despite his best efforts, the Covenanters' activities were proliferating. He was not receiving much assistance from the local lairds, many of whom were secret supporters of the Covenant. In his letter of 8th February 1679 to Linlithgow, there is a sign of his growing impatience. He had travelled to Thornhill the previous day for a meeting of the Commissioners who were to provide him with hay and fodder for his horses. Instead, he found 'only Queensberry and Craigdalloch, and not being a coram they could not proceed'. Later, he bluntly informs Linlithgow that if he requires hay he will go to any of the Commissioners' lands and take it – offering them the going rate.

In his next letter he expresses irritation at the lack of secrecy of his actions. He had arrested the messenger who brought him Linlithgow's reply, believing that the letter had passed through his enemies' hands. In the same month, one of his soldiers has actually been kidnapped by the townspeople of Stranraer and he asks for advice.

At last, recognising the difficulties Claverhouse and the others were facing, the Government began to act and the King, by express warrant on 18th January, empowered the Council to name extra Sheriffs and Bailies as required, to deal with the disturbed areas. On 11th March, Claverhouse and his second-in-command, Captain Andrew Bruce of Earlshall, were appointed as Sheriff Deputes of Dumfries and Annandale. This gave them wider powers over armed Covenanters. Now they could actually apprehend them for trial elsewhere.

The epithet 'Bluidy Clavers' which he was given by the Covenanters has largely been refuted through the research of Mark Napier and Professor Terry. The biography of A. & H. Tayler contains an excellent summation of the evidence. As will be seen later, most of the research has involved the disproving of groundless claims made in a host of contemporary pamphlets and histories written by those with a vested interest in creating a myth of evil and cruelty with which to justify their own creeds. Claverhouse's actions are demonstrably at odds with the activities of a heartless monster. For example, in a letter dated 21st April, Claverhouse expresses concern for an elderly and infirm prisoner, Francis Irwin, who 'is extreamly troubled with the gravelle . . .' His plans will be delayed for five or six days, and in fact this turns into fifteen days. In the same letter, he complains that a prisoner has been languishing in prison for one year: 'This is a great abuse . . . the man oght not to be suffered any longer here . . .'

In the same letter, he expresses doubt that the militia 'in the hands of the country people' will prove loyal in the event of open rebellion. He believes open rebellion is planned. His troop are now living on credit. He will have to take free quarters 'for I can not pay money if I get none'. Sir William Sharp owes him £600 and Lord Queensberry 'has been very unkynd to us'.

The first act of rebellion occurred at White-Kirkhill in East Lothian when a mob, 1200 strong, refused to disperse upon order by the Governor of the Bass, then assaulted him and his twelve men, killing one and wounding the rest. Only one man, a pedlar by the name of Learmont, was ever convicted for this crime – and hanged.

Three days after this, an event occurred which was to send shock waves around the country, and which upset Claverhouse deeply. His friend and patron, Archbishop Sharp was brutally murdered on 3rd May 1679 on Magus Muir in Fife, in the presence of his daughter and the Bishop of Orkney. The bullets 'burnt his coat and gown, but did not go into his body; upon this they drew him out of his coach and murdered him barbarously, repeating their strokes till they were sure he was quite dead'.[22]

A reward of 10,000 merks was offered for information

leading to the capture of the 'ten or eleven fanatick assassins'. Sharp had been a Covenanting minister, and when sent to make representations at Court as an emissary, returned as Archbishop of St Andrews, and with an entirely different set of principles from those with which he had set out. Nevertheless, the assassins had actually been searching for a Regality official by the name of Carmichael – a somewhat lesser target – and on encountering instead Archbishop Sharp felt themselves to be blessed by Divine Providence.

According to contemporary accounts, when the Archbishop was buried at St Andrews, a man preceded the hearse displaying his bloodstained gown on a pole. This was to prove to the superstitious that his body had been pierced by the bullets of the assassins. There were also widespread rumours that his pockets were found to contain many items believed to be 'magickal': a little purse containing two pistol bullets; a little ball made up of all colours of silk; parchment a finger's breadth in length with two words written on it which none could read although the characters were like Hebrew Shaldaic. Another witness said nail parings were in his tobacco box, from which, when opened, a bumble bee flew out – which they believed to be his familiar spirit.

The murder of the Archbishop was a signal for an increase in 'outrages' and disturbances throughout the country. A Covenanter walked up to the barracks in Falkirk where the dragoons were eating a meal and fired two shots in at them. After a chase the man was captured and interrogated by Claverhouse, who learned of a mass rally of eighteen parishes planned for the next Sunday on Kilbride Moor, four miles from Glasgow. His suspicions had been proved correct. Matters were rapidly coming to a head.

A large armed force of Covenanters had been patrolling the South-West since December protecting the vast field conventicles, and many of the leading preachers such as John Welsh, grandson of John Knox, and Richard Cameron, had armed bodyguards of their own.[23] They chose 29th May, the King's birthday, as a significant date for a major act of defiance. Claverhouse's unexpected march to Glasgow forced them to divert to Rutherglen, where they burned the Acts of Parliament and extinguished the celebration bonfires. At the conclusion of their rally they nailed their 'Declaration And Testimony' to the market cross.

Claverhouse received information of their activities and left Lord Ross in Glasgow to advance to Rutherglen, where he captured a notorious minister named John King. In an interesting digression upon the moral character of this preacher, Captain Creighton's *Memoirs* relate that he was arrested no fewer than three times, each time being released on the surety of a serving-woman whom he had made pregnant, and his own promise not to preach in the future. King was hanged at Edinburgh Cross on 14th August 1679. Claverhouse then made a detour to Kilbride Moor where he came upon the main force of Covenanters 'drawn up in batell, upon a most advantagious ground . . .' He concludes ironically – 'they wer not preaching . . .'

His letter, written from Glasgow that evening, has a postscript: 'My Lord, I am so wearied and so sleapy, that I have wryten this very confusedly.' The letter is, nevertheless, a succinct report of the battle afterwards known as Drumclog or Loudon Hill. Claverhouse was defeated by a force which outnumbered his own many times over. In many general works such as Fitzroy Maclean's *Concise History of Scotland* the Covenanters are described as being outnumbered. This was not so. Claverhouse did not have more than 'a hundred and twenty dragoons' according to Captain Creighton, an eyewitness, while the Covenanters were 'eight or nine thousand strong'. Other estimates of the forces are offered, but the Covenanters were certainly several thousand strong within the next two days. They were led by John Balfour of Burleigh, Hackston of Rathillet, both of whom had participated in the assassination of Archbishop Sharp, Sir Robert Hamilton and other lairds. Another of their leaders was the teenage poet William Clelland, whose heroic death-in-victory at Dunkeld in 1689 mirrors that of Dundee himself.[24, 25, 26]

Despite the odds, Claverhouse – the professional soldier – expected an easy victory and advanced rather recklessly after a preliminary skirmish in which a party of dragoons had chased off a battalion of infantry.

The Covenanters grimly advanced to meet them, coming down the slope in regular order, lustily singing psalms. 'They came through the lotche [loch], and the greatest body of all made up against my troupe; we kept our fyr till they wer within ten paces of us'.

> But up spak cruel Clavers then,
> wi' hastie wit an' wicked skill,
> 'Gae fire on yon Westlan men,
> I think it is my sov'reign's will.'[27]

Unfortunately for Claverhouse, in this, his first pitched battle in command of soldiers, 'a pitch fork made such an opening in my sorre horse's belly, that his guts hung out half an elle'. His horse bolted and removed him unceremoniously from the battlefield. 'He carryed me aff an myle; which so discoroged our men . . . that they fell into disorder.'

Despite the almost farcical nature of this engagement, about ten of his men were left dead on the field – including his Cornet, Robert Graham – whose head was mashed to jelly by the Covenanters in the belief that it was Claverhouse's. Many more were wounded. Claverhouse did manage to save his flags, but got no time to rally, and, receiving a fresh horse, fled with his men in ignominy, enduring taunts and worse from all sides. As they retreated, the townspeople of Strathaven rushed out of their homes and attacked them, but these they managed to repulse with a rearguard action. 'This may be counted the beginning of the rebellion in my opinion,' he concludes.

Back in Glasgow, Claverhouse, with the Earl of Home and Lord Ross prepared to defend the town and erected barricades in the streets. Glasgow was then an insignificant town of small size clustered around the Cathedral. Claverhouse sent his orderly, Captain Creighton, with six men to observe the movements of the Covenanters at the gates, and when he was sure their army had divided, he attacked one section and chased them from the town, then quickly regrouped and chased off the others. He did not have the numerical strength to pursue his advantage, and the government forces were soon ordered to rendezvous with the main army at Stirling under the command of the Earl of Linlithgow. The local militias were mobilised by proclamation. Large numbers also flocked to the Covenant army who elected Sir Robert Hamilton as their leader.

Upon the withdrawal of government forces, the Covenant army entered Glasgow and busied themselves in vandalising the Cathedral and quarrelling among themselves upon doctrinal matters. They dug up the bodies of two children of the Bishop and despoiled their remains.

When news of events circulated there was a full-scale panic in the Government. The army was ordered back to Edinburgh. A strong force was sent from England under James, Duke of Monmouth, on 11th June. Edinburgh Castle was provisioned, and a search made in Leith for ships' cannon. The Privy Council ordered out the militia of the Shires of Haddington, Berwick, Linlithgow, Peebles, Stirling, Fife, Perth, Forfar and Edinburgh, and appointed rendezvous. Any militia which failed to turn up was to be fined. Soldiers' pay was increased by half-a-crown.

Claverhouse was among the Government force which marched from Edinburgh on the Monday and on Tuesday to Kirkhill Park – a distance of about nine miles. The Duke of Monmouth, the King's illegitimate son – an able soldier – arrived at Edinburgh on the Thursday and joined the army late on Saturday night or early Sunday morning at Bothwell Brig on the Clyde 'where 12,000 rebels were encamped'. He apparently then 'by his Majesties special commission offered them every third church in the kingdom, with many other priviledges, provided they would lay down their arms, and . . . live quietly'. This had no effect.[28]

The inevitable clash of the two armies occurred on Sunday 22nd June. Claverhouse was in charge of the Marquis of Montrose's troop of cavalry. He distinguished himself by personally capturing two standards, expiating to a large extent his lack of diligence at Drumclog. The Covenant army was heavily defeated and over 1200 prisoners were marched to Edinburgh, where, tied in twos, they were herded into the inner Greyfriars Churchyard to languish without shelter for many months. Some were eventually shipped to Barbados as slaves, others died, and some managed to escape or bribe their way out. The main leaders, Balfour, Cameron and Hamilton escaped to Holland.

> Then wicked Claverhouse turn'd about –
> I wot an angry man was he –
> And he lifted up his hat
> And cry'd, 'God bless his Majesty!'[29]

The day after the battle Claverhouse, reinforced by a detachment of English troops, marched through Ayr, Dumfries and Galloway, calling at the homes of those believed to have been in arms. This led to a further skirmish at Bewly Bog near Ayr when, with a troop of eighty dragoons, he surprised 350 armed Covenanters. According to 'the officer of the army' who wrote the *Memoirs of Lord Viscount Dundee*, seventy-five Covenanters were killed and many taken prisoner, though this cannot be corroborated.

Two days later Claverhouse was ordered to accompany his Commander-in-Chief, Linlithgow, to the Court in London to give an account in person of the situation and to represent the wishes of the Convention in procuring an abandonment of the mild policy inaugurated by Monmouth. During this visit, which was to last for almost a year, he had many occasions to talk with both the King and the Duke of York but at the first audience, he apparently exceeded his authority with the King, and made Linlithgow extremely nervous by his blunt assertion that the rebellion was not over, and his forthright opinion that a strict policy should be adopted to deal with the lawless. Seated amid a flurry of his beloved spaniels, which he was feeding with sweetmeats, Charles was more amused than annoyed by the plain-speaking sincerity of the junior officer. But, the business over, there was time for the social events and pastimes of courtly life.

In July he wrote to Menteith that he was going to Dunkirk 'with the envoyes to see the Court of France. I am only to be away aight days . . .' We have no information on this trip. There is indication of his increasing frustration at the frivolity of London life, nevertheless, he remained in London until June or July of 1680. Most of his letters to Mentieth were sent from London.

A new Commander-in-Chief of the army in Scotland was appointed. General Thomas Dalyell of the Binns, known as the 'Muscovy Beast' since he had learned the 'art' of war in Russia and was reputedly the man who had introduced the 'thumbikins' to the country, was no soft-hearted liberal. A regime of unrelenting severity began. Lang, in his *History of Scotland*, claimed that the cruelties were mainly due to carelessness and inefficiency rather than to any deliberate ferocity of administration.[30] It is interesting to note, however, that the original seals of the Dalyell family are a design of a naked man hanging from a gallows. Dalyell, or 'Old Tom' as he was widely known, was very curious in appearance. He had refused to shave himself in protest at the execution of Charles I, and consequently his white beard reached to his waist yet his head was completely bald. While he certainly seems to have been a harsh disciplinarian – and relations between him and Claverhouse were somewhat less than cordial – he also seems to have had his more appealing aspects, and was very much a commoner, more at home with the common people than with the nobility.

At this time there were three main Protestant factions in the country. There were the 'Indulged' or vast majority of Scots, who had been allowed to follow their religion apart from the English Episcopalian tradition. Then there was the faction of Welsh and Muir who refused the Indulged religion but would not declare themselves against the King. Lastly, there were the followers of Richard Cameron and Donald Cargill who wanted to depose the King and forcibly set up the Kingdom of Christ in Scotland. There were other 'Saints' and prophets too, each espousing their own messianic faiths. There was a plethora of sects such as the 'Wild Whigs' the 'Wanderers', 'Glancing Glass-ites', 'Faithful Remnants', 'Hillmen' and 'Macmillanites'. John Gibb, for example, gathered his 'Sweet Singers' – twenty-six women and three men in the Pentland Hills, where, for days, they grovelled in a peat bog, 'confessing sins that the world had not heard of . . . praising the Lord from morning till night . . .' and fornicating! Gibb carried a brace of pistols to use should husbands arrive to enquire after their wives' spiritual welfare.

But the Covenanters were becoming increasingly desperate. Exactly one year after Bothwell Brig, the followers of Richard Cameron rode into Sanquhar in Dumfries and issued a declaration of war on the King and all who supported him, and just for good measure they also renounced the Rutherglen Declaration of 1679. A month later, in July 1680, seventy of these 'Cameronians' as they were now known, under Hackston of Rathillet, were surprised at Aird's Moss by Claverhouse at the head of a detachment of dragoons. In a swift and brutal encounter, Cameron was killed and Hackston made prisoner. Claverhouse was given the unsavoury task, with his deputy, Bruce of Earlshall, of rounding up and executing the rebels – those who had been in arms at Bothwell Brig. Bruce removed Cameron's head and brought it to Edinburgh with the prisoners, to claim a large reward. Hackston was executed in a particularly barbarous manner at Edinburgh Cross after trial.

James, Duke of York, the King's brother, visited Scotland in October 1680, and replaced Lauderdale as Lord High Commissioner. He was persuaded by the Privy Council to authorise the use of torture, the thumbscrews or 'thumbikins', the rack and the boot, to deal with the Cameronian prisoners. Some were despatched as slaves to the plantations of Barbados or Carolina, having 'a piece of their lugg cutt off'. Women were drowned, or burned on the shoulders with red-hot irons, or stripped almost naked and publicly whipped through the streets. Some men had their ears torn out by the roots, and their fingers and legs shattered.[31] Torture was of course already widespread in Scotland for the trying of 'witches and warlocks'. Hundreds of mainly elderly women had been tortured and executed in the most revolting and appalling manner. Records suggest that in Scotland the mania against 'witches' raged with a ferocity equal to any other country. Torture was also used to punish runaway coal-miners, who, being slaves – and regarded as much lower than the lowest peasant – were indentured to the mine and wore shackles on their legs throughout their miserable lives, which were mercifully short.[32] But the ferocity of the punishments meted out to the Covenanters was on a new level of barbarity for political offences. It was painstaking and brutally thorough.

The great nobles and Lords now seized the forfeited estates and goods of the Presbyterian lairds, and levied large fines which they used to their own benefit. In the share-out, Claverhouse received the modest lands of MacDougall of Freuch in Galloway. Queensberry and the others, who had richer pickings, refused, typically, to authorise this until he gave them an account of the monies and fines he had seized in Wigtownshire. When Claverhouse protested that it would take him some time to provide the accounts – he was in Edinburgh at the time – Queensberry flew into a rage and demanded then and there the sum of 569 pounds Scots. Claverhouse returned to London with the Duke of York's retinue and took the opportunity to petition the King. The grant of the land was authorised by royal decree. The King also demanded that Queensberry return the money he had taken from him, and on 11th May Claverhouse received a further sign of the King's good favour. As a reward 'for the good and faithful services and sufferings of John Grahame of Claverhouse and his predecessors', his estate at Glen Ogilvie became a free Barony in perpetuity, on payment of 'forty pounds Scots together with the sum of one thousand merks for the marriage of the heirs and successors of the said John Grahame'.

These events were a result of the patronage – and undoubtedly the growing friendship – of the King's younger brother, James, Duke of York. Claverhouse had travelled to London to escort the Duke north, and many viewed their association with envy and suspicion. Claverhouse played golf with James, went to Leith races with him, and accompanied him to Court Banquets and even the occasional stage play at Holyrood. Plays by Dryden and Molière were then all the rage, and

James had brought some of the actors from his Household Company with him. The Duke was unable to indulge his favourite sport of stag-hunting, 'for where the stags are there are such hills and bogs as 'tis impossible to follow any hounds'. In fact, 1681 was one of the best years of Claverhouse's career; he was enjoying success and popularity, and as yet he seemed to have no enemies, although Queensberry was hardly a friend.[33] He spent a substantial portion of the year in London, enjoying the favour of the Royal family.

On 7th October he was granted the Freedom of the Burgh of Stirling, the same honour being conferred also on his brother, his deputy Bruce of Earlshall and six others.[34] After the ceremony, Claverhouse and his brother returned to Glen Ogilvie where he was allowed to remain until the first week of December before returning to Edinburgh for the trial of Argyll. Claverhouse was on the jury, and his friend George MacKenzie was chief Prosecutor. Argyll, the 9th Earl, was on trial on a charge of treason, having refused to subscribe to the new 'Test Act' – or rather, he had taken the oath, but in such a low voice that few heard him, and he refused to take it a second time. The charge was really a fabrication devised to reduce Argyll's power, and the jury was carefully selected to include only loyalists. Argyll knew defence was pointless and so, when he was unanimously convicted of treason, made preparations to escape abroad.

On the journey to Edinburgh for the trial, Claverhouse himself had a narrow escape – from drowning in the River Forth. He was on a passage from Burntisland to Leith in a boat inappropriately called *The Blessing* when a storm blew up and nearly caused the vessel to capsize. The storm was commemorated in a poem written several years afterwards entitled 'The Tempest'. It includes the following references to Claverhouse:

> He who can boldly kill dares bravely die,
> Yet he whose ire hath smil'd on seas of blood,
> Looks pale on water, in his coolest mood
> Soldiers stern fire abhorrs the death of slaves;
> It can't resist, nor vengeance wre(a)ck on waves . . .[35]

This certainly seems to suggest that Captain Graham was seasick during the storm!

The system of government in Scotland pleased the Duke of York. This was because there was no Parliamentary opposition – merely loose factions grouped around prestigious figures. As Sir George MacKenzie remarked with some surprise: 'If the burghs had liberty to choose whom they pleased to represent them, the factious and disloyal might prevail to get themselves elected.'[36]

Samuel Pepys the diarist had travelled north with the Royal party, and he also admired the Scots way of running things: 'Their government', he later wrote, 'seems to be founded upon some principles much more steady than those of ours.' At this time, the policy of the government wavered between outright repression and uneasy toleration. The Test Act was as much an attack upon Catholics as upon Presbyterians, and in this way, James, a Catholic himself, sought to reassure the Scots. The Duke claimed that he was 'careful to give offence to none and to have no partialities'.[37] All the nobility and clergy were to take the Test, and Claverhouse among others did so on 22nd September.

A Proclamation was issued by the Privy Council making the landowners or heritors responsible for informing on any Conventicles held on their lands. The landowners' diligence was to be observed bi-annually, and large fines would be imposed on those found wanting. This measure was followed up by the Act For Securing The Peace Of The Country, passed on 29th August. This made masters liable for the fines of their servants and heritors for their tenants. Claverhouse strongly objected to this Act, and in a letter to Queensberry wrote later: 'It is unjust to desire of others what we would not do ourselves; I declare it a thing not to be desired that I should be forfeited and hanged if my tenant's wife, twenty miles from me, gives meat and shelter to a fugitive.'[38] According to Andrew Lang, Claverhouse 'was a more merciful man, despite his reputation, than the civilians'. This was certainly borne out by his later actions.[39]

Shortly after the passing of this Act, Claverhouse was

appointed full Sheriff of Wigtown, Bailie of the regality of Longlands, and Sheriff Depute and Steward Depute of the Shire of Dumfries and the Stewartry of Kirkcudbright and Annandale. His deputy, Captain Bruce, was commissioned for the same areas, with about a dozen others. These new officers were in addition to the existing officials, and were specifically appointed to punish Conventicles, and irregular baptisms and marriages. According to the Privy Council Register the special Commissioners were 'to apply the one halfe of the fynes . . . to your owne use and such as yow shall employ'.[40] The Sheriffs had powers only to arrest and try prisoners – but not to pass sentence on them – which was left to the Privy Council. The Council also supervised the use of torture to extort confessions in which the victims were made to implicate others.

One of the most prominent members of the Privy Council, Sir James Dalrymple, 1st Viscount Stair, noted in his *Memoirs* that 'while most men shrank from the sight of torture, the Duke of York was so far from withdrawing that he looked on all the while with an unmoved indifference'.[41]

Claverhouse returned to his duty in Galloway. He was now reporting to the Earl of Queensberry, whose fortunes were on the rise, and on 16th February wrote him 'the first account I have given to any body of my concerns in this contry'. He described his *modus operandi*: 'I will threaten much, but forbear severe execution for a whyll, for fear people should grou desperat and increase too much the number of our enimys.' Before promising to 'wryt often and much' he puts in a plea for three months' pay arrears.

In his next letter, a week later: 'I have so far preferred the publik concern to my owen, that I have not so much as called at Freuch [his new estate in Galloway], tho I passed in sight of it.' Queensberry's reply, three days later, grudgingly informed him that the Duke of York was 'pleased with youre procedeurs'.

Gratified, Claverhouse expands his theme:

> The way that I see taken in other places is to put lawes severely against great and small in excicution; which is very just:

but what effects does that produce, but mor to exasperat
and alienat the hearts of the wholl body of the people; for it
renders three desperate wher it gains on; and your Lordship
knous that in the greatest crymes it is thought wyse to pardon
the multitud and punish the ringleaders.

This policy seems to have the desired effect, and in the same
letter Claverhouse notes somewhat smugly that there were
'about three hondred at Kilkoubrie Church: some that for
seven year befor had never been there . . .'

On 5th March he considers it 'more of consequence to
punish one considerable laird than a hondred little bodys'.
He also asks permission to 'give the bond to little people' –
whom he proposes to let off on condition they promise good
behaviour in the future.

He visited Edinburgh on 24th March to give a report in
person on his activities, and to convey some prisoners to
the Tolbooth. These included Barscobe, a man who had
been at Bothwell Brig. Barscobe retracted in due course, was
pardoned, and would have been allowed to live peacefully
till old age had he not been strangled in his own house by
some men of 'wild principles'.[42]

But the Privy Council had another matter in hand, for
Claverhouse had sent in a complaint on 12th February to
them against Sir John Dalrymple, son of the 1st Viscount
Stair:

. . . the said Sir John did caball and meitt with severalls of
the gentry and endevour to make them combine with him to
sustain his false representations . . . he had the impudence
in their name to draw a most seditious, false and malitious
representatione against forces both officers and souldiers,
came deliver it by way of instrument to Mr David Grahame,
brother to the said John Grahame, complainer . . . designeing
thereby to stirre them up to sedition.

There had been a simmering dispute between the two over
which had the strongest legal authority. Stair had previously
complained of Claverhouse's 'meddling' and the dispute came
to a head when Claverhouse presided at a special court at
Strathaven. Dalrymple stormed in and began to take over

the court, leading to a furious public row with Claverhouse. Claverhouse began to prepare a legal case against Dalrymple. As the Council prepared to hear the case, Dalrymple's father, Sir James – who was by this time in exile in Holland, having refused to take the Test oath – tried to enlist powerful support for his son. He wrote to Queensberry and claimed 'his [Sir John's] own people do frankly engage against Conventicles and keep church as I believe Claverhouse will signify. I have been much obliged to him for his civility'. He makes no mention of the complaint or the fact that they had earlier attempted to bribe him at Glenluce. A week later, Sir John himself wrote to Queensberry: 'Claverhouse came to this parish and by some mistake went away without doing anything concerning disorders in this regality.' He continues, compounding the lie with an attempt to pull strings: 'I have the honour to be related to your Lordship . . . and I am fully confident of your favour and that you will not believe harsh representations of us . . .'[43]

Stair is described in Burnet's *History of His Own Time* as 'a false and cunning man with a particular dexterity of giving some plausible colours to the greatest injustice'.[44] He was of course later to acquire notoriety as the prime instigator of the Massacre of Glencoe in 1692 as Secretary of State, for which he was rewarded with an Earldom. Stair, feeling confident of his power and influence, now pursued a counter complaint on the grounds that Claverhouse was interfering with his jurisdiction as Sheriff.

The Council met on 29th August, and while postponing their decision, reprimanded Sir John. He had been sheltering Covenanters and imposing derisory 'mock' fines, in order, Claverhouse alleged, 'that he might take them off complainer's hands'. He had even pretended in this way to fine his own mother, father-in-law and sister.

Claverhouse brought an action for libel. On 29th September, the Council wrote to him that they were well satisfied with his actions and gave him a vote of thanks. They were also ready to concur in anything he might propose. Sir George MacKenzie, by now the Lord Advocate, wrote to Lord Aberdeen on 10th October: 'Clavrose has brok a caball that was designing in Galloway . . .'[45] The Duke of York assured Claverhouse that he 'need not fear anything that Stair can say against him'. And so, on 14th December, Claverhouse presented his bill of complaint against Stair for weakening the hands of the Government. In the ensuing heated debate, Stair alleged that his people of Galloway were orderly and loyal. Claverhouse turned on him with a haughty denunciation: 'There are as many elephants and crocodiles as loyal and regular persons there!' This was an amusing topical reference to an elephant which had recently been exhibited in Edinburgh for the first time, and it provoked laughter in the Court. Other witnesses claim that he offered to give Stair 'a box on the ear'![46]

While Dalrymple had made a rapid rise to fame, his fall from grace was as sudden. He was fined £500 sterling (£1 sterling was equivalent to £18 Scots) and deprived of his regal offices. Early the following year he was arrested and committed to the Edinburgh Tolbooth, where he languished for three months. Four years later he was pardoned, and such were the exigencies of politics, duly became the next Lord Advocate!

Claverhouse had spent most of the year on active duty, and on 15th May the Privy Council again expressed their thanks to him for his diligent service. In April he was able to inform Queensberry that 'this contry nou is in parfait peace . . . it is beyond my expectation', and later: 'All things ar here as I could wish in parfait peace and very regular.' Unfortunately this was not the condition of the rest of the country, for on 16th June Claverhouse had a very narrow escape. He had stayed two days longer than expected at Edinburgh and, as it was late, spent the night at The Bille or The Crook Inn, eighteen miles from the city on the Bille Water, a tributary of the Tweed. Here he was told he had missed by only a few hours a party of over a hundred heavily armed Covenanters, who had been terrorising the district for several days, and had been lying in wait for him. The armed band disappeared as mysteriously as they had appeared.

On 29th December, Claverhouse's promotion to the rank of Colonel was gazetted and – what was even better – a new regiment was to be created for him devised entirely from his own proposals, to be named the King's Royal Regiment of Horse. This regiment was to become his pride and joy, and he busied himself importing cloth and ordering uniforms and equipment for his 240 troopers. He did not want them kitted out in the second-hand cast-offs of other regiments. He wanted them to be the best regiment in the country – and the best-dressed.

Further honour came his way when he was entrusted by the Privy Council to represent their interests at Court. Since he had special influence with the Duke of York, he was their ideal representative. The main business in hand was the delicate matter of the forfeited estates of Charles Maitland, Lord Hatton, brother to the 1st Duke of Lauderdale. Hatton, who had just become the Earl of Lauderdale, had been ruined for tampering with the coinage, and his peers greedily eyed his estates, calculating what they could get from them. The Privy Councillors did not wish to be involved personally in the matter. Far better to employ someone else to do the dirty work. Queensberry, who was now a Marquis, coveted the higher title of Duke. Huntly also coveted the Dukedom. The Earl of Aberdeen hoped to get a grant of £20,000 for himself, and Claverhouse hoped to gain for himself the Lauderdale lands of Dudhope and the Constabulary of Dundee that went with it.

He set off on 1st March 1683. The winter had been mild and spring had come early. Already there were signs that the summer would be long and hot. The previous year had seen a great drought and plague among the cattle in all parts of the country. None of this greatly concerned the Court society at Newmarket. A letter sent by Claverhouse on the 9th complains: 'It is hard to gate any business don here. I walked but nyn mylles this morning with the King, besids cock faighting and courses.'

Claverhouse clearly disliked such idle pastimes, and would have found his days at Court, the continuous round of masques, balls, stage comedies and banquets exceedingly irksome. The pretensions of the sophisticated society fops offended his plain-speaking Church of Scotland soul. In another letter a few days later: 'It is very hard to doe any thing here either with King or Deuk [of York], for the Deuk hunts, beseids going where ever the King goes.' On 20th March, he was in London, unable to return to Scotland because the matter had been further delayed. He adds his thanks to Queensberry for recommending him for membership of the Privy Council. A week later, he has been having private discussions about Queensberry's Dukedom. The subject of the Dudhope Estate has also come up. Claverhouse again assures Queensberry that he is 'willing to buay a pairt of the land'.

Following a further meeting with the Duke, it becomes clear that the King is not willing to confer the honours as Claverhouse wishes. He is at pains to assure Queensberry that he is doing his best. 'If it had been for my lyfe,' he declares, 'I could do no mor. But, my Lord, I hop you will bear patiantly a little delay . . .' The tone of the next letter, 26th April, is brisker. Decisions are at last being made. Queensberry's Dukedom will be delayed only 'till the Deuk hears from your Lordship and the Chancellor'. Queensberry is to be granted the heritable lands of Stirling Castle. Claverhouse is granted Dudhope and the jurisdiction of Dundee. But Queensberry must have concluded that he was being fobbed off, for in a letter two days later, Claverhouse is 'sorry to see that the world is not wyser, and I must say that I think your Lordship gets hard measeur'. It is from this point that Queensberry's attitude to Claverhouse seems to alter to outright emnity. But when Claverhouse returned to Scotland in the second week of May, he was confident that his representations would ultimately be adopted. The mission had been a resounding success and one in which he had enjoyed an intoxicating proximity to the highest levels of power.

He had further cause for celebration when a letter arrived at the Privy Council from Charles appointing him Commander of the Royal forces in Scotland except where the Commander-in-Chief, General Dalyell, was actually present. It was also the King's wish that he attend the Privy Council 'in consideration of the loyaltie and abilities of our right trustie and well-beloved John Grahame of Claverhouse'. Here was rapid promotion for a man in his early thirties.[47]

There were considerable delays and time-consuming negotiations over the ownership of the Dudhope Estate, although the King had indicated that it was to be sold – not given – to Claverhouse. He particularly wanted – needed – the Estate, as it bordered his own lands at Mains, and contained a large fortified mansion on a hill overlooking the town of Dundee. The country house was no longer quite suitable for a Privy Councillor and Deputy Commander of the Scottish Army. His rapid rise had created new enemies: nobles who began to view him and his influence at Court as a potential threat. The disgraced Earl of Lauderdale found the Earl of Aberdeen a willing participant in a devious scheme to withhold the Estate from Claverhouse. After a great deal of litigation, King Charles interposed and directed Lauderdale to sell to him. The purchase was to take place over two years, although the King had assured him he should pay nothing at first, and the change of the terms meant that Claverhouse could barely manage to afford the Estate. He did not obtain possession of Dudhope until 23rd April the next year, 1684.

In the meantime he was directed to Roxburgh to deal with a threatened conspiracy. The Test Act had been extended on 31st August the previous year, and now all the King's subjects were to take the oath 'solemlie upon their knees with uplifted hands, repeating each word' to prove their loyalty to Church and King, and they also had to declare all Leagues and Covenants unlawful.[48]

Claverhouse wrote reports to the Lord Chancellor in June 1683; on the 5th from Jedburgh. He had forty dragoons at Langholm, twenty at Annan, more at Moffat and Dumfries, and had three troops of ten traversing the borders. He is liaising with Colonel Struthers on the English side of the Border, and is well in control of the situation. 'All the comons here have given obediance, and most of the gentry.'

It is possible to read in his letters of this time a growing self-assurance and confidence. His competence in military and diplomatic skills was marking out a new role for him – one in which he would play a bigger part in framing policy and guiding the ship of state. It was a role he had earned by diligent and able service.

On 9th June he is at Stirling attending the Circuit justiciary. He writes two letters: to Aberdeen and to Queensberry. These are no longer simply reports of his doings; they are filled with opinions and advice, and reveal much of his nature:

> I am as sorry to see a man day [die], even a ghique [whig], as any of themselfs; but when one man days justly for his owen faults, and may save a hondred to fall in the lyk, I have no scrupull. I understand not that . . . the Lieutenant General . . . hunting people for only stealing koues . . . when the King's service and peace is so neerly concerned.

A man by the name of William Bogue, who had been an armed rebel for four years was called to take the Test and pretended he had already taken it. He refused to admit Bothwell Brig was a rebellion or the murder of Archbishop Sharp truly a murder. He refused to take the Test. When he was then sentenced to death, he begged to take it, 'as far as it consisted with the Protestant religion and the glory of God'. When that was refused, he offered to take it in any way the Court demanded. This came too late to save him from being hanged.

It is difficult to have anything but respect and awe for those martyrs, many of whom did not break down under torture, who refused to speak the few words that would save them from death.

A further letter to Queensberry, on 13th September, concerns the business of the Privy Council which has been considering where to deploy the troop of horse. Claverhouse declares himself indifferent: '. . . where-ever it went I thoght mayself no ways oblidged to march with it, because that was the Capt Lieutenant's business.'

He expresses his obligations to Queensberry: 'I shall never forgait hou generous it was in your Lordship to alou me your friendship in a tyme that you was offered concurrence of persons who oght to have been my friends.' This is a clear reference to the growing number of his enemies, or can perhaps be seen as an attempt to ingratiate himself with a man whose untrustworthiness he suspected. He continues in similar vein:

> There ar people who think I have lost by the change, but I am far from it, for they knou not so well as I what I had or what any man can have there to loss. But whatever there had been in it, I would not have regraited it, and think my self very happy whyll I am asseured of your Lordship protection and friendship.

On 23rd April 1684, Claverhouse received the Crown Charter of Dudhope and lands and the office of Constable and First Magistrate of Dundee. The citizens of Dundee deeply resented this interference by the King in their right to elect these officials. For long the power of the Constables and Town Council had been in conflict. The Earl of Lauderdale, the previous Constable, had dealt summarily with municipal protest and had succeeded in fining the Provost, George Brown of Horn, 3000 merks and jailing him for six years. The Town Council drafted a Protest against the appointment of the new Constable, that Claverhouse might:

> . . . noewayes militat agt or be prejudiciall unto ye rights, liberties, & priviledges belonging & appertaining unto ye sd burgh of Dundie; And particularlie of cognoscering upon & decyding all ryotes, bloods, batteries, pettie thifts, and other lesser crymes comitted within ye bounds & jurisdictiones of ye sd towne be ther originall wrytes and evident, and ych ye sd magistrats & ther predicessors possessed formerlie without any interruptione; And that ye sd Collonell JOHN GRAHAME, as Constable, should have noe priviledge of being first Magistrat, it being express contrair to ye toune's priviledges & liberties and constant custome, But that ye toune's rights, liberties & priviledges should stand firme, & in full force, strenth, & effect notwithstanding yrof . . .[49]

Although Claverhouse received the house and lands of Constable, he did not assume the office of First Magistrate, in the face of implacable opposition from the Town Council under Provost Fletcher. The Council also refused to implement the later Royal Warrant (of September 1686, signed by King James VII), which listed the King's nominees for all civic posts. On 2nd December of that year James tried again; he appointed Alexander Rait as Provost, John Graham and others as Bailies, and a list of Councillors and Deacons of Crafts. The office-bearers were to continue in office 'untill Michaelmasse next', and there was a recommendation that 'Majour General Grahame [was] to be present thereat, to the end that he may see his Majestie's royall pleasure aforesaid regularly and effectually put in execution'. This also was ignored.

One of the first commissions that James VII was to order in Scotland on his accession was the formal ratification of Claverhouse's position as Constable and First Magistrate:

> . . . That is our will and pleasure that in all time coming the Constable of Dundee and his successors in that office be the first Magistrat of the said burgh. That is that he will have the procedeury and first Honours paid him befor the provost by all persones . . . we will Doe Require yow to send ane Extract of this our letter to the Provost of Dundee who is hereby ordered cause it to be registered in the Town Books . . . and to warrant you to punish any who shall upon any pretext whatsoever refuse obedience hereunto . . .[50]

The Council remained obdurate. King James then appointed Claverhouse as Provost in an attempt to bring the burgh to heel, and Claverhouse did, indeed, preside as Provost over several meetings for some months in 1688, but by 1689 Fletcher had resumed office where he remained more or less secure.[51] But this was in the future.

Now that Claverhouse had a house worthy of his higher role in political life, he needed only a wife to install in it. Quite co-incidentally he had fallen head-over-heels in love with the grand-daughter of the Earl of Dundonald, whom he had met for the first time in Edinburgh. His business in Ayrshire had brought them into contact on several occasions. He married Jean Cochrane on 10th June 1684 at Paisley. The marriage, which I intend to cover in a later chapter, was not without incident. The arrival of a dragoon messenger from General Dalyell cut short the ceremony and Claverhouse had to leave his bride in undignified haste to ride in search of a Conventicle reported on Blacklock Moor.

He returned to Lady Jean on the 13th, but again, after a matter of only two hours, had to leave her. His letter on that day concludes, with a fine touch of irony: 'I am just taking horse. I shall be revenged sometime or other of this unseasonable trouble these dogs give me. They might have let Tuesday pass.'

Two letters, dated 15th and 16th of June, to General Dalyell and the Archbishop of St Andrews, Dr Alexander Burnet, from Kilbryde and Paisley respectively, detail the extensive movements of the next few days. He has scoured from Paisley to Kilmarnock, Mauchline to Airdmoss, Dumfries to Strathaven, by Greenock-head, Douglas, Lesmahagow, from Cumnock to Gap. He has left 'no den, no knowe, no moss, no hill unsearched . . . the troops complain mightily of this march'. He is convinced that the Conventicle, all fifty-nine members armed, have escaped to the hills of Moffat: 'We examined all on oath, and offered money, and threatened terribly, for intelligence, but we could learn no more.'

Shortly after this, Claverhouse managed to snatch a visit to his home and wife to 'injoy the fruits of your [Queensberry's] faveur . . . and eat the bread of idleness'. He attended the Privy Council on 9th September, where he requested authority to commute the death penalty for several prisoners in Dundee Tolbooth. He claimed that their crimes of petty thefts or 'pykeing' did not warrant such an excessive penalty. They would be 'fitter to be punished arbitrarily than by death'. No doubt the prisoners were grateful for Claverhouse's humane intervention on their behalf.[52]

He participated in a rather unusual event on 29th November. The town of Edinburgh was searched from top to bottom by order of the Privy Council, at less than twelve hours' notice. The town, which at this time had about 30,000 inhabitants crammed into high tenements or lands between the Castle and Holyrood House, was divided into sixteen quarters, and all citizens were ordered to remain indoors until the search was over. The search began at 4 a.m., with officials laboriously checking the names, house to house, street by street, against the Householders' Roll. Claverhouse waited with some soldiers at Haddocks Hall to guard any fugitives who might be sent in to him.

Another commission had come his way and he was to travel south to Galloway in early October. A letter written to his brother (the only letter to his brother in existence) asks him to begin making arrangements:[53]

Edinburgh, Sept. 9, 1684.

Dear Brother,

My Lord Treasurer hes bene pleased to take me in with himself and his sone in a commissione which the Councill has given us of justiciary and Councill, and he, being desyrous all should be exactly done that relates to the King's service in these partes, hes allowed me to write to yow to prepare some things for us. I doubt not but, seeing yow have bene busie these severall weeks bypast in the shyre, yow can give ane exact account of it. My Lord Treasurer will expect to know from yow quhat heritors have bene slak in attending divin ordinance, for, I supose, there are non withdrauers altogether, and particularlie concerning the ladies of which I know some are yet obstinat. Besides this, we will expect that yow can give us account of all resetters or conversers with rebells, especiallie since the circuit in that shyre. As to the steuartrie, wher, I supose, yow now are and wher most disorders have bene, yow most take the paroch of Minigaff, the four paroches of the Glenkens, Partoun, Kirkpatrick and Irongray, and examine everie man concerning all maner of church disordors. The commons yow may judge according to your ordinary method, but heritors, onlie take there depositions, and make report therof to my Lord Treasurer quhen he coms as to resett. Examine all the commons on oath except some against quhom yow have any informatione, and in that caice examine there servants and neighbours, becaus, if they be found guiltie since the circuit, they must hang, which cannot be done if it be once referred to ther oath. Soe yow wold doe best to take of the ministers and honest men informatione concerning resett befor yow proceed to referr it to ther oath. Any yow find guiltie since the circuit of comons of this cryme, whither it be by probation of wittnesses or oath of partie, secure in prison and doe all dilligence to aprehend all who refuse to apear befor yow or are in the fugitive rolls, Examine not onlie who hes resett in ther houses but all who hes resett on there lands since the circuit, and, if anie heritors have resett declared rebels in ther housses or conversed with them, secure them quhatever they be, but examin noe heritor concerning his oun guilt in that cryme, becaus we will doe it, but examin all the comons against them and there oun servants. Acquaint the moderators of all presbiteries to intimat to there respective ministers that they make readie lists of all persons duelling within there parochins, heritor, tennent, cottar, sons or daughters above tuelv years of age or other persons reciding with them, alse welle women as men, and that they make readie ane account who of them withdraues as yet or keeps not the church ordinarlie or are guiltie of any fanatik disordors and all this upon oath to the best of there knouledge. Everie heritor most be acquainted by the shereff to doe the like within there oun lands, soe they most bring lists of all and account who of them are disorderlie or resettars upon oath according to there knouledge, and they most depon befor us, both ministers and heritors, that they have done there endevor to discover and inform themself all they could efter this intimation was givene. The minister will onlie need to swear as to there lists and church disordor. Inquire alsoe upon oath of the comons if the soldiers have payed ther localitie, particularlie those two years bypast. Be exact in this and precipitat not, for, though our dyett be the tuentie fifte of this moneth, yet my Lord Treasurer will may be allow yow to the thirtie, quhill he is going on in uther jurisdictions, Lag will doe the rest in the Steuartie. Adieu. Sic subscribitur,

J. GRAHM.

Queensberry, Drumlanrig and Claverhouse commenced the court on 2nd October. They passed an edict for the public not to crowd the courtroom. It must have been difficult to prevent this happening, as on one day alone, 145 persons appeared on the charge of harbouring, resetting and conversing with rebels. Of those who were punished, five were banished, one was fined 500 merks, seven were fined 100 merks, two women were scourged in public, and three men after an appeal were allowed to 'acknowledge their faults in the kirk'. The court lasted for two weeks, examining hundreds of suspects, and is extensively reported in the Privy Council Registers.[54]

Around the same time, a troop of soldiers escorting sixteen prisoners to Dumfries were ambushed by armed rebels in the narrow pass beneath Enterkin Hill, and in the mêlée fourteen of the prisoners escaped. Extremists had taken over Covenanter activities, and the acts of their supporters had grown more desperate. James Renwick, a seventeen-year-old student from Edinburgh, who had also studied at Göttingen University, was the new leader of the 'Cameronians' and published his 'Apologetic Declaration' in November. This was a direct challenge to the Government and called on the people to rise and kill all the enemies of God: 'especially the bloody soldiers and viperous Bishops and Curates.' In response, the Privy Council passed an Act 'that any person . . . who owns or will not disown the late treasonable Declaration on oath, whither they have arms or not, be immediately put to death, this being done in the presence of two witnesses and the person . . . having commission to that effect'.

Thus began a period of brutal repression known as the 'Killing Times' by the Whigs, and immortalised in a hundred furious pamphlets and on dozens of tombstones. Captives were shot as they knelt in prayer, sabred in their own houses, Conventicles of men, women and children were fired on, whenever and wherever they were discovered. The Cameronians fought back, murdering the curate of Carsphairn and invading Kirkcudbright – where they 'broke open the jail and carried away such persons as would go with them'.

Claverhouse attacked an armed band of Covenanters in Galloway, killed five and took three prisoners; some whom were the murderers of the Carsphairn curate. In the last week of January 1685, an Edward Maxwell of Hill was liberated from Kirkcudbright Tolbooth, and his fine reduced after he was examined by Claverhouse and Drumlanrig (Queensberry's son). Maxwell had appealed to the Privy Council, and it looks as though his refusal to go with the perpetrators of the prison raid may have stood in his favour. Claverhouse was quite willing to give prisoners the benefit of the doubt if they promised good behaviour in the future.

Scotland was informed in the early hours of 10th February by an exhausted, mud-spattered courier that Charles II, 'our late gracious soveraigne of ever-blessed memory', was no more. In the flyleaf of the Privy Council Register for the meeting held that day is scrawled: 'This Register begines the reign of King James the 7th the most august and serene Prince of Scotland, England, France and Ireland etc. . . .' The Privy Council had already booked apartments at Holyrood Palace for early March when James (as Duke of York) was due to visit, and this visit would now be postponed indefinitely, although it was expected that the new King would travel north for his Scottish Coronation within the year. Previous Kings had been crowned at Scone, including Charles II who had travelled there in 1651. James was, however, destined to be the first King who did not take Scottish Coronation oaths. And, in the eyes of the Scottish population, there was one important difference between Charles and James: James was a Catholic. He also lacked the intelligence or perceptiveness of his brother – and his choice of advisers was to be little short of disastrous. His avowed policy was religious toleration for all sects and creeds, but this was widely understood as a licence to re-introduce the hated Catholicism.

Thus the Privy Council, meeting on 10th March in the absence of James who had been due to preside, turned to other matters. The prison population was discussed, and a Committee was appointed to make reports and to set those at liberty whom it considered appropriate, and to list those still detained. Claverhouse was appointed to the Committee to visit Edinburgh Tolbooth and visited the same day, releasing thirteen prisoners and ordering that nine should continue in detention.

The nation was still in the grip of disorder. There were reports of Conventicles all over the South of Scotland and in Dundee, Forfar and Stirlingshire. Claverhouse was soon back in action:

On Frayday last amongst the hilles betwixt Douglas and Plel-
lands, we persued two fellows a great way throu the mosses,
and in end seised them . . . The eldest, John Broun, refused it
[the oath], nor would he swear not to ryse in armes against
the King, but said he kneu no King; upon which, and there
being found bullets and match in his house and treasonable
papers, I caused shoot him dead . . . the other, a yong fellou,
and his nephew . . . offered to take the oath, but he would not
swear he had not been at Neumilles in armes at the rescuing
the prisoners. So I do not knou what to do with him. I was
convinced he was guilty, but sawe not how to proceed against
him.

The boy provides Claverhouse with some information which
he passes on to Queensberry: '. . . and if your Grace thinks he
deserves no mercy, justice will pass on him, for I having no
commission of justiciary myself have delyvered him up to the
Lieutenant Generall to be disposed of as he pleases'.

While this letter does not imply that Claverhouse himself
pulled the trigger – which is unlikely – in the circumstances
he could not do otherwise according to his orders. In the
situation of a lengthy pursuit, the evidence found in the home
and the prisoner's defiance, Claverhouse merely acted with
meticulous attention to his orders. Many lesser men would
have peremptorily executed *both* the fugitives without trou-
bling their consciences in the least. Nevertheless, Claverhouse
did promise to alleviate the punishment of John Brown's
nephew by putting in a word for him with the Lieutenant
General – which he plainly did not do.

One of Charles's last edicts, dated 12th December 1684,
had revealed his impatience and despair at the Scottish situation: '. . . the many endeavours used by us to reclame the
disaffected and disorderly people in severall of the shyres . . .
have not been so effectual as the gentleness of our government
and the interest of all concerned gave us hope, but that on the
contrair they continued in rebellious convocations, seditious
conventicles and other disorderly practises . . .' The Privy
Council acted on this and sent 'delegates' to the troubled
areas to try to regain control of the situation. Claverhouse
and Colin Lindsay, the Earl of Balcarres, another friend of

his, were sent to cover Fife and Kinross. Delegates were also sent to Mid, West and East Lothian and Bathgate, Edinburgh itself, and the north district between Spey and Ness. The delegates were to act as if a 'quorum of yow our Councill wer present'.[55]

Claverhouse and Balcarres appeared at the Circuit Court in Fife and proposed that the oath should be extended to all men and women over the age of sixteen. It is hard to countenance this as anything other than a pragmatic measure, although it certainly seems repressive.

Claverhouse has received blame for the drowning of Margaret McLachlan and Margaret Wilson near Wigtown on 11th May 1685. This episode has been so inflated by the embellishments of later historians that the facts have been obscured. It is known that the two women were tied by the banks of the Solway Firth, and thus drowned when the tide came in, but Claverhouse had no authority over the area at the time, and although there was a David Graham on the jury that convicted the women, this was not Claverhouse's brother. In fact, Claverhouse was known to have been in Eskdalemuir at the time and it is hard not to see the execution as yet another of the atrocities of Sir Robert Grierson of Lag. The most unusual thing about the incident is why it took place at all.[56] Grierson, the judicial authority at Wigtown, did not possess powers of execution, and in fact, royal pardons from Edinburgh arrived too late to avert the tragedy. There are numerous similar incidents in such Whig histories as *Men of the Covenant, Life of Alexander Peden, Second Vindication of the Church of Scotland, The Cloud of Witnesses, Faithful Contendings, God's Judgement on Persecutors, Short Memorial of the Sufferings and Grievances, Martyr Graves* – and behind most of these one can discern the baleful glare of the Reverent Robert Wodrow, author of the *History of the Sufferings of the Church of Scotland*.[57]

It is generally accepted that there are three incidents in which Claverhouse can be held partly, or fully responsible. Of these, the case of Andrew Hislop, a seventeen-year-old lad, is an example of the value accorded to hearsay evidence. It was,

in fact, the case of Hislop which was occupying Claverhouse
on the very day that the two women were drowned in the
Solway. He handed Hislop over to Sir James Johnston of
Westerhall who was the judicial authority for that area. When
Westerhall decided to shoot him, Claverhouse protested to
the limit of his authority, and on being unable to prevail
upon Westerhall, turned away saying: 'This poor man's blood
be on your head, Westerraw; I am free of it.' There is no
other evidence in the case of Mathew MacIlraith save for his
tombstone near Girvan, which declares in letters of stone: 'by
bloody Claverhouse I fell, who did command that I should
die for owning Covenanted presbytery.' If indeed MacIlraith
had 'owned Covenanted presbytery' and refused to swear the
oath, then his death, like that of Brown, would have been a
military execution, justified by Claverhouse's orders. But even
the Reverend Wodrow, the source of so many of the stories
of Claverhouse's 'atrocities', does not relate the incident.
There is no real evidence against Claverhouse in the case of
Brown, Hislop or McIlraith, or the Wigtown women that
can justify the tales of atrocity and terror. In many ways the
burning desire of Whig historians to blacken his name has
been counter-productive to their cause.

By the end of the year Claverhouse was to fall temporarily
from favour because of his support of some ordinary soldiers'
claim against their commander, Colonel Douglas, brother of
the Duke of Queensberry. Douglas had taken the men's pay
arrears for his own use, justifying his theft on the grounds
that these soldiers had 'gotten coats on their entry for nothing
and so should pay for them'. He then expelled the men from
his regiment because of their shape and size. They did not
look soldierly enough. The normal practice was for officers
to pay for uniforms and equipment, which Claverhouse had
done at great personal expense. He criticised Douglas's action
on the grounds that it was contrary to natural justice and
furthermore would be prejudicial to recruitment. Claverhouse
was a little naive in this, for most of the military leaders
indulged in this kind of extortion, which was regarded merely
as good business practice, and when the matter came to the

Council it was pursued with 'some heat' by the Councillors. Claverhouse lost his temper and an account of the debate was forwarded to the King. James wrote back that he was 'sorry Claverhouse was so little master of himself'. The quarrel was used as an excuse for his enemies to vilify him for their own purposes. Many had already begun to mark his 'hye, proud and peremptory humour'. Claverhouse was excluded from the Privy Council meetings in February, March and April, but restored in May by order of James VII.

The King's new adviser, Drummond of Melfort, appointed barely a month after his accession, disliked Claverhouse intensely, and rarely missed an opportunity to intrigue against him. Thus while the King himself wrote to Queensberry, 'I am confident they do him [Claverhouse] much wrong . . . he is not a man to say things which are not; and this justice I must do him, that, whilst he was here, no man was more your friend than he, and did presse all your concerns with more earnestnesse', Melfort was writing a letter with a different message. He wrote numerous letters to Queensberry, which usually end with the imperative: 'throw my letter, after reding, in the fyre, as I doe yours' (which he plainly had not done!). In these letters he uses an elaborate system of numbers and codes to prevent his devious schemes being revealed should the letters miscarry. He talks of Claverhouse's 'insolence': 'ye know my opinion of him,' he says. On 4th April he assures Queensberry that he has persuaded the King not to restore Claverhouse to the Privy Council: 'It was in my humble opinion most unfitt . . . I told him he knew Claverhouse to be of a hye, proud and peremptory humour . . . he would certainly talk of it with intolerable conceit and vanity . . . a great deal more I say'd . . .', he concludes. In a further letter: 'I have been urging this four and twenty hours a tyme to speak with the King of Claverhouse . . . I whispered in his ear this morning . . .' Clearly, Melfort was a most unsavoury politician, even by the standards of the Scottish Privy Council![58]

The Council snubbed Claverhouse by sending Colonel Douglas to quell a rising in the Western shires instead of him, and his office of Sheriff in Wigtownshire was temporarily removed. Because of the threat of the Argyll Invasion, Claverhouse was made Major-General – but not however given precedence over Douglas, who had been his second-in-command, and was now made up to Major-General himself – one day earlier – to give him the seniority. Just before this, on 17th August, Claverhouse was made a Guild Burgess of the City of Aberdeen, although no reason is given for this honour. In the Burgess Register he is styled 'Master of the Horse and Clerk of the King's Council' – a title which is not applied to him elsewhere.

The growing insecurity of his position in Scotland, due to the envy and jealousy of the Scots lords and nobles, was further exacerbated by the growing unpopularity of King James himself. James was a more active King than his brother, but his religious toleration was unpopular, being feared as a plot to re-introduce Catholicism. The vast majority of Scots clung to the Indulged Episcopal Church of Scotland, though a few, unscrupulous souls in high positions made quick conversions to the Catholic Church in the hope of favours to come. Foremost among these were the Drummond brothers: Drummond of Melfort, James' chief Scottish adviser, and Drummond of Perth who was to be Secretary of State for Scotland. Both were to prove highly unpopular, and Melfort particularly was a factor in James' downfall.

Claverhouse was warranted to convey prisoners from the Bass Rock and Blackness gaols to the Edinburgh Tolbooth for trial – a minor task – and, on 11th December, was added to the Commission of Treasury and Exchequer, to supervise taxes and feu duties.[59]

Thus, by the end of 1686, Claverhouse had clearly entered upon the final and more important phase of his career. In the Council and in the country he had become a significant figure, an able soldier who could be trusted and relied on by the King despite the monarch's waning popularity. His abilities were widely recognised by those in power, resented by some and feared by others. From being a good policeman he was becoming an able politician.

3

The Revolution

There was a period of relative peace from the end of 1686. A respite from 'outrages' and savage reprisals. The 'Killing Time' had been replaced by a breathless unbroken stillness in the glens and valleys of the South-West. The leaders of the Covenant were toiling in the plantations of the West Indies or languishing in prison, and many were dead or in exile. According to one source, the number of persons transported was 1700, the number exiled was 7000, and 2800 were reportedly in prison – which is almost certainly an over-estimate, and is uncheckable. Certainly it was a time of very great misery for many – even by the standards of Scottish history – and for the time being the power of the Covenant was broken.[60]

James was now firmly established on the throne. In itself this was surprising when one considers that he had not been crowned like previous Kings of Scotland – even Charles II – at Scone, nor had he taken any Scottish Coronation oaths. He is now referred to in history books as 'James II' although of course in Scotland there had been six previous James'. The influence of the larger nation was already eroding the independence and sovereignty of the Scottish state. James had spent fifty-two years in the shadow of his brother – twenty-five while his brother was King – and was impatient to push through a range of 'improvements'. He was an idealist with some very decided views. He had spent his childhood amid the turmoil of the Civil War and the uncertainties of foreign exile, and had inherited his father's suspicion of Governmental institutions. He was not, in general, a warm or trusting person, and tended to take his responsibilities very seriously. Nell Gwynne referred to him as 'Dismal Jimmy' although he was more handsome than his elder brother. He seemed however to lack the ability to enjoy himself freely without suffering the pangs of guilt the day after. Yet he was quite unable to control his passionate urges. He shared his brother's sexual energy and barely allowed his two marriages to interrupt the course of his affairs. Pepys had already noted with pride and alarm that the King 'did eye my wife mightily'. Indeed some wives were sent into the country by their husbands to save them from the rapacious attentions of the King. His first wife, Anne Hyde, had grown large and fat, seeking consolation in food while her husband's appearance became gaunt and wasted as a result of his debauchery. She sought consolation also in political intrigues and Pepys remarked (in 1668) that 'The Duke of York, in all things but his codpiece, is led by the nose by his wife'.[61] Tall, skinny Arabella Churchill had been replaced by Protestant Catherine Sedley as his current mistress under the very nose of his second wife, Mary of Modena, whom he had married in 1673, two years after the death of Anne Hyde. Charles had often quipped that his brother's mistresses seemed to be selected by the Jesuits, and several of them were extraordinarily plain – almost as if to ensure he did not enjoy his liaisons quite as much as he might. It was a fact that many were also Protestants. Perhaps James felt that sinning with a Protestant was less objectionable to his Catholic principles? Charles had been a popular King, but too indolent and bent on pleasure to bother overmuch with the business of Kingship. He had distrusted most of his advisers and was a considerable cynic. James, who inherited an enthusiastic and excessively loyal Parliament, did not possess the charm to convince them of the quality of his political schemes. He also caused irritation by overtly procuring benefits for the Catholics, and by a gullible trust of, in the main, untrustworthy advisers and conniving and ambitious clerics.[62]

James' great interest had always been the navy, which he had built up to be the best in Europe. He laid the foundations for English naval superiority for the next 150 years. This caused a boom in overseas trade, and the English merchant classes prospered. His attempts to build up the army were, however, misunderstood as a plot to threaten Protestantism, and many people feared that James would take England into a war against the English ally, Holland, to help the Catholic French. Perhaps James was genuine also in his desire to end religious persecution; perhaps he did want complete liberty of conscience for all creeds (including the Quakers) for its own sake – and these certainly seem laudable motives – but they were totally impossible in a time of widespread ignorance and superstition. He would also be unable to prevent Catholics rising to positions of authority – or to prevent rapid conversions to Catholicism by the ambitious as the path to favour and fame.

Major-General John Graham of Claverhouse, now thirty-eight, was probably fairly unique in the politics of the time in that he had a genuine rapport with James, whose idealism he shared to some extent. More importantly, he had a fondness for the King, and there was a mutual respect between the two men. Both were fired by the royalism of the Civil War Cavaliers; both were romantics. Although Claverhouse was Episcopalian, he could see the good points in what James was trying to achieve, and was determined to remain his loyal servant in Scotland. He had a strong belief – unfortunately proved wrong by history – that James would develop into the best and ablest of Stuart kings; the least corrupted, the most efficient. And of course he was aware that his own career could hardly suffer during the reign of his patron.

He had improved the family fortunes remarkably in the ten short years since his days as a young cornet enjoying the reckless bravado of European warfare. Now he had numerous duties and responsibilities. He was head of the Graham clan, possessor of lands and holdings which stretched from his mansion at Dudhope, ten miles north to the country seat in the Sidlaws, where he had been born and south to the banks of the Tay at Broughty Ferry and Monifieth. He was Constable of Dundee, Privy Councillor and member of half-a-dozen committees, Deputy Commander of His Majesty's Forces in Scotland. He had risen spectacularly, but few would deny that his promotions were deserved. He had after all spent a good part of those ten years in the saddle, building a reputation for capable and incorruptible efficiency and hard-headed practicality. But he had a wide romantic streak, and it was this which prevented his compromising his support for James. It was galling nevertheless to see lesser men scrambling for honours, titles and rewards they did not deserve. Sycophants and connivers clustered around James. Scotland could be more efficiently managed if these Court fops and clerical toadies were swept away. Claverhouse had painfully learned the lesson that very few of those in high places had as much honour or loyalty as the humblest soldier who served in his troop. The Covenanting martyrs whom he had harried and pursued – though wrongheaded – had been men of fierce loyalty and honour. The great nobles and Privy Councillors had few beliefs or ideals – other than to serve their own interests – with some notable exceptions. The soldiers of Douglas' regiment had been unjustly treated (p. 45) – and Claverhouse had been nearly ruined for defending them. The Privy Councillors had all turned on him. They had even poisoned the King against him, and he had been forced to apologise on bended knee to that deceitful buffoon Queensberry.

Claverhouse had been commanding officer of the Scottish Horse in 1686, a year in which we have little record of his activities. We know that he was still engaged on military duties because there exists a letter to the elderly Earl of Airlie, whom he now commanded, dated Edinburgh, 20th May, instructing him to move his troop to Kilsyth, Campsie or Strathblane. But the incompetent James Douglas, Queensberry's brother, strutted at the head of the regiment Claverhouse had trained and equipped at his own expense. Claverhouse had no highly-placed relatives to help his career like Douglas, who, in addition to being Queensberry's brother, had as kinsman the Duke of Hamilton who had been sworn onto the English Privy Council on 14th October 1687, so that he was a member of the Privy Councils of both countries. This made Douglas practically impregnable at the head of the Scottish army.

By contrast, Claverhouse's position was anything but secure, due to the growing unpopularity of James' policies. His old enemy, Sir John Dalrymple of Stair, was Lord Justice Clerk. Drummond of Perth was Lord Chancellor, and though friendly to Claverhouse, was not popular. His brother, John Drummond of Lundin, the Earl of Melfort, had the King's ear continuously in Whitehall, and he disliked Claverhouse and always had done. The Drummond brothers' meteoric rise to power was partly due to their conversion to Catholicism on the accession of King James. They declared that papers found in the strongbox of Charles II after his death had converted them – which seems an unlikely story. This of course made them such favourites with James that they were easily able to depose Queensberry as Chief Administrator of Affairs. Melfort was already widely hated in Scotland and England. The fact that he exerted such an influence over James – and for such a lengthy period of time – is simply one more example of the King's disastrous choice of advisers – and his resistance to sacrificing them (as his father had sacrificed Strafford when the mob were at the gates of the Palace) on the grounds of expediency. James' kingship was motivated by two political maxims which he had deduced from his father's downfall – and which were to lead to his own: his abhorrence of weakness made him reluctant to compromise, and his obsessional fears of republicanism made him grossly exaggerate the dangers of that, by now thoroughly discredited, creed. Both made him entirely unable to differentiate between loyal subjects' modest criticisms and the implacable opposition of his bitterest enemies. He tended to regard both as one and the same.

Of the other political leaders, Queensberry, though temporarily powerless, was skulking at home and in a dangerous mood. The Duke of Hamilton was playing a risky game with the King, hedging his bets. He had received a letter from James on 25th February 1688 demanding an end to his prevarication: '. . . you may as well now as at any time give me an account if you can comply with what I desire . . . now I must do it and expect your positive answer.' Hamilton replied on the 25th, expressing extreme surprise that he had mistaken the time allowed for consideration of the matter. He had been ill. 'I can give your Majestie a positive answer, he states, and does not do so: 'I have been ever and still am of the opinion that none should suffer for conscience sake . . . but how is this to be done with securety to the Protestant religion, our laws and oaths, is, in my humble opinion, what will desairve serious consideration, and is above what I can presently determine myself in.' He ends with an ambiguous assurance that 'no earthly consideration would make me lose the King's favour'. The subject being, of course, almost purely spiritual in content.[63]

Breadalbane, in London, while supposedly assisting Queensberry to recover favour, developed the keen interest in the politics of toleration for Catholics which was to see his own fortunes improve, while scheming to supplant the authority of Atholl in the highlands. Atholl himself was involved in a bitter dispute with Locheil whom he accused of being in league with Argyll.[64]

Claverhouse had no liking for these politicians. There were few friends in Council he could rely on, and those closest to him were the Earl of Balcarres and George MacKenzie the Lord Advocate. MacKenzie had published, the previous year, his *Defence of The Antiquity of The Royal Line of Scotland* which he had dedicated to the new King. It was a patriotic onslaught in defence of Scottish identity against those English professors who had dared to refute the lineal claim of the Stuarts that they had been Kings of Scotland for over 1200 years, and included over a 120 monarchs. This was highly dubious, even then, but that it was asserted at all indicates the measure of engrained support for the incumbent monarch and the degree to which the Stuart dynasty was associated, rightly or wrongly, with the Scottish 'national' identity, such as it was.

At the Privy Council meeting of 28th January 1686, the Chancellor moved that 'notice should be taken of a seditious sermon preached the Sunday immediately before, in the High Church, by Mr Canaires, lately Popish, and now Minister at Selkirk. He had given his opinion freely against Popery . . . Claverhouse backed the Chancellor in this, but there being a deep silence in all the rest of the Councillors, it was passed over at this time; but he [Canaires] was afterwards both suspended, reponed and *pro-secunda*, suspended.'

At the same Council, Watson, a Catholic and a Printer, whose goods had been seized by a landlady, was 'violently taken back and brought down to the Abbey, and he protected there'. There was a rumour that King James had written to Chancellor Perth and his Catholic friends, 'checking them for their too open Masses, and recommending to them to be more cautious and private'.[65]

The jailed Covenanters were now to be released, and those who had been fined released from their obligations, by order of the King. James hoped that if he showed mercy, they would gratefully accept his offer to become decent, law-abiding citizens. It was a serious mistake.

A fencing master in Edinburgh named Keith was less fortunate. Despite a large amount of popular agitation, he was hanged on 5th March at the Edinburgh Cross by order of the Lord Chancellor. His only crime was that he had drunk to the confusion of the Papists and approved an anti-Catholic riot which had taken place in the city on 1st December the previous year. Perth personally took the decision not to allow a reprieve, flying in the face of mass opinion.

There is an interesting report on the Council of 4th March: 'the narrative of the late tumult against the Mass, being read in Privy Council, is extended [exaggerated], and swelled to a great bulk and sent to the King . . . one design was, to load Colonel Douglas as negligent, and to get Clavers put in his place.'

It is doubtful whether Claverhouse knew anything about this devious little plot, and whether he would have had anything to do with it had he known of its existence. He was rather more engaged in the continuing court drama between his Chamberlain, David Graham of Duntrune, and a neighbour, Thomas Fotheringhame of Powrie. It seemed that these two could not live together in peace. There had already been one High Court case, and this was the second – not to mention actions raised in the Magistrates Court in Dundee. Duntrune had previously charged Powrie with rioting. Powrie denied it and counter-charged Duntrune with rioting. Now Duntrune was complaining that Powrie had damaged his green corn 'rather of designe to damnifye and abuse his neighbour than to seek after sport'. He alleged that Powrie and two friends had 'continued to ride up and down destroying the grain and whipped the complainer with a horsewhip then bragged of it, and lay in wait for him'. He accused Powrie of 'the height of insolence', meaning: 'he in ane undiscreet and uncivill manner bid him kiss his arse . . .' Outnumbered three to one, he had been soundly horsewhipped across the buttocks. Powrie admitted the whipping, but claimed self-defence. *He* had been outnumbered three to one. He denied the foul language. Duntrune, he alleged, had called him 'villain and rascal, and spat in his face'. The judgement of the court was that Powrie was to be jailed for a short term. Barely a year later, he was to take Claverhouse to court on another matter.[66]

A letter from Melfort at Whitehall to Queensberry shows the effect that the report of the proceedings of the Council on 4th March had had at court: 'The account we had yisterday of the tumult that hapined laetly at Edinburgh was verry surprisinge, and maks abundans of talk hear . . .'[67] The King now called the Duke of Hamilton (who went rather reluctantly) and General Douglas down to London, which further weakened the stability of the Council, and appointed the Duke of Gordon as Captain and Constable of Edinburgh Castle. As Gordon was a Catholic, he was admitted to office without having to take the 'Test' oath. This was seen as a dangerous precedent, but was justified by the King on the grounds that it might make the Catholics in Edinburgh feel safer to know that the Castle was in the hands of one of their faith. Later in the year, the Earl of Seaforth, another Catholic, was nominated to the Council, again dispensing with the oath, and the Duke of Gordon also was nominated. Another Catholic, Niddry, was added on 16th December. The tide was turning. The Archbishop of Glasgow, Dr Alexander Cairncross, was removed from the Council, and from his Archbishopric, in January 1687, for the crime of paying the Reverend Canaires' fines and publishing his sermon. There were many who saw this as a rather one-sided form of religious toleration!

On St Andrews Day, 30th November, 'the Papists consecrated the Abbey-church [at Holyrood] with Holy water and listened to a sermon by Withrington . . . and seeing such multitudes flock to them, they behoved to have a larger place for worship . . .'

A man called Reid the Mountebank, who had been in court two years earlier for cruel treatment of a child acrobat known as 'the tumbling lassie', was, on 17th January, received into the Catholic church, and one of his 'blackamores' was also baptised as a Christian Catholic and given the name 'James' after the King. Lauder of Fountainhall notes sourly that this is a coup for the Papists.[68]

A letter from the King was read at the Privy Council on 17th February 1687, which attempted to introduce toleration to the statutes. The 'Test' oath was abolished and replaced with a simple oath of loyalty to the King. An Indulgence was granted to all moderate Presbyterians, Quakers and Catholics, and all penal laws against them were dispensed with. The new King's Commissioner to replace Queensberry was announced – Alexander Stewart, the 4th Earl of Moray, who had recently become a Catholic. Ironically, it was Moray's great-great-grandfather, Regent Moray, who had introduced the very penal laws which his descendant was now attempting to abolish.

Several days later, on 24th March, Claverhouse and the other Councillors – with the notable exception of the Duke of Hamilton – signed this 'Declaration of Toleration' and wrote to the King: 'We are very willing that your Majestie's subjects who are peacable and loyall may be of case and securitie, notwithstanding of their professione and privat worship.'[69]

But of course, this was not their true opinion as later events were to prove, and Hamilton was not alone in his opposition. In private rooms there were many voices raised in indignation.

Claverhouse was spending much of his time in the courts. Firstly, there was the case against Lin of Larg, a former Covenanter, whom he was pursuing for payment due to the MacDowalls of Freuch, whose forfeited estate Claverhouse had received in 1680. This was a complicated litigation, and obviously fascinated the legal-minded Lauder of Fountainhall who dwells on it at some length in his *Decisions*. Claverhouse eventually won the case, and presumably received the money. The other case, before the Criminal Court in Edinburgh on 10th June, had been brought against him by Fotheringhame of Powrie, who alleged that Claverhouse 'had violently stopped his possession of some Assize fish due to him by the infestments in Broughty Castle of nine fish per boat for their liberty of anchoring there on the rocks in storms'. Claverhouse won this case by declaring that, as Constable, he had allowed the fishers to refuse him payment. Not only did Powrie lose the case, he was now obliged to produce his Charters before an Inquiry to discover why he had ever had the right of taking nine fish per boat in the first place!

The case over, Claverhouse travelled south to London on 27th June 1687 with his wife and Balcarres. They remained in the south till late November. They visited the fashionable town of Bath where his wife wrote to her brother, Lord John Cochrane. The letter is not dated, but was presumably written sometime in the early Autumn. This letter is the subject of some controversy, since the original seems not to exist. For those interested in such minutiae, I outline the controversy in the Appendix of the Letters collection. Meanwhile, I include the letter extract from Katherine Parker's book, whose orthography has been modernised:

Dear Brother,

I received yours at the Bath three or four days before we come
from thence. It is the first that I had from you since we come
from Scotland. I should have been very impatient till I heard
from you had I not heard from our mother of your Lady's
being safely delivered of a son. I am glad that she does prove
so fine a nurse, and shall wish for the continuance of it.

As for our two pictures [portraits], Claverhouse has sat to
his with the best that was in England [Sir Godfrey Kneller –
the 'Glamis Portrait'], so that he is not to sit at this time, and
for mine, if I sit, you should have one, but I am resolved [not]
to sit for fear it should keep us too long here.

After two more paragraphs, the letter ends on a postscript:
'Claverhouse gives his humble service to you, and we both
to your Lady.' This is the seventeenth-century equivalent of
the holiday postcard – and presents a fascinating glimpse
of another side of Claverhouse – the picture of the man in
domestic bliss, able to relax and enjoy the company of his
loving wife.[70]

Upon his return to Scotland he was again in the courts, this
time as a prosecution witness against James Renwick, the
author of *The Apologetic Declaration* of 1684. Renwick, who
had just turned twenty, was an educated and inspiring leader,
and at the conclusion of his trial, went to his inevitable death
nobly and with great dignity, the last of the Covenanting
martyrs.

Several days earlier, King James had issued his list of nominees for Dundee Council, as he had in September and in
December the previous year, which being ignored, Claverhouse was now appointed Provost in an attempt to bring the
burgh to heel. The King's letter of the 5th refers to making
him 'absolute there'. The Earl of Balcarres was delegated
to instal Claverhouse as Provost, and on 29th March 1688
he was duly installed. There are unfortunately no records
remaining that might reveal the citizens' response to this,
and the Council meetings of 29th and 31st March at which
he presided are a list of elections of the new Bailies and
Magistrates. It seems that many of the existing Councillors

were re-elected for different duties, although several new names were added. Claverhouse seized the opportunity to introduce some new municipal statutes, mostly concerning rebellion and conspiracy.[71]

Later that month, much to his relief, the King finally began to recognise the danger of the situation and took stock of the widespread rumours of imminent invasion from Holland. He issued a Proclamation to the Privy Council, as he had already done in the English Parliament, calling home all Scottish soldiers and seamen, especially those in the service of the Dutch. There seems to have been a mixed response to this but at least some of the mercenaries did return. Some, like Hugh Mackay of Scourie and Sir James Dalrymple, 1st Viscount Stair, remained in Dutch service.

Drummond of Perth returned from London on 15th May with letters from the King. One of these was a warrant to reduce the size of Claverhouse's company from 120 to 50, to ease the financial burden on the city of Edinburgh. The city was becoming a haven for agitators and rabble-rousers released by the promise of toleration, and people of all creeds and denominations crowded into the capital in an attempt to influence the proceedings of Parliament. There had already been one major riot – and the King's answer was to reduce the standing army. No doubt Claverhouse felt disquiet at this measure which was so contrary to James' personal policy of expanding the army. Possibly he knew that the Earl of Melfort's influence was behind this and other ill-advised schemes.

Melfort is described in a later letter by the Italian Ambassador who knew him well as 'not yet accused of anything touching his loyalty, but it is certain that he was always too much attached to his own private interest'. Melfort's influence was so insidious that the King's closest supporters, to a man, soon demanded his replacement, and many felt that Melfort could not survive such unanimous opposition. The Earl of Balcarres in his *Memoirs* indicates that he felt he would be the one to replace him, and comments critically upon Melfort's employing James Stewart (of Goodtrees) in drawing up all the public papers, 'who was looked upon as an inveterate enemy to the established government, both in Church and State'. Then there was Melfort's fantastic scheme to require all those with a King's commission – which meant most of those in public office – to surrender their commissions and buy new ones from Melfort for £7 20s. 'This was thought hard, even by the loyalest of your subjects, to be paying for remissions for obeying your commands . . . a great many gave their sentiments very freely against it', Balcarres relates. The King when he heard about it dismissed the scheme, but 'it gave such bad impressions of those [who] were the contrivers of it . . . the advisers, who to the prejudice of your interest and dishonour of your servants, would have reaped a profit from it', Balcarres wrote.[72]

Another letter from James' Court allowed the Catholics to retain the revenues of Trinity Chapel in Aberdeen. Shortly after this, Lauder of Fountainhall notes that 'the rules of the Popish College in the Abbey were printed inviting all children to be educated there gratis'; he comments disgustedly: 'as Mountebanks promise great things with their programmes.'[73]

A further Indulgence was read out in Council on 15th May, but no vote was held on it. A week later, another of James' pet projects for improvement of trade was put forward, and a Council was elected for 'advancement of Trade and Manufacture'.[74] Since some of the Councillors were slow in volunteering to serve on this committee, Claverhouse put his own name forward, although the body does not appear to have done anything, or held any meetings. It is apparent that at this stage most Scottish politicians were willing to sign or say anything to keep the King happy, and most were already looking over their shoulders to Holland, and the invasion which now seemed inevitable. A number were involved in correspondence with the Prince of Orange by this time.

On 14th June a Thanksgiving was ordered for the birth of a son to James and Mary, but this was marred by the number of published tracts and obscene cartoons which appeared, most of them emanating from Holland, sanctioned – although he denied it – by William of Orange and his wife Mary, James' own daughter. Foul slanders that the newly-born Prince of Wales was the son of a herb-woman and had been smuggled into the Palace at dead of night in a warming pan were drawn out as cartoons on handbills, and given out freely in the London streets. There were jokes too about Queen Mary being the daughter of the Pope. When William of Orange had married James' eldest daughter, one of the things uppermost in his mind had been that one day he would gain the throne of England. Legally, of course, he could never be more than Prince Consort. But now that a son and heir had been born to James, his slender chances of legitimate succession were destroyed, and there was the prospect of a continuous dynasty of Catholic Stuarts. Once William received corroboration that the child was healthy, he resolved to attain the throne by violent means. He had nothing to lose. He assembled a large army, and built up his armaments, at the same time writing long letters to James assuring him of his loyal friendship, and encouraging his wife to do the same. The army he assembled for the supposed purpose of freeing the English and Scottish Protestants from the Catholic yoke was composed almost entirely of Catholic mercenaries! In the *Memoirs* of Lord Ailesbury, a Protestant friend of the King, it is noted that when the King went to church in Rochester after the invasion fleet had landed, some Dutch Guards came in to hear Mass. The King wryly remarked to their Colonel that while not 1000 in every 180,000 were Catholics in the English army, the invading army, brought in professedly to vindicate Protestant liberties, was two-thirds of it composed of Catholics.[75]

William assembled a vast fleet of fifty men-of-war and 500 transport ships for the invasion. Matters reached such a head during the summer months that the Privy Council was suspended. The last business Claverhouse heard discussed was in a Committee he had been elected onto that was examining the case between Lord Duffus and the late Ross of Kindeace. This dragged on in a desultory manner for two weeks and was finally postponed indefinitely. There was a long hot lull during which nothing at all could be done except to wait for news. Claverhouse returned to Dudhope where he found a letter, dated 20th July, waiting for him from a John Coutts of Montrose. This letter refers to a visit Claverhouse had made to a man called John Walker – presumably in, or near, Montrose burgh. Who or what John Walker was, or why he was unfit 'to be sett at liberty unless hey haed been manacled for a tym', can only be guessed at. Was he a murderer, or perhaps suffering from some form of mental illness?

> I account it wass both my honour and hapines that yow came to this place to take notice of John Walker his humor and condition, and as at that tyme I found your honour haed werrey just apprehensions of his unfittness to be sett at liberty unles hey haed been manacled for a tym untill it should be found to quhat dispositiones his releasment from prison wold bring him, so I was most willing to refeir myself solly to your honours determination, being convinced by all dutiful sense of your honours just inclinations not only towards my family but for securitie of other neighbours. I thought my self not a littill unfortunat that your honour wass not at Counsell when thos gentelmen the scheriff deputt and the Laird of Dunn thair report concerning that man was called for, I ame persuaded their wass non that could give a more just and distinct accompt of his cais then your Honour, and as I was bound to your freindly expresions to me when you wass hier, so I doe in all humilitie intreat yow wold honor me with the continwanc of your favor and friendschip in justice.[76]

The Privy Council met on 13th September and Claverhouse received a warrant for '200 horse and carabines and 200 hulster pistols from Holland(!) for his regiment of horse'. On 1st October he was further warranted for '160 of the best carrabines'. On that day, the Privy Council issued an order that 'servants travelling must have passes from their master.

The text of Fountainhall's *Decisions* stops abruptly here, and there are no further reports until 1692. There is an explanatory paragraph: 'N.B. We may count it a surcease of justice from August 1688 to the 1st of November '89 for albeit the Session sat during November '88, yet by the Prince of Orange's arrival then in England, no business was done, save on a few bills.'

The reports of the November Session are not available, beyond what occurs in the manuscript of some members who attended the meeting.

The Scottish army was already mustered on the borders in advance of the King's letter of instructions. This was made clear in a letter from General Douglas to his father, Queensberry, written from Moffat on 7th October: 'Yesternight I came here with difficulty enough, considering the badness of the weather. I'm not resolved to stir until I see the ammunition, which some say will be here this night. I met with an express from Carlisle, with the King's orders that I should march to Preston, and there remain till further orders . . .' The letter has a postscript: 'I'm much obliged to you for the concern your Grace has in me; but as to what can happen to me through people's malice, I'm very indifferent of it. No honest man can guard against villainous attempts.' This may be a reference to the growing rumours in Scotland that General Douglas was secretly in the pay of William of Orange. This was not actually the case, though Douglas, of all the Scottish leaders, changed sides perhaps the most often; five times within nine months.[77]

Just after Claverhouse's fortieth birthday the Revolution began. On 6th October the militia of all the Shires and Burghs were called out and the standing army was ordered to rendezvous in Salisbury. The letter from the King was advised by Melfort's assistant, James Stewart of Goodtrees, a man who had been sentenced to death for participating in the Argyll Rising, and who was a notorious plotter and schemer. 'The order', according to Balcarres, 'was positive and short . . . and written upon the back of a plate during a drunken debauch.' It was received in Scotland on the 10th, and the Scots appear to have considered action independent of the King, but were angrily commanded to obey by Melfort, acting largely on his own initiative.

It was a widely-believed rumour that William would attempt to land at Torbay in the south-west of England, although at this stage few could envisage the invasion proving successful. In the face of invasion by foreign mercenaries, the religious differences of the English would take second place to national unity. William could succeed only if there were wholesale defections of leading politicians and the military, and as yet there had been no sign of this. James had ample time to organise his armies and gather all his subjects under his banner.

The King was ill-prepared for the struggle, however. He was suffering from a form of apoplexy with persistent haemorrhaging that left him exhausted and depressed. The apothecaries had no idea how to treat the illness except by applying leeches to draw off vast quantities of blood, which left him even weaker. He was also depressed at the prospect of permanent separation from his daughter Mary – who had been his favourite – and whose company he was sorely missing. Instead of trusting himself to the hands of his own large and efficient army, he ordered the 3763 men of the Scots army south. The Privy Council regretted this move, which left Scotland entirely unprotected – and made little or no difference to the situation in England.

Balcarres noted that 'as soon as your Majesty sent orders that the army should . . . lie in readiness to march into England, all the discontented in the nation thought they had met with their just time, believing your affairs must be in a miserable condition in England when you was obliged to bring up so inconsiderable a force, and by that to leave a whole nation exposed to your enemies'.[8]

Letters sent to Queensberry from General Douglas track the movements of the Scottish army, and the conflicting orders it received:

Aleson Bank, 10th October

May it please your Grace: – I'm now in haste going from this place, having just got orders to send all the horse and dragoons to York, which accordingly I do by Major-General Grahame. I march myself with the foot there, as Dumbarton writes to me; but the King's letter mentions not that I go any further than Preston. How to reconcile the orders I know not; but be as it will, I shall do my best; though I never did see this practised before, to send away all the horse, and leave two regiments of foot open to the insults of foreigners, who are expected to land horse and dragoons . . .

Penrith, 11th October

. . . This morning I sent Major-General Grahame with the horse to York . . . He will be there speedily . . . Some people would make me believe that Major-General MacKartie joins me about Preston with a considerable force. But . . . I do not much credit it. However, if my Lochaber party come to me in time, I will be able to deal with the Dutch, if they overpower me not extremely by their number.

A note written by Claverhouse to William Blathwayt, Secretary at War, on 10th October, from Dudhope, tersely states: 'I have received the ordor for marching those troops under my comand to London which I shall doe with all convenient dilligence.'[79] Claverhouse's troopers arrived in London nearly two weeks before the infantry arrived, and quartered in Westminster, Tower Hamlets and the Minories to await the rest of the army. On the 5th, William of Orange had landed, as expected, at Brixham in Devon.

Claverhouse and Douglas had a meeting with the King on 9th November. Whitehall was in an uproar of comings and goings in preparation for the march to Salisbury. The King had received a letter from William with the preposterous claim that he was merely on a visit to his father-in-law, and had been forced to bring a large force with him because of the danger of crossing the Channel while at war with the French. James had hoped that his prized navy would scatter the invasion fleet during the crossing – but a storm had obscured the Dutch ships from sight. He now had no excuses for refraining from all-out defensive procedures.

Directly after the meeting the Scots army marched west to Salisbury, and arrived on 10th November. The camp was busy with rumours and rife with confusion and allegations of important defections. Two days after his arrival, Claverhouse was called back to London by a royal messenger. The King was by this time in the grip of illness, exacerbated by anxiety and stress. He was troubled by more than his health, however, for he must have begun to suspect that many of his command-ers and nobility did not have their hearts in the campaign. His suspicious nature was becoming more paranoid day by day. The reasons for his desire to see Claverhouse are uncer-tain; possibly he wanted to discuss the campaign with him in private, or simply to engage him in one of those lively conversations they had enjoyed during his stay in Scotland, to take his mind off the depressing affairs of State. Whatever the reason, at the end of the meeting, as Claverhouse was about to take his leave, the King presented him quite casually with a rolled parchment which had the Royal Seal attached to it. Only outside the King's chamber did Claverhouse realise that it was a Charter, dated that day, 12th November, that made him a Peer of the Realm with the title of Lord Graham of Claverhouse, Viscount of Dundee:

> For the many good and eminent Services rendered both to His Majesty and his dearest Royall Brother King Charles II (of ever blessed memory) by his right trusty and well-beloved Councellor Major-General John Grahame of Claverhouse in the severall offices and Stationes of publick Trust as well civill as military in which he has been employed for many years past; Together with his constant loyalty and firm adherence (upon all occasions) to the true interests of the Crown.[80]

The King held a Council of War at Andover on 24th Novem-ber. He informed the meeting that there had been a skirmish outside Winchester, and two high-ranking officers of the army, Lord Cornbury and Lieutenant-Colonel Langton, had defected with some of their regiments to William of Orange. James had trusted both men and the meeting was horrified to hear of defections so close to the King. All the officers present voiced loud condemnation of the defectors, and vowed their own loyal support for the King. Next day, however, it was discovered that a great many more defections had occurred, including some of those loudest in their protestations of sup-port the previous evening. Scots such as Lord Drumlanrig, Queensberry's eldest son, General Douglas, William, Earl of Annandale, and Lord Ross had sneaked away in the middle of the night. And there were mightier defectors: the Duke of

Ormonde, Lord Clarendon, Colonel Kirke and Lord Churchill (later to become the Duke of Marlborough). Even the King's other daughter, Anne, and her husband Prince George of Denmark had deserted. There is a story that, hearing of each new desertion over dinner, George of Denmark continually exclaimed 'Est-il possible?' as each name was mentioned. When the King heard of his own desertion, he is reported to have exclaimed: 'What? Has Est-il possible gone too?'

The result of the defections meant that Claverhouse, Viscount Dundee, awoke to find himself in command of the remnant of the Scottish army, with the Earl of Dumbarton who also remained, and few other officers of any significant rank. Even now, James possessed the military capability to drive the Dutch with their English and Scottish defectors back into the sea, but, incredibly, he ordered the armies to disband and returned forthwith to London leaving utter confusion at Salisbury.

The situation in Scotland was also deteriorating. The Chancellor, Drummond of Perth, had taken the disastrous step of ordering the Scottish militia to stand down on 16th October: 'give these gentlemen, who so chearfully convened in his Majestie's service, their hearty thanks, and to allowe them to returne home . . .' He had then fled from Edinburgh and attempted to sail from Burntisland to France. He was overtaken by an armed boat, and brought back to the 'common Tolbooth' at Kirkcaldy, from where he wrote a plaintive letter to the Marquis of Atholl: 'My Lord – I was retiring from Brittain, never to have seen it more, when the people of Kirkcaldy pursued me and took me. I entreate yr Lordship to call the Council, and sett me at liberty . . .'[81]

Perth was shortly afterwards removed to Stirling Castle, where he remained in custody for five years.

The Duke of Hamilton was dropping broad hints that he was considering transferring his support to William, and as later events proved, he had at this time already done so. Lord Breadalbane had declared his support for William, and Viscount Tarbat seemed about to join him. The situation in Scotland was highly volatile:

> The rabble, having nothing to resist them, entered Holyrood House, pulled down all they could find in the private chapel, demolished all things within the Abbey church . . . and plundered the house the Jesuits had lived in . . . they opened the Chancellors cellars . . . and made themselves as drunk with wine as before they had been with zeal. Two or three days rambled about the town, and plundered the Roman Catholics, who were very few. Some of their Ladies they treated with the utmost barbarity, nor did the Council anything to hinder these disorders. Those who hated such barbarities wanted power, and those who had, rather augmented than diminished them.[82]

The situation was described by another witness, Sir George Lockhart, Lord President of the Council: 'The mob, instigated by the Saints, had driven away the Privy Council, and made the Lord Chancellor a prisoner'. A third version of events is found in *The Lives of The MacKenzies* – Viscount Tarbat had formed an alliance with the Marquis of Atholl and Sir John Dalrymple. The plotters thought it advisable to disband the forces which kept order, seeing that the Prince of Orange had already made plain his views on standing armies. Perth naively fell for their proposal and the militia were dismissed. The cabal, who were now joined by the Earl of Breadalbane, thought that they could control the mob and use it for their own ends. The mob, however, knew otherwise and broke into their homes, forcing them, on threat of instant death, to sign a warrant authorising them to sack Holyrood House. The designs of the cabal did not even win the approval of the Prince of Orange, which had been the main aim.[83]

At Salisbury, the section of the Scottish army which had not defected, re-assembled and marched to new positions at Reading and Watford to await orders. The King had disappeared, and it was rumoured he was about to sail, or had already sailed, to France. When this rumour reached the Scottish army, Dundee uncharacteristically burst into tears – according to the wildly enthusiastic and unreliable *Memoirs of Captain Creighton* – dictated by Creighton, Dundee's orderly since 1678, to Jonathan Swift many years later. It would seem highly unlikely that he would have reacted in such a fashion under any circumstances.[84]

The Earl of Balcarres had been sent from Edinburgh on 4th December to meet with Claverhouse. His precise orders were 'to attend his sacred Majestie and to receive his royall commands at this juncture'.[85] He met Claverhouse at Watford, and was astounded to hear of recent events. They decided to attempt to persuade the King to make a stand before it was too late, and rode together in haste to London, leaving the regiment of Royal Horse intact and armed at Watford. They were convinced that even at this late stage the situation could be saved and felt sure the King had been wrongly advised. Before they left Watford, a note arrived for Claverhouse, delivered by a Dutch messenger, in which Claverhouse was guaranteed safe conduct if he would lay down his arms and order his troop to stand down. He barely glanced at the note before mounting his horse. Dundee and Balcarres attended a Privy Council meeting in the London house of the Duke of Hamilton, which ended in confusion and bitter argument. The Duke had decided to support William, but on learning that the King had not sailed to France and had in fact returned to Whitehall, he sent a note to Dundee and 'desyred that all might be forgot'.[86]

Meanwhile the Scottish Convention assembled under the Presidency of the Marquis of Atholl who proposed that an address be sent to the Prince of Orange, thanking him for his promise to free them from Popery, and offering their service. In the face of considerable opposition this motion was defeated, but the Assembly did vote to send him a short letter, in general terms, which was taken by Lord Glamis to the Prince. This letter did not receive a warm welcome, the Prince having been assured of something more effusively subservient.

On 7th December, the King, once again in the grip of panic, ordered his armies to disband, and again fled from London. An observer noted: 'I never saw a more disconsolate house than Whitehall, all pulling and destroying, some one thing and some another, and the souldiers stand looking one at another with their hands in their pocketts without a head or commander.'[87] Since there were at this time some 2000 rooms in Whitehall, the confusion can be easily imagined. But on the 16th, the King returned to Whitehall and was welcomed 'with all the usual demonstrations of loyalty, bonfires, bellringing, the people shouting "God Bless Your Majesty!"'[88]

Dundee and the Earl of Balcarres managed to gain entry to the King's bedroom early in the morning of the 17th. The meeting is described by Balcarres.

'He [the King] said it was a fine day, he would take a walk. None attended him but Colin [Balcarres] and Lord Dundee ... When he was in the Mall, he stopped and looked at them and asked how they came to be with him, when all the world had forsaken him, and gone to the Prince of Orange? Colin said their fidelity to so good a master would ever be the same, they had nothing to do with the Prince of Orange. Lord Dundee made the strongest professions of duty.'

'Will you two, as Gentlemen, say you have still attachment to me?'

'Sir, we do'.

'Will you give me your hands upon it, as men of honour?'

The three men solemnly shook hands. The King spoke after a minute's silence:

'Well, I see you are the men I always took you to be; you shall know all my intentions, I can no longer remain here but as a cypher, or be a prisoner to the Prince of Orange, and you know there is but a small distance between the prisons and the graves of Kings. Therefor, I go for France immediately; when there, you shall have my instructions. You, Lord Balcarres, shall have a commission to manage my civil affairs, and you, Lord Dundee, to command my troops in Scotland.'

And then the King walked away from them down the tree-lined avenue of the Mall, a disconsolate, stooped figure followed by a single lean greyhound.[89]

Later that day, the Prince of Orange arrived in London and the King was obliged to leave Whitehall for the coast. This was exactly what Orange wanted. The last thing he wanted was a confrontation with the King. Far better if James left his Kingdom and his Crown of his own accord.

Most commentators relate that the King left directly for France but there is a recurring suggestion of a further meeting between Dundee and James. Before the King reached the coast it is said that he stopped at Rochester, and Dundee and the Earl of Dumbarton, and Major James Middleton, an experienced soldier, visited him there. Quite how or why this meeting should have occurred when Dundee and Balcarres had already expressed their sentiments at Whitehall seems unlikely and its only authority seems to be a servant attending the King, who related the tale to the author of *Carte's Memorandum Book*.[90]

The servant saw that the fire in the room needed to be put to rights and renewed, but the King was so deserted that there was not a single servant in the vicinity. The Earl of Middleton went out to look for one – and found only his own servant, who duly came in to tend the fire. This servant overheard the discussion in progress. Lord Dundee was speaking: 'Sir, the question is, whether you shall stay in England or go to France? My opinion is, you should stay in England. Make your stand here, and summon your subjects to your allegiance. 'Tis true, your army is disbanded by your own authority; but though disbanded, not so dispersed but, if you will give me your commission, I will undertake to get ten thousand of them together, and march through all England with your standard at their head, and drive all the Dutch before you.' The King said he believed it might be done; but it would cause a civil war, and he would not do so much mischief to the English nation, which he loved, and they would come to their senses again.

Middleton thereupon said that since his Majesty rejected the party of force, he should stay in the Kingdom at any rate, though the remotest quarter. For though his going abroad might put them into a confusion for some time, it would not be more than a six-week affair, by which time a new Government would be settled, and he would be ruined.

Unfortunately, the servant having completed his task, left the room and heard no more of the discussion. Whether this unlikely meeting took place, what is known to be fact is that the King sailed for France on the 23rd.

Dundee and Balcarres remained in London for some weeks and during this period Balcarres was interviewed by William of Orange. He claimed to have refused to support him and to be grudgingly dismissed with a warning to 'beware how he behaved'. This loyalty to James is rather contradicted by the fact that he attempted to obtain an English peerage a month later. Dundee does not appear to have been interviewed, although, in the light of William's apparent willingness for reconciliation with all, he sent a note to William advising him that 'unless he were forced to it he would live quietly' – the height of ambiguity, but William seems to have chosen to overlook this. Dundee, was, with Balcarres, MacKenzie, Tarbat and Queensberry, one of five politicians who, William's supporters demanded, should be permanently banned from office.

The situation for Dundee and Balcarres was now highly dangerous. Neither had publicly renounced his support for the King – and there was the small matter of the Royal Regiment of Horse at Watford – still in arms. There is little doubt that up to the point of the King's departure, Dundee had not considered any course other than continuing support for the King. He arranged for a cleric Gilbert Burnet, who was married to his wife's aunt, and whose history of the times is an important source, to visit William 'to know what security he might expect if he should go and live in Scotland without owning the Government'. Back came the reply that 'if he would live peacably and at home he [William] would protect him'.[91]

Since there was now nothing that could be done for the King's cause, Claverhouse took the precaution of disbanding his regiment and sent them home in good order, keeping fifty troopers with him to escort himself and Balcarres back to Scotland in due course in early February. The Scots Dragoons and Lord Dumbarton's regiment who had attempted to return to Scotland *en masse*, had been forced to surrender due to the hostility of the country people. Dundee and Balcarres, by pretending to keep the peace, did not suffer such ignominy, and Dundee, escorted by his scarlet-clad troop, returned safely to Dudhope Castle.

4

Shades of Montrose

By the time Viscount Dundee returned to Dudhope, his wife was well advanced in pregnancy – into her eighth month. The State affairs of Scotland might be going badly, but there were compensations in the success he had made of his private life. As a man with a developed sense of family loyalty, he was more than normally pleased about the prospect of becoming a father himself. He had dynastic aspirations for the Grahams, and should the child by some happy chance be a boy, he would in time become the 2nd Viscount – and all that he had achieved would be consolidated and preserved for future generations. Perhaps now was the time to withdraw from public life; to turn his back on the intrigues and the politicking. Certainly the child would need a father's hand. Then, too, he enjoyed being about the place; strolling in the orchards, or in the well-laid-out gardens. How far away seemed the turmoil and anxiety of Whitehall or Watford.

Dudhope Castle was erected in 1450 on the site of a more ancient fortalice, and was extensively renovated in 1600 by his predecessor, the Earl of Lauderdale. One of the windows still bears this date carved into the lintel. The Castle had housed royalty in 1617, when James VI stayed for a night during his return visit to Scotland. A clock tower and belfry give Dudhope its characteristic appearance: a fortified house rather than a castle proper. The lands adjoined the Mains estate of the Grahams of Fintry and the estates of the Grahams of Duntrune. The estates of Glen Ogilvie came down to the suburb of Bonnethill, so that Dundee's estates extended from the Tay ten miles north into the Sidlaws.

He now enjoyed a period of respite and relaxation at Dudhope with his heavily pregnant wife. He had spent little enough time with her in their four years of marriage. His family life must have been compensation for him: a pretty wife, a child on the way and a spacious home, worthy of his illustrious name, in which to relax. After their initial meeting in Edinburgh, he had met Jean Cochrane at her father's house near Paisley, a slip of a girl then with long red hair and an honest freckled face.

He had ridden out there one day in April 1684 when he was still a Colonel and plain John Graham of Claverhouse, to question the elderly Earl of Dundonald on the whereabouts of some Covenanting fugitives. The family had strong Presbyterian connections, and the old Earl was under threat of prosecution for harbouring fugitives on his lands. Both his sons had been involved with the Covenant – one had fled to Holland after participating in the Rye House Plot to assassinate the King in 1683 and had a price on his head, and his daughter-in-law, Lady Catherine, Jean's mother, was widely-known to be a rabid Covenanter.

Claverhouse had found the company of the old Earl congenial – he was no rebel – and had been re-introduced to Lady Jean Cochrane, his grandchild, then twenty-two, whose unaffected naturalness quite made him forget the purpose of his visit. It was only after leaving that he realised he had not cross-examined the Lady Catherine, and so would have to make a return journey. In fact, he returned many times to the Cochrane mansion, and his visits began to assume an altogether different purpose, as he found himself more often alone in the company of Lady Jean than his business might have called for. He underwent an entirely new experience during two spring months; he fell head-over-heels in love, and very soon he found that he could no longer pretend otherwise. He was smitten – for once his head was overruled by his heart. It was a crazy match; a match that might destroy his career, but such was the strength of his feelings that he felt compelled to take the chance. Their relationship grew almost in spite of his political differences with her family. This was so different from his wooing of Helen Graham, which had consisted almost entirely of long business letters and discussions of the gains and losses of a marriage contract. The two women were greatly different too; Helen Graham had been the sophisticated Court lady, whereas Jean Cochrane preferred outdoor sports and healthy country pursuits.

The Earl of Dundonald welcomed the match. He had loyally served the Crown all his life, but the actions of his family were threatening his ruin. If he died with his son a declared rebel, the largest part of his estates would revert to the Crown. By marrying his grandchildren to those who, like Claverhouse, were above suspicion, he could save his inheritance.

Claverhouse took the precaution however of sounding out some of his friends and allies on the match. The affair had attracted a great deal of adverse comment, and he sought reassurance from Queensberry on 19th May 1684: '. . . the neu alleya that I am lyk to mak is not unusfull to me in the Shyr of Air and Ranfrou. They have the guying (guiding) of those shyrs and they doe strenthen my hands in the King's service . . . For my owen pairt,' he adds, 'I look on myself as a cleanger. I may cur(e) people guilty of that plague of presbytery be conversing with them, but can not be infected, and I see very little of that amongst those persons but may be easily rubed of[f]. And for the young ladie herself, I shall answer for her. Had she been right principled she would never in dispyt of her mother and relations made choyse of a persecutor, as they call me.' He ends the letter with a plea to defend him against malicious gossip. In the second letter to Queensberry later the same day, he complains that the Duke of Hamilton is refusing to allow the match until both the King and Duke of York agree to it. He clearly regards Hamilton's actions as hypocrisy: 'The Deuk knows what it is to have sons and nephews that follou not advice.' This was a barbed remark, since at the same time Lord Cochrane, Jean's brother, was actually seeking the hand of Lady Susannah,

Hamilton's daughter! He then takes up Dundonald's case: 'nobody offered to medle with him till they heared I was lyk to be concerned in him.' Dundonald, he feels, is clearly being singled out as a rebel purely to 'get at' himself. He continues in full flow: Dundonald should have favour shown to him 'considering his aidge and the imployments he has had'. He has cases prepared against many others whom he feels have been let off more lightly than Dundonald. 'I can give lists', he declares, 'and prove them, of persons ten times guiltier than Dindonald and able to pay . . . lait not my enimys misrepresent me . . . it is not in the pouer of love, nor any other folly, to alter my loyalty.'[92]

The marriage ceremony was held in the Cochrane mansion at Paisley. This was a considered move to present an outward show of family unity, and prevent embarrassing religious differences becoming obvious during the ceremony. The bride's mother, Lady Catherine Kennedy, dourly refused to attend, and did not sign the marriage contract, and Jean's father was dead. Her brother John, and the grandparents, William, Earl of Dundonald, and his wife Euphane Scott, the Countess of Dundonald, and William Cochrane of Paisley and Ochiltree, son of the fugitive Sir John, signed the contract from her side of the family, and Lord Ross and Lord Montgomery and Colin (younger brother of George) MacKenzie were witnesses for Claverhouse. The marriage contract contained a clause for the event of Claverhouse's early demise without children, in which case Lady Jean would inherit the entire estate. The list of properties ascribed to the bridegroom seems impressive at a glance: besides the Glen Ogilvie estate, he owned Claypotts and lands, Dudhope, the lands of Claverhouse, Ballargus, Myreton, Monifieth, Broughton [Broughty Ferry], Pokello, Polcambock, Tealing, Balgray, Sheilhill, Ballumbie, Warieston Creig – all in Angus, and Polgavie in Perthshire.

The displeasure of others made itself felt during the ceremony. General Dalyell, the crusty Scottish Commander-in-Chief, expressed his by deliberately sending orders to Claverhouse forcing him to leave his bride minutes after the service and ride the Blacklock Moors for two days. No sooner had he returned to Jean than he was again called out two hours later.

Viscount Dundee could smile now at these recollections. It was pleasant to know that he had made the right decision. His career had not been damaged. He had had four and a half years of marriage – and shortly would be a father.

Although he was pleased to be back at Dudhope for some peace and quiet, there were duties to perform. He must attend meetings of the Town Council, and sit in the Provost's chair. He had not in fact attended the Council since 4th September 1688, and he was aware that some of the Magistrates had made an attempt to have him replaced because of his non-attendance, presenting a petition of sorts to the Council meeting on 17th January, taking advantage of the political turmoil in the country.

The Dundee Town Council Book records that Viscount Dundee sat as Provost at meetings on 24th and 27th February. On the 27th, there was a protracted debate on the national situation and how the town should act. Last business transacted on that day was a vote on an oath of loyalty (presumably to King James) – which was carried 'except the convenor Wedderburn'; a vote of 12 to 1. Wedderburn was a leading Dundee merchant whose family pioneered the Baltic trade routes. The history of the Wedderburn family is almost the history of the burgh itself. The business then would seem to have been interrupted following the vote, and there is not even a full stop. The remainder of the page, and three-quarters of the next, is blank. The next recorded minutes are for Saturday 20th April – a considerable gap – made more significant by the knowledge that paper was always in short supply, and the Council Book, like all official registers, normally utilised every millimetre of available space. On the 20th of April James Fletcher has resumed the Provost's chair and the Council had now decided to support William of Orange.

Towards the end of February, it was clear that the national crisis was deepening, and that Viscount Dundee did not have the patience to ignore it. He would have to intervene. He had received several letters urging him to take a public position and give a lead to those still loyal to the King. He was already being regarded as the only man who could provide the necessary leadership for the loyal party. It was no longer possible for him to remain at home and ignore the situation.

Viscount Dundee rode to Edinburgh on 13th March 1689, filled with apprehension, and not just for the state of the Government, or what was to happen in Edinburgh – his fears were also for his wife. He was forty and desperately wanted a son to continue his line – he wanted to be with Jean at this time – and certainly had little desire to be on the Edinburgh road. Even worse, he was riding to attend a Convention that had been called by the illegal authority of William of Orange. Circular letters had been sent to 'The Lords of the Clergie And Nobility And To The Sheriffe Clerks For The Severall Shyres And To The Toune Clerks For The Royall Burghes'.

The English Parliament had already accepted William of Orange as joint sovereign with his wife, Mary Stuart, and the Convention had been called to see whether Scotland would follow suit or remain loyal to the exiled King James. The issue was far from decided, and few politicians had fixed opinions that could not be swayed by signs that they were in a minority. Most were attending the Convention purely to see what was going to happen and because they dared not stay at home lest they were proclaimed traitors. Dundee would have given a lot to be able to absent himself, but he knew that could not be. He had responsibilities to his King, but could not have been aware of just how large a part he was to play in the drama that was to unfold.

On arrival in Edinburgh, he met up with the 'Gentlemen officers' of his troop of dragoons, whom he had sent from Watford to find private lodgings in the town. They had exchanged their uniforms for civilian wear, but Dundee had no intention of disbanding them entirely until he should see how things went at the Convention.

He found the capital town swarming with armed men from the disbanded regiments and mobs of Presbyterian supporters from the South-West, including at least a thousand armed Cameronians. It was barely safe to walk the streets, and he quickly became aware that, for him especially, Edinburgh was highly dangerous. Among the rabble were Covenanters he had himself arrested, who had since been pardoned. He received angry glances from the crowds in the streets, and occasionally was jeered from the doorways of taverns. Yet no-one dared to approach him face-to-face.

The Convention of the Three Estates began at 10 a.m. on 14th March in the Great Hall of Parliament House. This majestic building still stands beside the National Library, but due to rather insensitive remodelling by Sir Robert Reid in 1824 retains barely a hint of its original opulence. Over the main entrance of the building two lifesize figures represented Mercy and Truth, and supported the Scottish Arms between them. Mercy carried a crown close to her heart, the seat of loving kindness, and Truth held a pair of gilded metal scales but, unlike other statues of justice, no sword of execution. With these figures was the inscription: 'Stant his Felicia Regna' – 'These virtues make Kingdoms happy.'

The Great Hall, whose lofty, magnificent ceiling was finished in hammer-beamed Scots and Baltic oak, is fully 122 feet long with a span of 43 feet. It was finally completed in 1640 and has survived intact. The walls were lined with green baize cloth and the interior lit by beautiful stained-glass windows.

The Earl Marischal presided at the table in the middle of the hall where the jewels of the 'Honours Thrie' winked in the muted sunlight. Raised on a dais was the elevated throne, adorned by a canopy of colourful velvet with the Royal Arms. It was a magnificent building, with a dignity entirely proper to the ancient Kingdom of Scotland.

The members of the Three Estates filed into the Great Hall, and when all were in their places, the scarlet-coated heralds blew a fanfare, which was followed by the entry of the Macer, who duly proclaimed the authority of the Convention. In this unique case, this was the letter from William of Orange. Then the Bishop of Edinburgh, Alexander Rose, mounted the steps of the pulpit at the far end of the hall, and led the assembly in prayer, asking God 'to have compassion on King

James – and to restore him'! It must have seemed confusing to many, that Parliament was convened by the authority of one King, so that prayers could be offered for the restoration of another!

Then came the long and tedious calling of the Rolls, and for a long time all that could be heard above the incessant murmur of agitated conversation was the solemn intonation of the name of each representative by the Macer. It was a formidable list: in the First Estate there were forty-nine names: Lords Spiritual – the Archbishops of St Andrews and Glasgow, Bishops of Edinburgh, Dunkeld, Moray, Ross, Dunblane, the Western Isles and Orkney; Lords Temporal – the Duke of Hamilton, the Marquises of Douglas and Atholl, twenty-eight Earls, Viscounts Kenmure, Arbuthnot, Oxenford, Tarbat and Dundee. The Second Estate consisted of fifty Commissioners for the thirty-three Shires; and the Third Estate of fifty Commissioners for the Royal Burghs. This meant that six Commissioners for Shires and fifteen Commissioners for Burghs were absent on the first day.

Several objections, most of them trivial, were heard and recorded by the clerks of the Parliament. Most of these concerned the order of precedency, or importance, of the nobles. The Earl of Mar protested against the Earl of Argyll because his father's title was still attainted, but Argyll resisted this, and the matter was merely noted. He was allowed to remain, it later turned out, purely because he was a supporter of the Duke of Hamilton.

The Convention then turned to the first item on the agenda, the election of the President. Normally, the President was considered to be impartial, and was usually one of the greater nobles who was in a sense 'above politics', but due to the almost equal balance of both factions, whoever was elected President would clearly be in a very strong position to control the Parliament. It would also be an indication of which faction was the stronger. There was a very great deal of negotiation and compromise going on among the members, very few of whom wished to be isolated from the majority opinion; the great bulk would support the faction that looked the stronger.

Two candidates had emerged for their consideration: the aged Marquis of Atholl, and the Duke of Hamilton. Hamilton was the choice of the Whigs, or Williamites. Though known as a strong supporter of William, he had not, in point of fact, openly declared for William. Atholl was sponsored by the Tories, or the James' Party, although he too had made overtures to William soon after the Torbay landing. This was the reason he was chosen by the Tories as their candidate – they felt that he would attract the vote of the Whig moderates. Privately, Atholl was terrified of becoming singled out as a leader. His supporters, however, felt certain of victory. 'We thought ourselves by far the strongest party,' Balcarres records. When it came to the vote, however, Atholl panicked and he and twenty of his supporters defected to the other side; consequently Hamilton was elected by the narrow margin of fifteen votes.[93]

The Earl of Balcarres recorded: 'This unexpected accident made above twenty forsake us, finding we had lost a vote so material, and that the other party would have both forces and authority upon their side.'[94]

The jubilant Whigs pursued their advantage immediately, and proposed a Committee of Elections. There were fifteen places on this Committee, and every one of their candidates was successfully elected, so that they held twelve of the fifteen places, amid the growing confusion in the hall. Perceiving their superiority, the Whigs in short order got their nominees elected to a Committee for Securing The Peace, and to a delegation to oversee the town guard. A debate then ensued as to what could be done to give 'securitie to the meeting from insults and tumults'. Despite the almost unbearable clamour of mobs of armed men surrounding the Convention, and in all the main streets of the town, whose presence was impossible to ignore, the Convention made the incredible assessment that the main danger to the peace of the realm came from Edinburgh Castle with its Catholic Governor, the Duke of Gordon, and tiny, beleaguered garrison!

The reason for this soon became obvious. It was revealed that it was the Duke of Hamilton and his allies who had been responsible for the arrival in Edinburgh several days before the Convention of the large number of armed men. These had been dispersed in lodgings throughout the town – and had assembled a great rabble of disaffected persons whom they paid to conceal themselves in vaults and cellars of the town's tenements, or 'lands' as they were called. Hamilton and his allies did not consider the mob a threat because they were the mob's paymasters. They considered the Castle a threat because it was the only strongpoint in Britain, apart from the Bass Rock, that held out for King James, and because King William had ordered them to capture it.

The James faction put forward a motion 'that the Town being full of people, from all parts of the Kingdom, and who generally were armed; it was thought fit, for preventing Disorders, to command all persons from Town that were not Inhabitants nor belonged to the Members of the Meeting'. But the House, with its Williamite majority was of the opinion 'that the Castle must be first delivered'.[95]

Accordingly, after a noisy but short and rather one-sided debate,

> The meeting of the Estates of this Kingdom, considering that the Duke of Gordoun and some others of the popish religion under him intrusted with the Keeping of the Castle of Edinburgh are not qualified by the Law of this Kingdom [this was a reference to the old 'Test' Act, which Gordon had not taken], they grant warrand to the Earls of Loathian and Tweedale to repair immediately to the Castle of Edinburgh and to require him and others of his persuasion ther, In name of the Estates of this Kingdome to remove out of the said Castle within tuenty four houres after this Intimatione and to leave the Charge thereof to the nixt Commanding officer being a protestant. And he and they doeing the same, the Estates give assurance that he and they are and shall be Exonered and secured as to anything they have acted in that or any other statione contrair to Law as being papists.

The two Earls set off on foot to the Castle with generous terms of surrender for the Duke. The Earl of Tweeddale was a good friend of the Duke, which was the reason he had been chosen for the task.

George, 1st Duke of Gordon, is described in Andrew Lang's *Characters of The Nobility of Scotland* as 'certainly a very fine Gentleman, understands Conversation, and the *Belles Lettres*; is well-bred; made for the company of Ladies . . . very handsome, and taller than the ordinary size, thin, dresses well, but is somewhat finical, resembling the French . . . is a Roman-Catholic, because he was bred-so, but otherwise thinks very little of revealed religion . . . the Priests and New Converts in King James' reign, represented him to be a Libertine and a Fop, because he would not concur in their measures for ruling the Kingdom . . .'[96] He was forty-six years old and had performed military service with the French, and with William of Orange. He had risen from being Marquis of Huntly to his Dukedom on Claverhouse's recommendation in 1684, although he was unassuming and unambitious. One of his contemporaries described him as 'possessed of physical and moral courage though tending to vacillate in the face of a conflicting situation'. He had several times attempted to resign his post of Governor, and after the landing of the Prince of Orange became eager to negotiate a surrender. He did not relish the intrigues and conflicts of Scottish politics, and his personal desire was to retire to the Continent. He had been on the point of surrender in February, when Viscount Dundee and Balcarres, returning home via Edinburgh, came upon him supervising the removal of his personal belongings and furniture from the Castle. They managed to persuade him to remain until he had word from James.

Gordon received Lothian and Tweeddale gratefully, and discovering that he was considered the principal threat to the Convention, asked for time to consider the ultimatum. Tweeddale added his own personal appeals to common sense, and believed that Gordon was on the point of surrender. Since the Earls had not been given the power to concede any time to the Duke, they returned to the Convention.

The Convention considered Gordon's reply, and presumably moved by Tweeddale's conviction that Gordon was about to surrender, ordered him to make his reply by 10 a.m. the next morning. The Earls once more ascended the steep hill to communicate this to the Governor.

For the party loyal to James, the likelihood of the Castle's surrender was yet another bitter blow. They had to do something to restore the fortunes of their monarch. The Castle itself was of minor importance in a military sense, but as the last fortress in Britain to hold out against William of Orange, its political significance was greater. This had been recognised by King William, who had written a friendly letter to Gordon requesting his surrender. Dundee, Balcarres and others of the loyal party held a brief parley, and immediately sent word to Gordon to 'put him in mind of his engagements to us'. Balcarres, in a letter to King James, continues: 'As irresolution had been the cause of his promise to the Earl of Tweeddale, so the arguments used by us for defending it, joined to an earnest desire to be faithful to your Majesty, brought him about again.'[97]

Shortly after this, the Earl of Dunfermline, a brother-in-law of the Duke of Gordon, ascended Castle Hill and conversed with him. He gave an account of the day's proceedings, informing the Duke that the Whigs, or Williamites, were in full control of the Convention, and that as he, personally, could do nothing to control the course of events, he intended to retire to his lands in the North and await word from King James.

It is not known what Gordon's thoughts were on this, but, whether freely or not, he did append his signature to a letter authorising Dunfermline to raise the Clan Gordon to arms if required. He also gave an order to his Master of Horse to provide horses so that the loyal party could escape from the Convention, should the situation worsen.

Late in the evening of 14th March, it must have seemed as if Dundee was at last making some headway. He had spent most of the afternoon negotiating outwith the Council Chamber, attempting to bolster the loyal party, building up support, giving assurances and guarantees, making promises to those not yet firmly committed. There was still a substantial body of support for the King, but clearly little could be achieved in

Parliament when the Whigs were so much in the ascendant. He foresaw that events would force them to withdraw, but there might still be a chance, he felt, if the loyalists stuck together and acted sensibly. If they remained for a few days more they could build up their own support and hope to provoke the disintegration of the Whigs into factionalism. If nothing else had been achieved that day, at least they had secured the Castle for James.

Dundee was unaware that several messages had been conveyed to the Duke of Gordon late in the evening, after Dunfermline's visit. The import of these messages was that if the Castle was not surrendered, a price would be put on his head. This badly scared the Duke. His already shaky resolve weakened yet again. He drafted a set of proposals which he hoped would save his fine sense of honour and yet satisfy both parties.

In the early hours of the 15th, Dundee hastily rose and slipped through the deserted streets to the Castle, and informed Gordon that a rival Convention, loyal to King James, was to be planned. This was as yet only a bare idea. They had to play for time so as to obtain the maximum possible support. After this short meeting, Dundee slipped back, unnoticed, to his lodgings.

At 10 a.m., business began with disputed elections. Balcarres remarked in his *Memoirs* that these disputes would have required a much longer time to settle if most of the loyal party had not yielded their claims, 'perceiving nothing of justice was so much as pretended to be done'.[98] He cites the remarkable case of Mr Charles Hume, who attained the title of Earl of Hume after the death of his elder brother. Since the Estate was heavily in debt, he did not assume it, having another Estate which he would have lost had he become the Earl of Hume. Thus he sat as a Shire Commissioner. Unfortunately, as he was loyal to King James, the Whigs rejected him. When he heard that he was refused as a Shire Commissioner, he told the President that, since they had taken one way of sitting in the Convention from him, he would try another which they could not take from him – so he took his place as the Earl of Hume, with the loss of his entire Estate, and consequent financial ruin.

The Duke of Gordon's letter was read. It explained that he was quite willing to surrender the Castle and comply with the Convention's demands, but he had received a personal letter from the Prince of Orange asking him to leave the Castle, 'which I promised to doe, but expected certain reasonable things to be first granted to myself and Garrison. I hope I have not merited so ill of my country, as that I may not be trusted with the Castle, until a returne come to this letter, which I expect every hour'. In effect he was telling the Convention that he could not surrender the Castle to them because he was already surrendering it to William of Orange!

This, not surprisingly, was received with mingled rage, amusement and incredulity in the Convention. The letter continued with an offer to put up hostages of £20,000 sterling as a bond of good will. Lastly, if these first two proposals were not acceptable, he wanted an indemnity for himself and his fellow Catholics, security for the Protestant members of the garrison, who might otherwise have been penalised for collaborating with him, and payment of all arrears of pay.

The Convention debated this letter at 10 a.m. on the 16th and decided against allowing Gordon to remain Governor of the Castle. They opted for the last of the alternatives he had proposed. The Earls of Lothian and Tweeddale once again climbed the Castle rock with the safe conduct which would allow Gordon to conclude the treaty of honourable surrender with the Estates.

They discovered, much to their astonishment, that Gordon now refused to agree to the terms he himself had arranged only the day before. Almost certainly the Duke was acting to a plan conceived in collusion with Dundee, the main intention of which was to gain time for the loyal party to organise. Gordon renegotiated the terms of the treaty along the lines of a general amnesty for himself, his garrison and 'his friends', with passports to be given to anyone who wished to leave the country.

This was not so radically different from the previous proposals and the Convention agreed, but sent the exhausted Earls to the Castle for a precise definition of the phrase 'his friends', whom they wanted him to name individually. The poor Earls had to make a further two visits before it became clear that Gordon had named all the clans in the Highlands as 'his friends'! This was a calculated insult, and the Earl of Lothian was so incensed that he was unable to get the words out to describe to the Assembly what had happened. Possibly the Duke of Gordon had received advance notice that the clans were stirring in the North in the name of King James. He had ended his vacillation, and was now resolved to defend the Castle, which his better half had always intended to do in any case.

After the furore had died down, Dundee intervened in the debate by producing a letter in which the Duke of Gordon offered to meet the objection to his Governorship by surrendering the Castle to the Protestant Earl of Airlie. The Earl had been captain of a troop of horse under Claverhouse's command, and was felt to have steadier nerves than Gordon, but this was angrily rejected by the Convention as a trick – which, of course, it was.

Dundee then sent a gentleman called Cockburne of Lanton (the younger) to warn the Duke that the Convention were about to formally proclaim him a traitor. 'And the same hour came two heraulds, two pursevants, and two trumpeters sounding their trumpets' and approaching the walls, read the summons, by which Gordon and 'all other Papists' were to remove themselves immediately, upon pain of treason. The proclamation also forbade subjects to converse with or assist the Duke, or any under his command, and promised a reward of six months' pay, to the Protestants in the garrison, if they would seize the Duke and other Catholics, and deliver them up with the Castle into the hands of the Convention.

The Duke answered the heralds, and 'bid them tell the Convention from him, that he keept the Castle by commission from their common master, and that he was resolved to defend it to the last extremitie'. Gordon gave some guineas to the heralds to drink the King's good health, and all honest men in the Convention, which they promised to do; and 'he advysed them, in drollery, not to proclame men traitors to the State with the King's coats on ther backs; or at least they might turne them'.[99]

When the heralds had gone, Gordon called the garrison together, got the young ensign to read the summons and told them of the dangers they were all running by defying the Convention. As far as he himself was concerned, he was not going to be threatened out of his duty and he would continue to hold the Castle for the King. He offered to anyone who might wish to leave the chance to do so, and one lieutenant, one doctor, a master gunner and his two gunners, two sergeants, one corporal, one sutler, two drummers and between sixty and seventy private sentries did take advantage of the Duke's offer, received their pay arrears and quit the Castle.

As the gates closed behind the last man to leave, the garrison got itself ready for a siege. There were barely enough men remaining in the Castle to defend it effectively. Besides Gordon and his Lieutenant-Governor, Windrahame of Nether Liberton, were an ensign, four sergeants, one of whom was sick, and just over 100 sentries. Shortly afterwards, Gordon made an inspection and discovered to his horror that most of the gunpowder was damp and entirely useless, and that there was an abysmal lack of provisions. Following the defections, this was well known by now to his enemies.

The Castle had been under a siege of sorts since the Convention started, loose groups of hillmen and soldiers keeping watch on the comings and goings on Castle rock. This had not until now greatly inconvenienced the garrison, and certainly the Duke of Gordon was fairly free to come and go, as a sighting of him in a hackney coach 'betwixt nyn and ten acloack yesternight [the 15th] betwixt the Cross and the Luckenbooths' confirms.[100]

Later that day, a letter arrived from James' military commander in Ireland, the Earl of Tyrconnel, which Gordon had scruples about opening as it was not addressed to him, but to the Chancellor (Drummond of Perth, who was in jail).

Windrahame, who was standing nearby, snatched it from his hands and tore it open. The letter revealed that King James had landed at Kinsale in Ireland with a fleet of thirty-seven ships, two hundred 'good officers' and £200,000 sterling. Tyrconnel hoped by 10th April 'to show him 50,000 men well armed and disciplined, of which number 10,000 are horse and dragoons'. But there were no instructions about the Castle. Gordon sent the letter on to Dundee and Balcarres [101]

Another, more important, letter arrived from King James a letter which was to have catastrophic effects on Parliament, and wreck the careful plans of the loyal party.

In the *Acts of the Parliaments of Scotland* the arrival of this letter is noted thus: 'The Maisser haveing signified that one Mr Craine was at the door and hade a letter from King James to present to the meeting he was called in and Did present the letter, And it being moved by some members, that the letter from the King might be read, The Lord President Did Resume the occasione of the meeting, being the address that wes made by the noblemen and Gentlemen of this Kingdome being at London for the tyme to the then Prince of Orange Desyreing his highness to take upon him the administration of the Government in respect of the Disorders that were here at the tyme and to call a meeting of the Estates, And did Represent that ther wes also a letter from his highness by whose authoritie they wer mett, to this meeting Brought hither by the Earle of Levine [Leven], which his grace Desired might lykewayes be read And it being argued, that it wes fitt first to read the princes Letter in regaird they mett by his authoritie and Call, and that anything therin Contained could not Dissolve the meeting as the Kings letter, might doe. It was resolved first to read the Princes letter.'[102]

The letter from William was then read. It is a model of conciliation and reasonableness, almost obsequious in tone:

My Lords & Gentlemen.

WE are very sensible of the Kindness and concerne that many of your Nation hath evidenced towards Us, and Our undertakeing for the preservation of Religion and Liberty. which were in such imminent danger, nather can Wee in the least doubt of your confidence in us, after haveing sein how farr soe many of your Nobility and Gentrie have owned our Declaratione Countenanceing and concurring with Us in Our endeavours, And desyreing that Wee should take upon Us the administration of affairs Civill and Military, And to call a meeting of the Estates for secureing the Protestant Religion the ancient Laws and Liberties of that Kingdome which accordingly Wee have done.

NOW it lyes on you to enter upon such Consultations as are most probable to setle you on sure and lasting foundations which Wee hope you will set about with all convenient speed, with regaird to the Publick good, and to the generall Interest and Inclinations of the People That after soe much trouble and great suffering, they may live happyly and in peace, And that you may lay asyde all animosities and factions that may Imped soe good a worke.

WE were glad to find that so many of the Nobilitie and Gentrie when here at London, were soe much inclined to ane union of both Kingdoms and that they did look upon it as one of the best means for procureing the hapines of these Nations setling of a lasting peace amongst them which wold be advantagious to both, They liveing in the same Island haveing the same langwage, and the same common interest of Religion and Liberty, Especially at this juncture when the Enemies of both are so restless, Endeavouring to make and increase jealousies and Divisions which they will be ready to improve to the oune advantadge and the ruine of Britain, Wee being of the same opinion as to the usefulness of this Union, and having nothing soe much before our Eyes, as the Glory of God the Establishing of the reformed Religion and the peace & happyness of these Nations, are Resolved to use Our utmost endeavours in advanceing everything which may Conduce to the effectuating the same So we bid you heartily farewell from our Court at Hamptone the 7th day of March 1689.

WILLIAM R.[103]

In his *Memoirs,* Balcarres gives an insight into the effect on the loyal party of the arrival of the letter from King James, and its reading at the Convention: 'His coming [Mr Crane] was joyful to us, expecting a letter from your Majesty to the Convention, in terms suitable to the bad situation of your affairs in England and as had been advised by your friends before we left London . . . but, in place of such a letter as was expected . . . came a letter . . . in terms absolutely different from those we had agreed upon, and sent to your Majesty by Mr Lindsay from London. Upon other occasions such a letter might have passed, if there had been power to have backed it or force to make good its reception; but, after the Parliament of England had refused to read [it] . . . because of the Earl of Melfort's countersigning it as Secretary, and considering that it was known you had none to sustaine your cause but those who advised letters of another strain, it was a fault of your advisers hardly to be pardoned. Mr Crane having neither letters nor orders to any you used to employ, made us suspect things were not as we wished; but, not knowing the contents of your letter, nor imagining any about you could have produced a letter so prejudicial to your affairs, we pressed Mr Crane's being brought to the Convention to deliver the letter.'[104]

David Lindsay was the man who had carried a letter prepared by Dundee and others for James to sign and send back to the Convention of Estates. This letter was carefully drafted to offer general amnesties and to be conciliatory and benevolent in tone. One of its major instruments was the removal of Melfort from office. Although Lindsay had orders to deliver the letter to none but the King himself; he was intercepted by Melfort, who prepared a different letter and supressed the original. None of this was known until the letter itself was read and by then it was too late to do anything.[105]

So Dundee and the others argued that the letter should be read and it was agreed on the conditions that, irrespective of its contents, the Convention would remain undissolved 'untill they secure the religione the Government lawes and liberties of the Kingdome'.

Balcarres described this as 'a pill to the loyal party so bitter it had never gone down, if they had not been persuaded your letter would have dissipated our fears'. Accordingly, Dundee's signature appears with the names of all the others on this document. The letter was then read to the meeting.

Bonnie Dundee

My Lords and Gentlemen,

Wheras ue hav bein informed that you the peirs and represent-
atives of Shires and Borrous of that Our Antient Kingdome
uer to meitt together at our Good toun of Edinborrough some
time in this instant March By the Usurped Authority of the
Prince of Orange, We think fitt to let you kno That as ue hav
at all times relyed on the faithfullness and affectione of you
our Antient People so much that in our greatest misfortunes
heartofore ue had recourse to you assistance And that with
good success yo our affairs. So nou againe ue require of you
to support Our Royall interest Expecting from you what
becomes loyall and faithfull subjects generous and honest men
That you will nather suffer yr selves to be cajolled nor fright-
ened into any actione misbecomeing true hearted Scotsmen
And that to suport the honour of yr Natione you contemn the
base example of disloyall men And Eternise your names by a
loyalty whereof you will choise the safest part since thereby
you will evite the danger you most neids undergo, The infamy
and disgrace you most bring upon yourselves in this world
and the Condemnation due to the Rebellious in the nixt And
you will Ikewayes hav the opportunity to secure to yourselves
and your posterity the gracious promises ue hav so often
made of secureing your Religion laws Propertys libertys and
rights which we are still Resolved to performe as soon as it is
possible for us to meit you safely in a Parliament of that Our
antient Kingdome. In the mean time Fear not to declare for
us yr Lawfull Soveraigne Who will not feal on Our part to
giv you such speedy and powerfull assistance as shall not only
inable you to defend yr selves from any forraigne attempt
but put you in a Conditione to assert Our Right against Our
Ennamys who hav depressed the same by the blackest of
usurpations the most unjust as well as most unnatural of
attempts Which the Almighty God may for a time permitt and
lett the wicked prosper. Yet the end must bring Confusione
upon such workers of Iniquity. We further lett you kno that
ue will pardone all such as shall return to ther duety befor the
last day of this moneth inclusive. And that ue will punish with
the rigor of Our Law all such as shall stand out in rebellion
against us or Our Authority. So not doubting that you will
declare for us And suppress whatever may pose our interest
and that you uill send some of your numbre to us with ane
accompt of yr diligence and the posture of our affairs ther
We Bid you Heartiely farewell.

Given on Board the St Michael first of March 1689. And of Our Reigne the 5th Year.

By His Majties Command. MELFORT.[106]

James' friend, the Protestant Lord Ailesbury, deplored this letter in his *Memoirs:* 'the style of which was very far from being gracious and sweet; and to cut his own throat . . . he could find nobody to countersign but my lord Melfort, a person abominated in that Kingdom'.[107]

No sooner was the letter read for a second time, Balcarres writes, 'and known to be Earl Melfort's hand and style, but the house was in a tumult – your enemies [the Whigs] in joy and your friends in confusion'.[108] The Whigs were delighted that the letter made no promises other than the threat of retribution and eternal damnation, with an insistence that all those adhering to William by the end of March would be regarded as traitors. The tone of the letter was all wrong for a monarch in the unfortunate circumstances which James found himself in. Balcarres knew that the Whigs had 'much feared many of their party would have forsaken them if your Majesty's letter had been written in the terms we advised from London'. The reception of the unfortunate letter forced the loyal party into a hasty decision to leave Edinburgh and call the rival Convention at Stirling 'as your Majesty had given the Archbishop of St Andrews, the Viscount of Dundee, and myself [Balcarres], the power to do by a warrant sent by Mr Brown from Ireland'.[109]

Rapid preparations were made to inform all those still loyal to King James of their plans, and Monday the 18th was appointed as the day for the ride to Stirling. Balcarres takes up the story: 'Before we could be determined, it was thought absolutely necessary to be assured of the Earl of Mar and the Marquis of Atholl, the Earl having the command of the Castle [Stirling], and the Marquis, that he might bring his Highlanders to be a guard to your Convention in the town, The Earl had early appeared forward in your cause, and gave us assurance of doing whatever the majority of your friends should judge fit for your service; the Marquis likewise agreed to leave Edinburgh and go to Stirling, but his irresolution to do this broke all our measures, which delays upon such occasions never fail to do.'[110]

On 17th March, the day before the rival Convention in Stirling, Dundee discovered a plot to assassinate him. He had suffered insults and threatened violence since his arrival in Edinburgh, and there may possibly have been other plans to kill him, but with the advantage of historical distance, it is possible to view his complaint to the Convention as a device to allow him to leave the assembly without giving the game away. Certainly the plot was real enough, and he felt justified in reporting it to the Estates, but he may have exaggerated the danger he was in – for effect.

Lord President Hamilton agreed to a motion made for the security of members of the meeting, based on a piece of information that two men intended violence on Lords Dundee and Rosehaugh (Sir George MacKenzie). The motion was put by MacKenzie who informed the meeting that he had a witness, James Binnie, a dyer, who had heard two men lodged in his house say they resolved to kill the two lords, and inquire the whereabouts of their lodgings, boasting that neither would escape, though it was not to be done for 'some nights'.

The house had little sympathy for their position, and the majority felt the matter was irrelevant to the business in hand. Impatiently, they howled MacKenzie down, and in the uproar many vented their spite on 'the Persecutor', who was now getting 'a taste of his own medicine'. Others thought the Lords were surely exaggerating, or indulging in timewasting tactics to delay the business. The President threatened to cut short the tumult by having Dundee and MacKenzie removed, and at this moment Dundee stood up to reply. He waited until the tumult had largely subsided, and his voice cut clear across the hall as he offered to leave – on the grounds that if the Convention would not guarantee the safety of its own members, and continued to allow armed mobs to gather in the streets, he could no longer remain. He informed the house in a calm, steady voice that in his opinion the Convention had been called illegally, and that it was his intention to obey a royal commission lately arrived from King James, which required him to adjourn the Convention to Stirling. He called upon all true and honest subjects of the lawful King to follow him, and then he stalked unhurriedly from the Chamber, without looking back.

This was a signal for most of the loyal party to leave – which would have left the Great Hall echoingly empty.

All was now going to plan, and Dundee sent three Highlanders through the siege lines to the Castle with a letter to the Duke of Gordon informing him officially that the loyal party were to travel to Stirling in the morning, then he sent a request to the Convention demanding that they send a reply to King James' letter.

A Macer was sent to his lodgings informing him that the Estates had no intention of replying to the letter. There had not been a single voice raised in the assembly in support of making such a reply to the King, since the loyal party had absented itself from the proceedings. Dundee sent the Macer back with a request for a permit to allow him to go to Ireland. Back came the Macer – his request was refused. He had exhausted all other courses of action, so, in the evening he visited the officers and men of his troop of horse in their quarters and ordered them to prepare. They were to act as a guard-party for the Convention members on the journey to Stirling.

At the very last moment, however, some members of the loyal party held a meeting (at which Dundee was not present), the Marquis of Atholl having suffered another attack of nerves. He insisted that they delay one more day and attend the Convention in one last attempt to persuade Hamilton and the others to pass laws against the mobs. Atholl was an old man and his son and heir, Lord Murray, was a prominent Whig supporter. He advised caution, largely on the basis of his own timidity. The upshot of this secret meeting was that Atholl and the others did not turn up at the rendezvous at dawn on the 18th.

Dundee, who had donned his uniform for the occasion, and

his thirty scarlet-clad troopers waited patiently, their horses snorting and pawing the ground. At last, word was brought to him of what had occurred. Despite all his efforts he had been unable to bolster their craven spirits for two consecutive days. For a few moments after MacKenzie's messenger had left him, he considered his position. He knew he had been seen by his enemies, and, merely by being in arms with his troop, he was running a grave risk. He could no longer remain in Edinburgh. He had played his part. Now he was forced to wait until the great lords finally made their move. Clearly he had to ride from Edinburgh. He must have felt revulsion at the cowardice and irresolution of his friends, the incompetence of James' letter and the total failure of the loyal party, potentially stronger than the Whigs, to retain some kind of unity. Some, like the Duke of Queensberry and the Earl of Dunmore, had not even attended the Convention. If the affair had been better organised, the Whigs would have been routed in the Convention, and the Scottish army, never having been sent to England, would have been a guarantee of loyal behaviour. But he had one last duty to perform.

He gave the order to ride, and the troop, with Dundee at their head, clattered over the cobbles of Leith Wynd, and along the Lang Gate to the North side of the town, towards the Castle.

As they rode towards the black crags, sentries on the Castle walls above observed them with interest. So, too, did the half-awake pickets in the siege lines on Castle Hill. The scarlet-jacketed troop galloped around the base of the rock towards St Cuthbert's kirk, and on the spur of the hill they halted. Viscount Dundee dismounted and climbed a hundred feet up the craggy, moss-covered slope to the Postern Gate, in the outer wall of the Castle's defences.

There is a plaque commemorating this climb, and a plaque also above the Postern Gate, where, alerted by a sentry, the Duke of Gordon appeared. It is a relatively easy climb nowadays for the average fit person as it has become grassed-over, but three hundred years ago, the crag may have been less eroded and certainly more difficult to climb in full uniform with cavalry boots and spurs. Dundee is reported to have sped upwards like a gazelle without once pausing for breath. Within fifty feet of the gate he shouted out to the Duke – who came down from the gate and met him.[111]

The purpose of the parley was to persuade the Duke to ride with him, so that his clans could be raised if required – in the event of hostilities. The Duke was more interested in the actions of the loyal party, and was alarmed when he heard that Atholl and the others had delayed for a further day. Already he was proclaimed a traitor, and Dundee too would now be outlawed for speaking with him. Surely Hamilton and the Whigs would not permit Atholl and the loyal Commissioners to ride to Stirling once the alarm was raised? What was in Dundee's mind to take so bold and dangerous a step? By his precipitate retreat from the town he would upset the carefully laid plans. But Dundee was in no mood for councils of caution and delay. He had come this far and he could not go back. He was weary of the politicking and the conniving – and glad to be back at the head of his troop of honest, diligent soldiers whose qualities of loyalty the great nobles seemed to lack.

He turned towards the wide estuary of the River Forth – the direction also of his own beloved Dudhope – and gazed upon the peaceful lands set out before him. In answer to Gordon's anxious questions he murmured: 'I go whither the shade of Montrose shall direct me.'[112] And he began to descend the crag. At the bottom, he gave the perplexed Duke a farewell wave, and once mounted, led his troop westwards.

THE BONNETS O' BONNIE DUNDEE

To the Lords of Convention 'twas Claver'se who spoke,
'Ere the King's crown shall fall there are crowns to be broke;
So let each Cavalier who loves honour and me,
Come follow the bonnet o' Bonnie Dundee.

'Come fill up my cup, come fill up my can,
Come saddle your horses and call up your men;
Come open the West Port, and let me gang free,
And it's room for the bonnets o' Bonnie Dundee!'

Bonnie Dundee

Dundee he is mounted, he rides up the street,
The bells are rung backward, the drums they are beat;
But the Provost, douce man, said, 'Just e'en let him be,
The Guid Toun is well quit o' that Deil o' Dundee.'

As he rode down the sanctified bends of the Bow,
Ilk carlin was flyting and shaking her pow;
But the young plants of grace they look'd couthie and slee,
Thinking, luck to thy bonnet, thou Bonnie Dundee!

With sour-featured Whigs the Grassmarket was cramm'd
As if half the West had set tryst to be hanged;
There was spite in each look, there was fear in each e'e,
As they watch'd for the bonnets o' Bonnie Dundee.

These cowls of Kilmarnock had spits and had spears,
And lang-hafted gullies to kill Cavaliers:
But they shrunk to close-heads, and the causeway was free,
At the toss of the bonnet o' Bonnie Dundee.

He spurr'd to the foot of the proud Castle Rock,
And with the gay Gordon he gallantly spoke;
'Let Mons Meg and her marrows speak twa words or three,
For the love of the bonnet o' Bonnie Dundee.'

The Gordon demands of him which way he goes –
'Where'er shall direct me the shade of Montrose!
Your Grace in short space shall hear tidings of me,
Or that low lies the bonnet o' Bonnie Dundee.'

There are hills beyond Pentland, and lands beyond Forth,
Be there Lords in the Lowlands, there's chiefs in the North;
There are brave Duniewassals three thousand times three,
Will cry HOIGH! for the bonnet o' Bonnie Dundee.

There's brass on the target of barken'd bull-hide;
There's steel in the scabbard that dangles beside;
The brass shall be burnished, the steel shall flash free
At the toss of the bonnet o' Bonnie Dundee.

'Away to the hills, to the lea, to the rocks –
Ere I own a usurper, I'll couch with the fox;
And tremble, false Whigs, in the midst of your glee,
You have not seen the last of my bonnet and me!'

He waved his proud hand and the trumpets were blown,
The kettledrums clash'd, and the horsemen rode on,

Till on Ravelston's cliffs and on Clermiston's lee,
Died away the wild war-notes o' Bonnie Dundee.

Come fill up my cup, come fill up my can,
Come saddle the horses and call up the men,
Come open the gates and let me gae free,
For it's up with the bonnets o' Bonnie Dundee!

Sir Walter Scott.[113]

Although this is an excellent folksong, Sir Walter Scott is wrong on two counts: Dundee's ride from Edinburgh was precipitate rather than defiant; and self-preservative rather than warlike. Dundee had not decided on anything other than a withdrawal from a place where his life had been threatened, and did not, at this stage, firmly envisage war.

The doors of the Parliament building opened on Monday the 18th, and the loyal party members duly trooped in and took their places. The session began, but they were entirely unable to put any motions to the house. Soldiers and hillmen had observed Dundee parleying with the outlawed Duke at the Castle, had watched him riding off at the head of his troop of cavalry, and were intent on making their opinions heard. The mob had taken up the clamour and the number of Dundee's horsemen was increasing as the minutes went by. The Whigs began to fear that there was an elaborate military coup planned against them. Some were for immediate defensive measures – calling out the militias; assembling a standing army – and surely any attempt to legislate against the mob would have been doomed to failure. The loyal party had to sit in silence while Hamilton and his acolytes denounced Dundee, the Duke of Gordon, all enemies of King William wherever they might be. It was high time, Hamilton roared, 'to look to themselves, since Papists and enemies to the sitting of the Government were so bold as to assemble in a hostile manner'.[114] Worse, Hamilton glaring in the direction of the loyal party members, declared that there were undoubtedly some amongst them in that very hall who shared the same views as the traitors. He demanded the doors be locked and the keys placed upon the table. He ordered those who, like him, had brought armed men to Edinburgh, to assemble them from the stables, cellars and vaults of the houses where they had been concealed.

Balcarres remarked: 'several others likewise bragged of men they had brought to town, and magnified their numbers; the Earl of Leven was appointed to assemble them, which when done, never was seen so contemptible a rabble, nor was it to be doubted if your friends [the loyal party] had known their own strength, or had not judged their enemies far more considerable than they were, but they might easily have accomplished their designs in declaring for your Majesty, and put themselves out of hazard from their enemies.' Balcarres is being wise after the event here, for he, like the rest, found his courage draining away when faced with armed men at all the doors of the Convention, and outside, a large and belligerent mob lusting for blood. The Marquis of Atholl lost his nerve and immediately renounced his support for the rival Convention. Subsequently he developed an attack of gout and travelled to Bath where he remained virtually incommunicado for months. The Earl of Mar, who was sick, declared for William, as did the Earl of Annandale and the Earl of Dunmore, followed by a number of Shire and Burgh Commissioners. Balcarres, who refused, was jailed, as was Lieutenant-General Douglas – who had initially deserted to the Prince of Orange at Salisbury. George MacKenzie travelled the next day to Oxford to conduct some extremely urgent study – and to glory in the intellectual climes of the Bodleian Library. He had always been something of a pacifist, and declared: 'I will live peacably and with great satisfaction under the present King for tho' I was not clear to make him a King, yet I love not civill warrs nor disorders and wee owe much to him.' His defence of the antiquity of the ancient line of the Stuarts was to remain purely academic in the face of possible personal injury.[115]

The loyal party did evolve a weak plan to get Gordon to fire upon the Convention building – which they hoped would cause Hamilton and his party to retire to Glasgow. The Duke of Gordon, however, refused to do this for fear someone would be injured! Viscount Tarbat sent the Laird of Alva to Stirling to help in setting up the rival Convention, but on arrival Alva found that the Castle was being held for William of Orange by the followers of the Earl of Mar.

The loyal party – those who had not been arrested – the Earls of Hume, Panmure and Southesk, the Viscounts of Stormont, Oxenford and Lord St Clair, the Sheriff of Bute, and many others then retired to their homes. Dundee was, with the exception of the soft-hearted Duke of Gordon, entirely alone.

Dundee's troop galloped along the Linlithgow road and the peacefulness of the countryside must have been a relief after the noisy clamour of Edinburgh. As they approached Stirling, Dundee was informed of the defection of the Earl of Mar and so he led his men through the town at full gallop – and out the other side. They halted for the night at a changehouse in Dunblane. After the excitement and tension of the last few days, Dundee must have suffered from a feeling of anticlimax and disappointment.

There was another overnight guest at the tavern – Alexander Drummond of Balhaldie, son-in-law to Cameron of Lochiel, who was actually on his way to Dudhope with a message for Dundee. The clans had already formed a confederacy on behalf of the King and wanted Dundee to join with them – and lead them.

The Viscount must have received this news with some excitement. The clans had never allowed a lowlander to lead them – with the honourable exception of his noble ancestor, Montrose. For Dundee, this comparison with his great kinsman would have been a source of delight. Perhaps he saw it as an omen, certainly he could only have construed the action of the clans as a sign of loyalty, and so their move decided his course. In the meantime he had preparations to make. He was chiefly worried about his wife and child-to-be, and so he travelled home the next day. He was to claim that he had written on that day to the Duke of Hamilton explaining his actions: a letter clearly intended merely to delay proceedings against him; but such a letter no longer exists among either the Hamilton Muniments or any papers of the Scottish Parliament, and it must be considered unlikely that he ever did write a letter on the 19th, although he alludes to it in a letter of the 27th which exists.

On the day that he rode home to Dudhope, the Estates, 'being informed that the Viscount of Dundee and the Lord Livingstone, with several others, are in armes, at or near the toun of Linlithgow, without any warrand from the Estates . . .', ordained a herald 'to charge the said lords to appear before the Meeting of the Estates, within twenty four houres under pain of treason'.[116]

On the 20th, a warrant for expenses for a herald and trumpeter were approved by the Convention, and Dundee was proclaimed an outlaw at the market cross that day. These heralds arrived at Dudhope on the 26th, where, before the Castle, they solemnly pronounced their sentence. It was this summons that forced Dundee to write to the Convention, whether or not he had already done so, on the 19th as he claimed:

Dudhop, March 27, 1689.

MAY IT PLEASE YOUR GRACE,

The coming of an herauld and trumpeter to summon a man to lay down arms, that is living in peace at home, seems to me a very extraordinary thing, and, I suppose, will do do to all that hears of it. While I attended the Convention at Edinburgh, I complained often of so many people's being in arms without authority, which was notoriously known to be true, even the wild hill men.' and, no summons to lay down arms under the pain of treason being given them, I thought it unsafe for me to remain longer among them. And because some few of my friends did me the favour to convey me out of the reach of those murderers, and that my Lord Levingston and several other officers took occasion to come away at the same time, this must be called being in arms. We did not exceed the number allowed by the Meeting of Estates: my Lord Levingstone and I might have had each of us ten, and four or five officers that were in company might have had a certain number allowed them; which being, it will be found we exceeded not. I am sure it is far short of the number my

Lord Lorne [Argyll] was seen to march with. And, tho I had gone away with some more than ordinary, who can blame me, when designs of murdering me was made appear' Besides, it is known to every body, that, before we came within sixteen miles of this, my Lord Levingston went off to his brother, my Lord Strathmoir's house; and most of the officers, and several of the company, went to their respective homes or relations; and, if any of them did me the honour to come along with me, must that be called being in arms? Sure, when your Grace represents this to the Meeting of the States, they will discharge such a groundless pursuit, and think my appearance before them unnecessary. Besides, tho' it were necessary for me to go and attend the Meeting, I cannot come with freedom and safety, because I am informed there are men of war, and foreign troops [General Hugh MacKay had just arrived in Scotland] in the passage; and, till I know what they are, and what are their orders, the Meeting cannot blame me for not coming. Then, my Lord, seeing the summons has proceeded on a groundless story, I hope the Meeting of States will think it unreasonable I should leave my wife in the condition she is in. If there be any body that, notwithstanding of all that is said, think I ought to appear, I beg the favour of a delay till my wife is brought to bed; and, in the meantime, I will either give security or paroll not to disturb the peace. Seeing this pursuit is so groundless, and so reasonable things offered, and the Meeting composed of prudent men and men of honour, and your Grace presiding in it, I have no reason to fear farther trouble. I am, May it please your Grace,

Your most humble servant,

DUNDIE.

I beg your Grace will cause read this to the Meeting, because it is all the defence I have made. I sent another to your Grace from Dumblein, with the reasons of my leaving Edinburgh: I know not if it be comes to your hands.[117]

This letter bears clear signs of sarcasm and certainly of pretended naivety, though it is certain that the main aim was to allay the fears of the Whigs and secure a delay while his child was born. Dundee was acutely conscious of Gordon's charge that he was acting precipitately. He needed time to be certain of making the right choice. He was aware that war looked the most likely option now that he had been outlawed and proclaimed a traitor. He needed time to obtain a reply from the clans, and for his commission from King James to arrive.

Dundee's letter was read to the Convention on 30th March, and had no effect whatsoever upon the remaining Convention members, who had now accepted the necessity of making an example of him in order to bring all the dissenting lords into line. Since the Convention had not yet proclaimed William King of Scotland, the declaration against Dundee was signed – with a fine sense of irony – in the name of King James!

On the same day, forty-eight miles to the north at Dudhope, Dundee became the proud father of a son. The child was named James – in honour both of the great Montrose and of the exiled King – and is possibly the only child to have been born and disinherited on the same day!

Dundee's actions had, so far, been prompted by necessity. The abandonment of the King's cause by a large part of the Scottish legislature had forced him into precipitate flight from Edinburgh – now construed as open rebellion. He could deal with these defections as long as the clans proved loyal and James' army triumphed in Ireland; and if that occurred, the political situation was likely to improve. But with Dundee now firmly committed to the restoration of King James, the last thing he expected was that his efforts would be betrayed within the Court of the King. No-one could have anticipated the scale of the treachery which caused Dundee's downfall and wrecked the fortunes of the Stuart monarchs – or that its source should be the King's own principle advisor, the odious Melfort.

5

Rebellion

Dundee had been declared a traitor by the Convention and William of Orange, but there was a large amount of support for James Stuart in the country. Many regarded the new monarch as unlawful, as a usurper proclaimed only by a self-serving minority. Though opposition was unorganised and unarmed, many would flock to Dundee's banner if he could provide an encouraging example of leadership. He was one of the most effective military commanders – although what little previous experience he had of pitched battle in Scotland was rather less than glorious – and he had never commanded troops to victory. Nevertheless, his expectations were high: the Highlanders would provide him with an army; King James would soon be master of all Ireland, and from there would return to Scotland with a large, victorious army. Together, master and dutiful servant, they would drive the Whigs back to Holland and end William's usurpation. But before these mighty events could take place, Dundee knew that he must in the meantime avoid capture, and use his time to unite and assemble the supporters of King James. The Convention would proceed rapidly against him, and it was unavoidable therefore that he should make a strategic retreat to the North.

He was to remain, however, at Dudhope for a further two weeks, having posted look-outs on Dundee Law to guard against surprise attack. On 9th April, his ten-day-old son and heir, James Graham, was baptised in Mains Parish Church. William Graham of Balquhaple, formerly Major in Dundee's regiment, was named as godfather. Only two days after this event, they learned that the Convention had, as expected, proclaimed William and Mary King and Queen of Scotland. In legal terms this was unconstitutional – quite apart from the fact that they had not, like previous Kings – except James – been crowned at Scone, or taken any Scottish Coronation oaths. If James could be regarded as having abandoned his throne, and if Mary was to be Queen, William could be Prince Consort only. However, the throne had been won by bloodless conquest, and such constitutional legalities were swept aside, The Stuart line had been supplanted by the House of Orange.

Dundee's reply was a swift and dramatic gesture of defiance: a declaration of war. Gathering a small group of troopers and kinsmen around him, he galloped up to the flat top of Dundee Law, where, in full view of the astonished townspeople, he unfurled the Royal Standard. He must have been aware that this provocative act would be reported immediately to the Convention and draw rapid retaliation. What may have worried him more than this was that his commission as Commander-in-Chief of James' army had not arrived; he was acting entirely on his own authority. He could not recruit, and had no official standing until it did arrive. This was perhaps the reason for raising the Royal Standard in such a public manner – so that there could be no misunderstanding about his motives, or his loyalty. He did not want the taint of rebel. The Whigs were the rebels. They had usurped the lawful King.

The next day, 14th April, Dundee and his entire household with all their personal effects and furniture moved out of Dudhope, and began the ten-mile journey to the country seat at Glen Ogilvie. Not a moment too soon, for barely twelve hours later Lieutenant-Colonel Thomas Livingstone, who had recently replaced the Earl of Dunmore in command of Dundee's old regiment, the Royal Regiment of Scots Dragoons, arrived at Dudhope with strict instructions to 'surprise his horse and seize his person, if possible'. He duly reported that the Castle was empty, and Dundee gone, and then settled into lodgings in the town to await orders.

Dundee had mentioned in his letter to Hamilton that 'foreign troops were in passage'. These comprised detachments from three regiments of the Scottish Brigade in Holland, led by General Hugh Mackay of Scourie and two subordinate officers, Brigadier Bartold Balfour and Colonel George Ramsay. Mackay had been displeased to receive a commission of service in Scotland, and only the day after landing proceeded to lecture the Convention on its incompetence. He had a rather officious manner and certainly regarded most Scots as incompetent and inefficient almost by definition. Mackay promptly issued a series of orders to prepare the country for the civil war he was convinced was in the offing. He distributed money to the three detachments and ordered them to recruit native Scots to bring their numbers up to full regimental size of 1200 men in each. He ordered the Earl of Annandale and Lord Belhaven to supply a troop of horse each, and the Earl of Leven and Viscount Kenmure each to raise a battalion of foot. He put the siege of Edinburgh Castle onto a business-like footing, and made it widely known that he was in command of all forces in Scotland. The Convention was not overjoyed at the cost of Mackay's new army, which had doubled in size since the march south to Salisbury the previous year.[118]

When Mackay heard that Livingstone had been unable to capture Dundee, he decided to take over operations himself. Clearly he held his own capabilities in some esteem, and did not want to incur the consequences of letting Dundee 'persuade men to his measures, and play his personage among the nobility and gentry of the north'. The Convention, especially Hamilton, were very much against his going north personally, but their opinions he disregarded contemptuously.[119]

In trying to inflate Claverhouse's already swollen reputation as a military commander, many writers have somewhat traduced General Mackay, accusing him of pedantry, dullwittedness and being of 'slow brain'. However, while Mackay certainly had a fine conceit of himself, and was in addition unused to Highland warfare, he was certainly an efficient commander with a good reputation and moreover had more experience than Claverhouse. The Editor of *The Melville & Leven Papers,* however, assures us that he had 'an everweening opinion of his own merits [which] rendered him querulous, tenacious and impracticable . . . With great self-complacency he determined that no Scotsman except himself had any regard for the public good, and that the King and the Earl of Portland were under a great mistake in never answering or noticing his letters . . .'[120] Probably a fairer description was offered by Gilbert Burnet: 'Mackay . . . was the piousest man I ever knew in a Military way . . . one of the best officers of the age, when he had nothing to do but to obey and execute orders, for he was both diligent, obliging and brave; But he was not so fitted for command. His piety made him too apt to mistrust his own sense, and to be too tender, or rather fearful . . .' Of course this comment was made some time after Killiecrankie, with the benefit of hindsight; history rarely favours a loser.[121]

Mackay wrote to various nobles in the North to attempt to have Dundee's escape routes blocked. The Marquis of Atholl was requested to raise 300 men to guard the Pass of Killiecrankie; the Earl of Mar was to raise the same number to keep watch on the Braes of Mar; the Laird of Grant was entrusted with the job of guarding the banks of the Spey. Thus, Mackay believed, Dundee would be unable to move to the Highlands without being observed and his movements noted. These careful plans, as we shall see later, were to come to nothing. Having offered his services to Mackay, Grant delayed too long in Edinburgh when Mackay believed he was already in position and fulfilling his duty. Nor did the Marquis of Atholl live up to Mackay's expectations, and Mar was to die at a very inconvenient time. But in the third week of April, it seemed to Mackay that it was only a matter of time before Dundee was cornered and captured.

The political climate was far from settled. There was an underlying tension and mistrust throughout the Lowlands.

Few were quite certain of their neighbour's allegiances should the situation change for the worse. As early as 23rd March, Sir James Dalrymple, Lord Advocate, had expressed fears about the threat of invasion from Ireland, and had attempted to persuade the English Privy Council to pay for a force of 10,000 infantry to be raised in Scotland. 'It would be a hopeless remeed [remedy] to send downe grein English from their plentiful lyf to merch 400 myls and get hard quarter . . . and new raised English from ther soft beds, will nether be proper in Scotland, nor so fitt anywher as our hard bred people,' he wrote. The armies would have to be raised in Scotland – and Scotland had no money. Dalrymple was highly suspicious of the 'ingratitude of this people, who ar apt to returne to Egipt many of them'.[122]

On 8th April, a messenger from Ireland called Brady was apprehended and found to be in possession of letters from King James and Melfort to Dundee, the imprisoned Balcarres and the Earl of Perth. One of the letters was Dundee's long-awaited commission:

> We have therfore resolved to send commission to you of Lieutenant-General, that you may raise as many of either as you can, with commissions blank for the inferior officers, to be filled up by you, and to command all forces as can be raised there, and to command likewise such as we shall send from this to your assistance. Being resolved to come ourself as soon as it is possible . . . we have thought of sending five thousand men, whereof 100 horse and 150 dragoons, believing that a greater number of horse and dragoons will be inconvenient to ship over to you . . .
>
> We have sent letters to the Chiefs of Clans to arm, and to most of the nobility we have reason to judge faithful to our interest, and by the forces we send over, commissions shall be sent to you and the rest of our friends. The officers of our standing forces we will require to attend you by proclamation, and such as are with us we shall immediately prepare for their journey as soon as we hear from you. As soon as our forces or any considerable body can be brought together, we think fit that the nobility and gentry should call the Bishops and Boroughs, and by our authority call themselves a Convention of Estates, to declare for us, and to put the

Kingdom in a posture of defence. We need not tell you the
necessity you lie under to defend yourselves. The Presbyterians are not good masters in any government, much less with
you, where their particular quarrels are revenged in those
public confusions . . . As for yourself, you may be assured
that as your services to us all alongst have been eminent, so,
when it pleases God to put it in our power, the reward shall
be the same.

The letters were dated Dublin, 29th March. Balcarres's letter
was substantially the same, except that his commission was
as a Colonel of Horse and Foot, which he was unable to avail
himself of, being imprisoned in the Edinburgh Tolbooth. The
letter to Balcarres puts King James' army at 500,000 (a slip
of the pen for 50,000) – the letter to Perth has their number
at 40,000. Melfort requests Balcarres's advice about landing sites and provisions. This letter, revealing Balcarres's
high level of involvement, was the principal reason for Balcarres's continued imprisonment. The letter from Melfort to
his brother the Earl of Perth details the money to be spent in
the campaign and requests he open all the letters and send
his advice, and 'nothing shall be ommitted which you shall
advise . . . I know not where you are; therefore this is short'.
Perth had been transferred by this time to Stirling Castle.[123]

Other letters intercepted at this time were addressed to the
Marquis of Atholl requesting his service in the name of King
James, and offering him compensation, and an indemnity to
all those who voted against James in the 'late illegall convention'. Atholl must have felt he was under suspicion, for he
wrote to William on 13th April, effusively protesting his
loyalty. 'None', he declared, 'shall be more readie to serve
and promot your Majesties' interest according to my duty
and capacity, as in the meeting of the Estates I have cheerfully
concurred in every thing I conceived truly conducive for that
end, and therefore to advance your Majesties' great concern,
I have heartily voted and consented that the throne of this
Kingdom be filled by your Majesty as the next most proper
and deserving Prince of the Royal blood.'[124]

Several commentators have remarked that much of this

The 'Melville Portrait' of John Graham of Claverhouse. Perhaps painted in the Netherlands by an unknown artist, or perhaps earlier still in Scotland before his departure for service with William of Orange. Clad in old-fashioned armour, he wears a melancholy expression of youthful innocence. Courtesy of Scottish National Portrait Gallery.

The murder of Archbishop James Sharp of St Andrews, 3rd May 1679. An engraving made shortly after the event. Courtesy of the British Museum.

John Maitland, Duke of Lauderdale, by Sir Peter Lely. When Maitland was ruined for tampering with the coinage, Claverhouse succeeded to the Estates of Dudhope and the title of Constable of Dundee. Courtesy of Scottish National Portrait Gallery.

Left A wax bust of William of Orange. 'The darling and glorie of our present age . . .' wrote the Master of Forbes. In pursuit of his ambitions he set aside his homosexual tendencies and married the daughter of James VII. *Right* Major-General Hugh Mackay, born in Scourie in Sutherland. 'The pionsest man I ever knew,' declared Bishop Burnet; 'one of the best officers of the age . . . diligent, obliging and brave; but he was not so fitted for command.' Courtesy of Scottish National Portrait Gallery.

Sir Ewan Cameron of Lochiel, a living legend throughout Scotland. He had successfully resisted Cromwell's invasion and had reputedly killed the last wolf in the country. Although the Camerons were a small clan, Lochiel's influence was enormous. At the time of Killiecrankie he was still active in battle, although an elderly man. Courtesy of Scottish National Portrait Gallery.

John Drummond of Lundin, Earl of Melfort, dressed as a Knight of the Thistle. '. . . nor is he much to be trusted himself, but where his ambition can be fed.' His politicking was to play a major part in Dundee's downfall.

letter, and especially the final line, is loaded with ambiguity. This would be quite in keeping with Atholl's previous timid behaviour, but his primary motive was the desire not to be implicated or involved – he was elderly and unwell – and it is doubtful whether he would risk giving deliberate offence in a direct letter to William.

Viscount Tarbat was another whose allegiance wavered. In a letter to Melville on the 13th, he apologises for his illness which had prevented him from attending the Convention. He admits to considerable anxiety for 'the interest of our King and Kingdom [which] are not yet so fixed as to be out of danger . . . many of this nation, who have too little religion, and several who consider not the danger of the Protestant Religion . . . will be too ready to join with the Irish . . . not only the greatest part of our Highlanders, but the far greatest part of the Low Country people benorth Tay, and very many besouth it, especially in the south borders, will concur in this'. Tarbat then enters a plea for compromise and moderation and criticises the leadership in Scotland, demanding that 'the chief trust should be put into moderate and serious hands', meaning, of course, his own.[125] Another suffering convenient illness was Breadalbane, who, though troubled by gout, was an active correspondent with James in Ireland, pressing the removal of Melfort, the restoration of Argyll and being involved through trusted subordinates in Jacobite intrigue, though falling short of declaring outright support for Dundee.

If the important and eminent lords were riddled with such doubts and anxieties, then Dundee's opposition could not be as united as it should have been. The Convention leaders must have felt dismayed at the evidence from the intercepted letters of a high level of organisation against them, and at the supposed size of King James' army in Ireland. Their response was to empower the Duke of Hamilton to imprison whomsoever he suspected of treason or conspiracy; then the Assembly adjourned itself to prepare for defence of the realm. Throughout his campaign, Dundee was to receive good information of the activities and decisions of the Convention from several Lowland Jacobites who carefully concealed their support for James.

Lord Melville, Secretary of State, wrote an account of the country to William on the 16th, assuring him that 'there has not been so general and cordially joy expressed of a great many years . . . there is a wonderful change in the countenance of people since from what was the day before'. He apologises to the King for the speed of the Proclamation which was made purely to unite the country against Dundee. 'Our actions', he writes, 'may just seem to be incomprehensible to those who live at a distance, and too many of ourselves does not well understand ourselves, our interest, or our duty, but I desire not to lay open the nakedness of my country.' Melville admits: 'I cannot be altogther satisfied with the methods we take. I will not say that some of us desire not to win to the bottom of the affair . . . but . . . we use not all the prudence in the world in managing our business.'[126]

Hamilton, Lord President, reported to King William the day after, considering the matter important enough to send his letter with his son, the Earl of Selkirk: 'Sir – seeing so great designes laid down against us, and many ready to lay hold on the occasion to disturb our peace, I judged it high time to press on the settlement of the Crown.'[127]

Thus can be seen the precarious position of the new Government. Even among its most prominent supporters there were doubts and anxieties. No-one was exempt from suspicion. Almost the only person with no conflict of interest was General Mackay, William's man in Scotland. But then, the military situation was clear and straightforward. Had the Convention been forced to pursue the civil war by its own actions, it is highly likely Dundee would have been ultimately successful. But Mackay was not to give him much room for manoeuvre.

Hamilton received a reply from King William written on the 25th, and believed to be in his own handwriting rather than that of Shrewsbury, his Secretary: 'Though it were to be wished that in some things the Convention has proceeded otherwise than they have done, yet I am persuaded that no pains nor industry of yours has been wanting to prevent those errors . . . your presence here would contribute so much to my service, that I hope you will make what haste you can hither . . .' The King then makes suggestions as to what should be done in Scotland: 'A distribution of money among the Highlanders being thought the likeliest way to satisfy them, I have given orders for five or six thousand pounds to be sent to Major-General Mackay for that purpose, as also for two frigates to cruise on the north-east coast as you desire.'[128]

Meanwhile at Glen Ogilvie, Dundee had been joined by several of the local gentry and minor nobility, his small band of troopers thus increasing to between eighty and ninety. Hearing word of Colonel Livingstone's advance, he took farewell of his wife and baby son, and assembled his men around the Royal Standard. His brother David was among them, as was William Graham of Balquhaple and other Grahams from Angus, obeying the call of loyalty to the titular head of the family. Dundee led his band northwards up the Glen, into the Sidlaws.

Hamilton was informed on 20th April that Dundee had left Glen Ogilvie. Mackay expected he would make for the lands of the Duke of Gordon, and decided to ignore the wishes of the Convention and pursue Dundee in person. The next three months were to become an elaborate military chess game, from which it is possible to compare and contrast the movements and decisions of Dundee and Mackay, and learn much of their respective characters: the flamboyant, imaginative Viscount and the phlegmatic and cautious General; the Lowlander who respected and admired the Highlanders, and the Gaelic-speaking Highlander who disliked them and their way of life. Certainly the campaign was to develop into a personalised contest between two able men – and a clash between two different ways of life – with Scotland as the prize.

Dundee and his band rode up the Glen and skirted the magnificent Glamis Castle, home of Patrick, Earl of Strathmore, a personal friend. They forded the Dean Water and rode through the farming hamlet of Kirriemuir, crossed the Isla, and continued across the wide and open Vale of Strathmore, through the Prosen Water and towards Glen Prosen itself, heading into the Grampian Mountains. This was a ruse, for shortly the troop turned back and skirted the foothills around Brechin to the North Esk, which they crossed at North Water Bridge. They rode up Glen Esk for some miles beside the river, passing through rocky defiles and thick pine woods, and then gradually they began to ascend the higher ground, crossing the Devilly burn and rising higher to the summit of Cairn O'Mount. This afforded them a panoramic view from its 1488-foot summit of the Mounth – the great barrier that cuts Strathmore off from Mar and the rest of the central Highlands. There was a wide track – the only convenient route across the mountains east of Glenshee – known as the 'Great North Road', widely used as a drove road for the great herds of Highland cattle moving south to market. It was useful to have this at their backs in case of a surprise attack. They had ridden nearly forty miles since morning, the last of these up the sides of a steep glen; so they made camp on the summit.

They woke early the next morning and set off down the winding route that leads to the Water of Freugh and the valley of Dee, across rolling heathery moorland, pine forests and swiftly flowing streams. They had moved out of the Howe of the Mearns, and there could be no mistaking that they were now in the Highlands. The air was sharper, clearer, with the scent of snow and pine in the wind. The Freugh Water joins the Dee at Banchory, swelling a magnificent crystal-clear river that ripples over a pink pebble bed. This was dangerous country for them. Just two miles east was Crathes Castle, home of Gilbert Burnett of Leys, who, only months before, had been created Bishop of Salisbury and Chancellor of the Order of the Garter by express order of William of Orange. He was to be known to a later generation of Jacobites as 'Leein' Gibby', but his *History of His Own Time is* a useful source of information on Dundee – to whom he was distantly related, having married the dour Lady Catherine, Dundee's mother-in-law.

Keeping to the middle of the wide valley, Dundee's troopers reached the tiny village of Kincardine O'Neil, the fording point for crossing the swiftly flowing Dee. There was an even bigger danger now in sight. Ahead of them, set in the midst of a thick forest, were the tall towers and budding turrets of Craigievar Castle, home of the Master of Forbes. The allegiance of Forbes can be inferred from the wording of a letter, written on 25th January 1689 in which he congratulated the King who had 'rescued these Realms from ane uneasie government occasioned by pernicious forraigne councillo ... Your Highness', he continued, 'is the Darling and Glorie of the present age. So you will be the admiration of the ages that are to come.'[121]

The Master of Forbes is described in Macky's *Characters of the Scottish Nobility* as being 'zealous for the Revolution ... a good-natured Gentleman, very tall and black'. Since his father was old and infirm, he was in control of a wide triangle of land from Fraserburgh in the northeast, to Aberdeen in the south, all the way inland to Braemar. The headquarters of the clan was Druminor Castle, on the borders of the Gordon lands. Forbes was thus in control of all routes north and northwest, and was to prove a useful source of information to Mackay. Mackay had written to William that he 'hoped to make [Forbes] useful to the service, though [he was] as yet bashful before his enemy, never having seen any'.[130]

Dundee and his troop managed to circumvent both castles and cross the Don without being detected – it is possible that they completed the journey by night. They reached the lands of the Duke of Gordon by Sunday 21st April. Here the people were mainly Catholics – and no friends of William of Orange – and guarded their frontiers zealously against Forbes to the south and east, and Grants in the west. Many of their castles, such as Glenbuchat, Kildrummy, Craig and Towie, bordered on Forbes territory. The headquarters of the Gordons was the magnificent Huntly Castle, then called Strathbogie, but Dundee and his men rode another eleven miles past this veritable palace to the small town of Keith. At Keith, he sent Major William Graham ahead with two letters to the Earl of Dumfermline, then continued for a further six miles to Fochabers, which stands on the edge of a large forest. The village was dominated by the lofty battlements of Gordon Castle east of the River Spey at Bog of Gight, with its magnificent views of Spey Bay. Only one tower remains; the rest was demolished in 1955. Many maps and guides do not even list the ruins, although it was later to become the ancestral home of Lady Catherine Gordon – Byron's mother.

Viscount Dundee was welcomed at the Castle on the 22nd by the Earl of Dunfermline who had quit the Convention to ride north and prepare the Highlands. Some Gordon gentry joined Dundee during his two-day stay at the Castle, Dunfermline promised to raise more men for him, and they arranged to meet again in a week's time.

Dundee was aware of General Mackay's move north with a sizeable force, and knew that Lieutenant-Colonel Livingstone had been sent to garrison the town of Dundee. He decided to pass the week by moving further north. He left Gight on Wednesday the 24th, and his troop were ferried across the Spey, then, as now, too fast-flowing and deep for a safe crossing by ford or by swimming. They passed the town of Elgin, where Dundee wrote to the Laird of McIntosh. Then they forded the Lossie and at last 'rested in the sweet fields of Forres' in Morayshire on land owned by the Laird of MacIntosh, his cousin; his mother, Jean Graham of Edzell, being Dundee's aunt.

Dundee had written to McIntosh the previous day from 'Kokstoun', which has been identified as Coxton Tower, two miles east of Elgin:

> Sir – I wrote to you the day before yesterday, concerning the present state of affairs, yet having the occasion of this bearer, I am so concerned that you make no wrong step to the prejudice of your family, or to your own dishonour, I would forbear to mind you of the just cause the King has, or the objections you have to him, and the happy occasion you have now by declaring for the King to oblige him and all honest men in such manner. As you will be sure to be established

in all your ancient rights, and rewarded according to your deservings, you may assure yourself ever of all the good offices and services lays in the power of, sir, your affectionate cousin and most humble servant.

DUNDEE.[131]

Family relations aside, Dundee was tempting providence by the promise to restore MacIntosh's ancient rights, for the Lochaber estates of Glenlui and Loch Arkaig were held by his staunchest ally – Cameron of Lochiel.

It has been claimed that the troop spent the night at Breackachie, one of three farms rented by Malcolm MacPherson, and there is still in existence a bond signed by Dundee at Breackachie on the 26th for 659 merks in favour of Cluny MacPherson; presumably in payment for goods received. It was here that Dundee received word from his wife by her messenger, Patrick Allen, that some of Livingstone's Dragoons, stationed in Dundee, were willing to defect. Lady Dundee had entertained some of the officers who had drunk a toast to King James and asked her to inform her husband they were ready to defect as soon as an opportunity arose. Some of the officers had been of this mind since the retreat from Salisbury, principally Lieutenant-Colonel William Livingstone (no relation to Sir Thomas), Captain John Livingstone, Captain James Murray and Captain Creighton – who had been with Dundee since Drumclog – Lieutenant George Murray, and Lord Charles Murray, the 1st Earl of Dunmore, who was the second son of the Marquis of Atholl and who had been the Commander-in-Chief of the Scots Dragoons until he was replaced by Thomas Livingstone. None of these soldiers had taken an oath of loyalty to William of Orange. Captain James Murray is supposed to have assured the disappointed Regiment on the return from England that they would not be fighting under William: 'What ails you, Gentlemen? Stick to me, and I will stick by you; I would wish to run this sword through my own heart, if ever I would desire you to draw your swords against King James.'

And earlier in the year Lord Charles Murray, the 1st Earl of Dunmore had invited 'all my ain lads' to meet him in an

Edinburgh tavern to discuss details of a mass defection, but he had made a fatal mistake. Despite warnings from Captain Creighton, he invited General James Douglas – the same who had defected to William at Salisbury – to the meeting, and scorned the suggestion that Douglas could not be trusted: 'My Lord Dundee has assured him that the General [Douglas] had given him his faith and honour to be with him in five days, if he marched to the hills to declare for King James.' Douglas was certainly at pains to prove his loyalty: 'dinner was no sooner done, than we heard that King James was landed in Ireland. Then Douglas, taking a beer-glass, and looking around him, said, – "Gentlemen, we have all eat of his bread, and here is his health," which he drank off on his knees, and all the company did the same. Then, filling another bumper, he drank; "damnation to all who would ever draw a sword against him".' This was Douglas' fourth (and penultimate) change of heart since the Torbay landing of William.

This was the sort of news for which Dundee had been waiting. He knew the officers personally and considered a rapid move south to meet them, but was dissuaded from this when a messenger from Mackay to the Master of Forbes was intercepted. Mackay's letter revealed that he hoped to be in Dundee with a much larger force on the 26th. He had with him Colchester's Regiment of English Horse, although he had brought only 120 of them, the remainder being too exhausted by their long journey from England. He had 200 infantry from one of the Dutch regiments, and these, plus the Scots Dragoons and Colonel Lauder's Foot, already at Dundee, put Mackay's force at well over 1000. Dundee knew now that Mackay intended to pursue him wherever he went, and instead of retreating further north, led his uncomplaining troop back to Cairn O'Mount, a distance of eighty-three miles. He was perfectly aware of Mackay's shortcomings in irregular warfare, and may have planned to draw him north to leave the south and west unprotected against landings from Ireland. One of the most invaluable primary sources on Dundee's Highland campaign is the epic poem, *The Grameid*, written in Latin in the Horatian style by James Phillip of

Amerlieclose near Arbroath, only two years after the events described. As Dundee's Standard Bearer – a position of which he was immensely proud – he rode alongside the Viscount for much of the time. He was Dundee's greatest 'fan', and apart from a tendency to over-glamourise, his account must be taken as an accurate, sometimes verbatim report.

Mackay arrived in Dundee, waited there three days, and on the 29th, set off north to Brechin.

Dundee waited on the summit of Cairn O'Mount, scanning the Mearns for troop movements, until, next day, Mackay came into view – just eight miles away. Then Dundee signalled his party with a sweep of his fringed gauntlet, turned about and rode north. Instead of crossing the Dee at Kincardine O'Neill, they crossed three miles further west at Birsemore, rode past Aboyne and up into the Cromar Hills by the Tomnaverie stone circle, down the other side, forded the Don at Kildrummy, rode at full gallop past Druminor Castle – which seemed deserted – and halted at Huntly Castle.

Huntly, or Strathbogie as it was then called, was a palace rather than a mere castle, perched high on the banks of the Deveron. Behind it, on a grassy mound, are the ruins of a tower house dating from the Middle Ages. Huntly itself was built in the mid-fifteenth century and redesigned in the sixteenth. It has some splendid carved stone panels above the main entry to the staircase tower at the rear of the building.

Dundee's disappearance baffled Mackay. He had detached his nephew, Major Aeneas Mackay, with fifty infantrymen, to hold North Water Bridge, believing that an attack south to Angus was intended. He had other problems to contend with: 'The General finding among the party of English horse but forty that could pass the hills, left his nephew, who was sickly, with eighty horse at Brechin, all sore-backed and in disorder.'[133] Mackay had tried to move his men through the Grampians at night – and this was the result. He had expected to hear news of Dundee at Kincardine O'Neill, where he had been joined by the Master of Forbes with 'forty gentlemen of his name on horse, and about five or six hundred country Foot'. The General thanked them for their loyalty but declined their offer of service on the grounds of their poor condition and lack of weapons. They had been unable to give him information on the whereabouts of Dundee's party. The Viscount seemed to have completely disappeared. There was nothing for it, under the circumstances, but to return to Fettercairn. He learned there, however, that Dundee had been within seven miles of him but had taken to the hills. He was unwilling to halt the pursuit, but was greatly hampered by lack of accurate information – and this was to remain his principal problem throughout the campaign. He sent spies, 'several poor countrymen, with money in hand (and a promise of more at their return with sure intelligence) upon country horses' to find out where Dundee had gone.

Dundee left Strathbogie at daybreak on 1st May and rode the nineteen miles to Gordon Castle to keep his rendezvous with the Earl of Dunfermline. James Seaton, 4th and last Earl of Dunfermline, described as 'middle-sized, well-favoured, high-nosed', was then forty-seven years old and had, like both Dundee and Mackay, served as a soldier of fortune in the Low Countries, some of the time under William of Orange. He was an ardent Jacobite, and one of Dundee's best officers, and had served with him in the South-West. The forty or fifty men he had brought with him for Dundee's service, chiefly Gordon gentry-soldiers, were apparently only an advance guard, and more could be expected to join them later.

The enlarged Jacobite force retraced its steps east across the Spey, via Elgin and Forres, Darnaway Castle and Auldearn to the Highland frontier town of Inverness. Perhaps the Viscount felt some stirring of his soul as they rode past the site of his kinsman's great victory almost exactly forty-four years earlier.

The Earl of Findlater was one of the Officers of Regality in the district where Dundee now was, and received a letter dated Innes, Morayshire, 2nd May, from one F. Ogilvie, an unidentified correspondent:

> Your Lord shall know that my Lord Dundie went by Elgin yeisternight to Forroes after sevin hours at night. He had about sixty hors. My Lord Dumfarling was halff our behend

him. He had about sixteen hors and sex bagedg hors. Ther is on[e] Mockay foiling them wt two redgments off hors and foot. He was yeisternight at Wheytloumes or thereby. My Lord Dundie did intersept ane packet of letrs that was coming over the carne [Cairn O'Mount] to the Master of Forbes with ane commission to reas men and severall other letrs and newes, which gave my Lord Dundie so heartie newes to remove for his auin saftie . . .

Mackay's regiments marched to Strathbogie. Dundee had gone but was a mere twelve miles ahead of them. This so encouraged the General that he ordered an immediate hasty pursuit, being particularly anxious to prevent his opponent meeting up with the Gordon men or having time to rally. In this he failed. Dundee was nearly at Inverness. Cameron of Lochiel had replied to his letter and MacDonnell of Keppoch had been delegated by the clans to meet Dundee at Inverness.

But Keppoch had ideas other than supporting Dundee in a pitched battle against Mackay. He had not waited for his leader to arrive before indulging himself in reprisals upon the town. Inverness had not replied to two letters from Dundee asking them to declare for James, and this was the excuse Keppoch needed. He had imprisoned the Town Council in his tent, and was holding them to ransom for 4000 merks.[134]

Dundee arrived to find Inverness in a state of siege. The Laird of Kilravock with 300 Rosses was on one side of the town and Keppoch on the other. Since Kilravock professed loyalty to James, Dundee allowed him to stand down and 'guard his country'. He then received a deputation of indignant Magistrates complaining of Keppoch's behaviour. This was a tricky situation for him, considering the size and ferocity of Keppoch's band of brigands, whose appetite for plunder had been well and truly whetted, but Dundee was equal to it. He told the burgesses that Keppoch had no warrant from him to be in arms, much less to plunder, but that 'necessity had forced him out'.[135] He gave them his bond that at the King's return (assuming Inverness did not declare for William in the meantime), their money would be repaid. Then he confronted Keppoch.

Coll na Ceapaich, Chieftain of the MacDonalds of Keppoch, was a man 'whom the love of plunder would impel to any crime'. He had no notions of discipline, or any conception of chivalry – except when it suited himself. He must therefore have been perplexed when a Lowlander, whom he outnumbered more than six to one, dared to 'expostulate the matter with him in very sharp terms', letting him know, quite bluntly, that his actions were those of a 'common robber' and would not help the King's cause. He listened in anger and amazement to this rebuke, and made some sort of blustering apology – which surprised his men and even himself. There must have been something in the manner of this Lowlander that suggested authority and compelled compliance. Or perhaps Keppoch's men were reluctant to engage in battle, being so loaded with spoil that they were likely to desert at the first opportunity. Thus Dundee was forced to allow them to return to their homes, which they did, plundering and looting all about them on their way to Lochaber and Glen Roy.[116]

The Highlands, like the Lowlands, were entirely feudal at this time. Clan chiefs like Keppoch were tribal princes with large retinues attending them wherever they travelled. It was an extremely hierarchical society. The *bladier*, or spokesman, was always on hand to announce the Chief's presence. A *gilliemore* carried his broadsword, and was responsible for keeping the blade sharp. A *gillieconstrain* led his horse. The *gillietrusharnish* bore his baggage, and the *gilliecassflew* carried him over the fords, so that his feet did not get wet. The Chief's piper was a gentleman in his own right and had a gillie of his own to carry his pipes. The piper played outside the Chief's window while he was dressing, during meals and at other times for entertainment of guests.

At night there would frequently be 300 or 400 of the Chief's followers and friends sleeping in the castle on straw. The Chief and his wife had a separate room, but they were the only ones to have such a luxury. The Chief presided over regular feasts, seated at the head of the table with his wife and older children. In the middle reaches of the trestle table sat the tacksmen and duine vassals; the commoners sat at the lower end, while outside on the green (or in the outhouses if the weather was cold or wet) the lowest orders waited for the leftovers. While the Chief and his guests would drink fine-quality imported claret, the tacksmen drank beer and the commoners picked at sheep's heads and drank whisky diluted with water.

Despite the rigidity of the system, and their wretched living conditions, the Highlanders bristled with pride and love of their clan, and carried themselves with an extraordinary dignity that was in total contrast to the shuffling gait of the European peasant. For, no matter how poor or humble, each clansman was aware that he was directly related to his Chief, and gloried in his Chief's success and importance.

The Highlander at this time was not much distinguished by his dress from poor Lowlanders, who also wore plaids, although whereas the Lowlanders wore trews, the clansmen's legs were generally bare. Tartans, of plaid cloth, were coloured with local dyes, and were rather dull with few, if any, checks or stripes.

Meanwhile, a letter written by Dundee to the Magistrates of Elgin had been intercepted by Mackay. The letter ordered the burgesses of the town to make quarters ready for his men and horses. It stated, partly as a threat, that he had met MacDonald of Keppoch 'with 900 or a 1000 brisk Highlanders' and now intended to pursue Mackay – whom, of course, he now outnumbered.

When Mackay read this letter, he remarked with unwitting humour that the citizens of Elgin were 'unwilling to receive a visit from such hungry guests . . . but being an open country toun they agreed, buying off the hazard of an attack at the loss of a little money'. The intercepted letter 'put the General first to some nonplus what resolution to take'. He was uncomfortably aware that Dundee had written it the day before and might even now be near at hand. He did not want to contemplate retreat with all its implications for morale, and believed that if he could arrive in Elgin before the Jacobites, his regiments with their experience of siege and defence in the

Low Countries would be equal to the task of defending the town. He was aware that his own army could not manoeuvre like Dundee's, and was determined to provoke an encounter before he exhausted his men. He kept his horse and dragoons 'at the trot for seven miles' and despatched a messenger to his nephew at Brechin ordering him to bring up the troopers he had left there to recuperate. He wrote in his *Memoirs* some time later that he was pleased to see his small party 'so desirous of action'.[137]

Mackay arrived at Elgin just before nightfall with enough time to survey the area and post lookouts in strategic positions. Once consolidated, he sent expresses to Lord Strathnaver, the Earl of Sutherland's son, Lord Reay, Ross of Balnagowan, and Grant to prepare to come to his aid. He summoned also the MacKenzies of Seaforth and the Frasers of Lovat, though neither made him any reply. He sent a courier to Brigadier Balfour in Edinburgh with an order to pick 600 of the best men from the three Dutch regiments and despatch them with Colonel Ramsay by the quickest route to Badenoch.

There is a possibility that Dundee had intended this letter to miscarry, since it was written on 2nd May when Keppoch had already returned home. Possibly Dundee was hoping to lure Mackay yet further from his base into the turbulent and hostile North by making him believe that he would soon be obliged with what he most desired – a pitched battle along standard European lines – fought according to the rulebook. Mackay was fond of the rules of combat, and had actually written such a manual himself: *Rules Of War For The Infantry, Ordered To Be Observed By Their Majestie's Subjects Encountering With The Enemy Upon The Day Of Battel.*[138] This was recommended to all 'as well officers as soldiers' of the Scots and English armies, and contained some twenty-three articles, ending with a specially written prayer for victory. Mackay considered himself a master tactician and strategist, but was to greatly revise his manual a few years later. He was also later to claim credit for the replacement of the 'plug screw bayonet' with a bayonet that could be fixed to the outside of the barrel to allow simultaneous firing. (This was a direct result of his experiences at Killiecrankie, when the time taken to fix bayonets after firing was a crucial factor in the defeat. Certainly that innovation was to shatter the success of the Highland charge and lay the foundation for British military supremacy in the eighteenth and nineteenth centuries.)

What was becoming apparent to many in the Highlands was the General's cynical disrespect for the Highlanders and their Chiefs. He had not wished to return to the land of his birth, and his memories of childhood, exacerbated by his distrust and fear of the clans, seemed to produce an almost obsessional dislike in him. He had remarked his disgust at the physical appearance of the heritors of Atholl in his *Memoirs,* and contemptuously dismissed the Master of Forbes and his 'country foot' as, likewise, the Laird of Grant and his followers. He felt safe in so doing now that his cavalry had arrived from Brechin, but these were real insults to the prowess of men who prided themselves on their bravery and fitness for war. Mackay's pride would not let him admit that his personal animosity to Highlanders was to affect his judgement and his conduct of the campaign.

Lord Reay and Ross of Balnagowan arrived at Elgin with approximately 500 men between them, and Mackay busied them in erecting palisades across the entries to the town. He reviewed the 300 armed citizens, and expected the arrival of Balfour's 600 veterans. Confidently he awaited Dundee's attack.

Viscount Dundee did not attack. Instead his troop rode away southwest along the banks of the River Ness in Stratherrick to Invergarry Castle on the shores of Loch Oich, a distance of thirty-eight miles. This was junction territory between MacDonalds, MacPhersons and Frasers. On the shores of the loch itself was the spot where, according to legend, seven of Keppoch's brothers had been decapitated by a party of MacDonalds from Sleat and the heads washed in a stream before being laid at the feet of Glengarry: punishment for crimes they had committed.

One of the reasons for the greater mobility of the Jacobites remarked earlier was the sturdiness of their Highland ponies or garrons. Short-necked and hollow-backed, these sturdy beasts never grew higher than ten hands (forty inches), being reared in large, semi-wild herds and foraging for themselves. They were used to hills and rocky terrain and possessed great powers of endurance. The routes over which the armies marched were indeed primitive. Eighty years later, after the coming of Marshall Wade, Bishop Forbes was to describe the 'roads' in his Journal of 1769 as 'the most rugged in the world – a narrow sheep or goat track winding around huge boulders'. Yet the armies, laden with equipment and weapons, garbed in ill-fitting, rough uniforms and fed on scanty rations, were expected to march long distances in all weathers, snatch a few hours of restless sleep in the cold night air – and be ready to march the next day at daybreak without complaint.

From Invergarry, Dundee's party turned back the way they had come for seven miles along the fringes of Inchnacardoch Forest to the Kirk of Kilcummin, so named after St Cummin, one of Columba's successors in the Abbacy of Iona. Later, Kilcummin – Cille Cumein in the original Gaelic – was named Fort Augustus as an insult to the Highlands after Culloden. Surprisingly, the original name has never been restored; the dark memories never quite expunged.

Once again, Dundee was stepping in the ghostly footprints of his famous ancestor, for it was here in 1645 that Montrose and the Highland Host signed their Bond of Association. Dundee's party spent the night here, and we are left to speculate whether he felt any inspiration from these dark, secretive hills. In that Bond are the names of the MacLeans of Duart and of Lochbuie, the MacDonalds of Glengarry and of Keppoch, the Captain of Clanranald, the tutor of Struan Robertson, Glendessary, the Stuarts of Appin and various MacGregors, MacPhersons, Gordons, Grants, MacDonalds and MacKenzies; a magnificent confederation who were shortly to unite under the leadership of another Graham, for these were the same clans to whom Dundee must appeal for his King's army.

Spring was beginning to make itself felt; grass springing up in even the rockiest defiles for the starved and pitifully thin cattle. This was the worst time of the year for food, both for animals and humans as the stocks of oatmeal and grains were nearly done. Sometimes in the spring the beasts would have to be bled so that the blood could be mixed with oatmeal to make cakes, rather like black pudding. Soon, however, there would be cheese, butter, milk and vegetables.

The countryside may have been peacefully awaiting the coming of summer, largely untroubled by the manoeuvring of Dundee and Mackay, but messengers hurried hither and thither carrying letters from both sides to the leading clans and gentry, demanding allegiance.

Cluny MacPherson, Chief of the MacPhersons of Badenoch, received a letter from the Earl of Dunfermline dated 3rd May, '. . . desiring ye may Immediately convein the haill Badenoch men and keip them on foot togither, and ye shall be advertised when and where to march'. He received a similar note from Mackay dated Elgin, 6th May: 'You are required to assemble your men together . . . as you shall be answerable upon the highest peril for all things that shall fall out contrarie to the interest of the service by your non-concurrence and disobedience . . .'[139]

Mackay wrote to George MacKenzie, Viscount Tarbat (no relation to the ex-Lord Advocate). Tarbat had been under suspicion, but had managed to extricate himself by promising to negotiate with the clan chiefs. It was his idea to buy them off, and he believed the entire Highlands could be bought for under £5000, which advice had been accepted by King William himself. Mackay, like the King, believed the scheme had possibilities, and had written to the Convention assuring them of Tarbat's loyalty and usefulness. Since both these gentlemen were themselves Highlanders, it is amazing how little they understood their fellows, or how little account they seemed to take of the clans' traditional and unswerving loyalty to the Stuarts. Seeking to buy that loyalty and the pride of the chiefs by open bribery was distasteful to the clans. Worse, it was regarded as an insult. But their views were widely shared by the élite who ruled Scotland, to whom the Highlanders were barbarians. Mackay's letter to Tarbat on the 8th instructs him to 'loose no tyme to gain Locheyl, assuring him from me of the King's favour and consideration if he shew himself active in breaking the Highland combination'.[140] With the benefit of hindsight, it seems incredible that Mackay believed Lochiel – undisputed leader and idol of the clans, a man famous throughout the realm for his honesty and, above all, his loyalty – could be bribed so easily. But it was widely believed in Government circles that the main motive for the clans' disaffection was fear of the Earl of Argyll and the Campbell clan. The Whigs felt that, like themselves, the clans had no higher motivations. Since the Argyll lands had been divided among the other clans, they feared that the Campbells would wreak vengeance on all around them now that their Earl had been restored, Thus Tarbat proposed that the Government pay compensation to the Earl of Argyll for his forfeited lands remaining in the hands of the clans presently holding them. He believed that the problem was merely one of confidence and economics. The plan's chances were totally dashed by the appointment, as negotiator, of the Laird of Cawdor, 'a Campbell to his name, and kinsman to the Earle of Argyll', a man 'in whom the Highlanders concerned could not be supposed to repose much trust, nor did his behaviour in after times, testify much that he meant very sincerely with the Government, tho' a Privy Councillor'.[141] On the failure of the scheme, Mackay wrote directly to Lochiel and Glengarry, offering them £1000 each, plus other benefits, but Lochiel did not even bother to read the letter, and Glengarry wrote a sarcastic reply suggesting that Mackay imitate the actions of General Monck and restore his King to Scotland. This association of himself with Cromwell's hated general infuriated Mackay and ended the correspondence forthwith.

On the morning of Thursday May 9th, the two armies were thirty-four miles – the entire length of Loch Ness – apart: Mackay at Inverness, Viscount Dundee at Kilcummin (Fort Augustus). There is an entry in the Burgess Roll of

Dundee for 9th May which names Dundee and his wife as witnesses, with others, at the baptism of 'Jean, daughter of Robert Davidson of Balgay and Elizabeth Grahame' in Mains Parish Church, Dundee's presence at Kilcummin at this time is so well-documented, however, that the Burgess Roll must be wrong.[142]

It was now nearly one month since Dundee had ridden north to the Highlands and the armies were no nearer a decisive battle, but this was clearly to Dundee's advantage. He was steadily building up support, and apprehension of his activities and irritation at Mackay's inability to halt his progress were growing in Edinburgh and London. While he remained at large, hope for the Lowland Jacobites and those in England remained high. Mackay was finding it difficult to remain so far from his base; the Highlands were becoming increasingly hostile; but he had no other course than to wait until Ramsay arrived with his battalion. He was in fact to remain at Inverness until the 26th, which gave Dundee the time and space to gather in the faithful clans.

Dundee left Kilcummin at daybreak, marching south-east through the Pass of Corrieyairick along the River Tarff to the point where the River Spey is formed from a host of tiny tributaries in the mountains above Strath Mashie. Crossing the river near the site of the modern Laggan Bridge, he made his way to Cluny Castle and halted for the night at Presmukerach on the Truim between Cluny and Dalwhinnie, a secluded farm belonging to Malcolm MacPherson of Breackachie, in whose home farm they had stayed several weeks before.

It was here that Dundee drafted a letter in the King's name to all the faithful clans, instructing them to meet him in Lochaber by May 18th with their men armed and ready for battle. The intervening nine days he resolved to put to good use. Mackay was at Inverness, confident that he was thereby sealing off the Highlands and that the central Highlands were safe in the hands of those he had empowered to secure them: Atholl, Grant, Sutherland, Lord Reay, Ross and the Earl of Argyll. As far as Dundee was concerned, however, Mackay was simply stranded, without adequate information, far from his home base. His lines of communication and supply were vulnerable and exposed. Dundee required supplies and ammunition himself in order to implement a brilliant plan that owed much to the operations of Montrose. That great leader had raided Perth, won the battle of Tippermuir and poised himself for an attack on the Lowlands, creating panic among the Covenanters. Dundee, led by the 'shades' of his great forbear, resolved to do the same. He knew that William Blair, son-in-law of the Duke of Hamilton, and the Laird of Pollock were drilling a Horse regiment there and he saw this as a wonderful source of weapons, ammunition and equipment. The move would raise the morale of his troopers and his lowland supporters. After a month of withdrawal, they needed something to celebrate. He knew that the hard riding in inaccessible places, the spartan rations and the humble lodgings had drained them. Another reason for the move was provided in a message from his wife brought by the faithful Patrick Allen. The Dragoons had sent Captain Creighton to Glen Ogilvie to inform her that two entire companies of the King's Own Regiment Of Horse were ready and willing to defect. Creighton had served with Dundee for years as his orderly and claimed afterwards to be a close friend. In his *Memoirs* there is a tendency towards exaggeration and gross overstatement of his own importance: 'The first night I got privately into the Castle (as it had been agreed between my Lord Kilsyth [Lt-Col William Livingstone] and me . . .'[143] Dundee realised that with Mackay in Inverness, there was a good chance of making a rendezvous with Kilsyth and the other Dragoon officers, and such a move would call into question the loyalty of the entire army.

Early in the morning of 10th May, Dundee and a band of about seventy troopers galloped south by the head of Loch Garry and followed the river down through the hazel forests of Blair to Blair Castle. The Atholl men were traditionally loyal to the Stuarts, and Blair Castle was being held for the Marquis of Atholl by his factor, Patrick Stewart of Ballechin, who welcomed Dundee warmly. After a brief halt, the Jacobites advanced down the Strath by the Tummel and the Tay to Dunkeld, seeing from a distance the Cathedral tower rising above dark oceans of pine forest on all sides.

Swooping in through the western gate, they encountered a bewildered tax collector whom they promptly relieved of his revenues and his weapons. There was a complaint later by Lord Rollo (in a letter to Lord Polwarth) against the conduct of the Bishop of Dunkeld 'who had incited others to take up arms for Claverhouse, who had taken prisoner three of Lord Colchester's troopers, who had prayed for restoration of King James, and had entertained Claverhouse'. There was little opposition to the incursion, and many of the inhabitants seem to have welcomed it.[144]

The troop rested in Dunkeld until nightfall, then Dundee ordered them to mount and link the horses together by the bridles, thus making it safer to cross 'the swollen, dangerous deep fords of the Tay'.[145] They rode through the dark, their path lit only by the stars. James Phillip, the Standard Bearer, records that when they reached the second last milestone from the town of Perth, Dundee halted and selected twenty men. This small party quietly entered the open gate and made straight for the market place where they dispersed and occupied the watch houses. A signal was then given, and the remainder of the troop clattered noisily over the cobbles of the empty streets. Half-asleep, the enemy soldiers were put under guard and all the arms and horses in the town were collected and piled in the market place. The townspeople woke to find Perth occupied. It appears that some of the gentry had been present the night before at a municipal banquet and could only be roused from their drunken slumber by the sharp points of cavalry sabres. The Laird of Pollock and William Blair were taken from their beds in this way, and when brought before Dundee they complained of their treatment. Dundee is said to have retorted: 'You take prisoners for the Prince of Orange, and we take prisoners for King James, and there's an end of it.'[146]

The two lairds, several officers and many soldiers were taken captive with their standards, weapons, ammunition and all their equipment. The cavaliers did not, however, rob or despoil the burgh and took no private property or money that did not belong to the Crown. There is a tale that Dundee took 9000 merks of public revenue but left behind in the same room the sum of £500 sterling, understanding it to be private property. 'He intended to rob no man, though what was the Crown's he thought he might make bold with, seeing what he was doing was purely to serve his master.'[147] All told, the spoil of the raid amounted to forty horses, some arms, ammunition, public money, numerous prisoners including two of Mackay's lieutenants, and two or three officers of the new militia regiment. Some sort of ceremony seems to have taken place at the market cross, when Dundee assembled his men and the prisoners, and removed the golden oranges from the standards of the captured regiment, the symbols of the House of Orange.

These prisoners were subsequently carried along through Angus and Perthshire into the mountains, and eventually over to Mull where they were incarcerated on the barren and rocky remoteness of the island of Cairnburg, one of the Treshnish Islands. After Killiecrankie, they were removed to Duart Castle, where William Blair died. Robert Pollock died in 1703, partly as a result of 'having been confined in the most barbarous and uncivilised places of the Highlands during the space of nine months'. One of these prisoners was Lieutenant James Colt, whose evidence at the Convention in 1690 remains an invaluable source of eye-witness detail of the events of the next two months.[148]

An unsigned letter to Lord James Murray written the same day claims: 'this will make a great noyse at Edinburgh, and its like the Shire may suffer for it . . .'[149] Indeed, Mackay, hearing of the raid some time later, was to conclude that Murray was a traitor on account of Dundee's passing twice through Atholl country with impunity.

Dundee's party now divided into two. The main party, led by the Earl of Dunfermline, herded the prisoners to Stobhall Castle by way of Scone. This was the scat of the Earl of Perth, then a prisoner himself, in Stirling Castle. An advance party was sent out to collect the revenue and cess that the unfortunate tax collector – now a prisoner – was unable to collect.

Dundee, accompanied by only a handful of officers, rode to Scone Palace where they dined with the 5th Viscount Stormont. Stormont, his father-in-law Scott of Scotstarvit, and his uncle Sir John Murray of Drumcairn were afterwards to plead with the Convention that they had been unable to refuse to provide Dundee and his officers with a meal. Stormont assured them that 'Dundee had forced his dinner from him on Saturday last'.[150]

After dining heartily they rejoined the army at Stobhall. Two experienced officers, Major James Middleton, who had served with Wauchope's Regiment in Holland, and a Lieutenant, Robert Charters, were waiting there for him, both having deserted from the regular forces at Edinburgh. Dundee's cousin, James Haliburton of Pitcur, described by Phillip as 'the flower of nobles', also joined, with two other local lairds, Fullerton of Fullerton and Fenton of Ogil, whose properties were in the vicinity of Kirriemuir.

The graphic account of *The Grameid* continues: 'when night had settled down upon the sky, and all things were finding repose, the wakeful Graham quickly arms and mounts, and calls up his men with trumpet sound. They soon gather around, big men yet taking the saddle at a bound . . . and, cheerfully following their leader, rode by Coupar Angus and Meigle and the Kirk of Eassie.'[151]

They arrived at Glamis Castle with its 'smoking chimneys, lofty porticoes and superb turrets' early in the morning of Monday 13th May. Here, 'on the green grass, Dundee rested his wearied limbs, and sent out in the King's name, light troopers to collect the revenues'. Although there is no documentary evidence of the visit to Glamis, there is a family tradition that the Earl of Strathmore rode out to meet him; there was certainly a cordiality between them, as befitting close neighbours. They rested at Glamis until early afternoon, then rode south to Dundee.

Four miles from the town, in the village of Tealing, a lady called Mrs Maxwell saw them riding down from the Sidlaws, and sent her servant, a man named Moir, to warn the town. This messenger was observed, but managed to elude capture and warn the citizens, who, fearing that the Jacobites intended to slaughter them and set fire to the town, retreated behind the gates. The bells of the churches rang backwards, the signal for a general alarm, and the militia began to barricade the approaches to the town with bales of hay and straw, carts and casks.

Dundee appeared before the town at about 5 p.m., and found the gates barred against him and militia musketeers on the walls. James Phillip narrates that Dundee, wearing a steel helmet covered in black fur (probably similar to the ceremonial headgear of a Hussar), armour breastplate and backpiece over his scarlet coat, rode forward 'surrounded by a brilliant staff of horsemen'. It was not his intention to attack the town, which, because of its defences and the large number of regular soldiers inside, would have been pointless in any case. He hoped to give the dragoons a chance to come out and join him. His troopers drove several outposts in the suburbs back to the town's walls. The suburbs stretched from the Westport up the Bonnet Hill, called in those days the 'rotten row' and now known as Hilltown. Local tradition has it that Dundee reduced the houses on Bonnet Hill to ashes in annoyance at the defiance of the burgesses, and indeed this common misconception has been repeated in local guidebooks and histories of the city ever since. It did not happen.

Dundee rode around the town walls with a spyglass, anxiously watching for any signs of support. Then he galloped his men up the Law Hill to await the dragoons joining him.

Lord Rollo had been commissioned to raise the militia among the gentlemen of Angus and Kincardine, and had encountered only disaffection and rudeness there. He returned and saw the Jacobites and only narrowly gained the sanctuary of the town walls ahead of his pursuers. There were certainly more than enough regular soldiers, militia and armed citizens within the town to send the Jacobites packing, but strangely, no-one seems to have made any effort to engage them in battle. Not even Brigadier Balfour, Sir Thomas Livingstone or Lord Rollo – who were to be reprimanded for cowardice. Proclamations were posted within the town, and in the market places in every town loyal to William throughout the country offering a reward of £1000 sterling for the capture – dead or alive – of Viscount Dundee. Even for this sum the above-mentioned gentlemen did not venture to leave the safety of the town walls.

The situation within the walls of Dundee was confused. Among the Municipal Papers of Dundee there is a petition by Robert Lindsay, a merchant, dated from the prison where he had been put for 'drinking King James' health, or for being in the company where the samen was drunken'. The dragoons who wished to join Dundee were unable to do so as long as the army remained within the town, and since Brigadier Balfour was unwilling to risk a sortie from the gates, they could only fret amongst themselves. Lieutenant-Colonel William Livingstone wanted them to fight their way out, but this did not carry a majority.

Without orders, four young soldiers of Dundee's troop attempted to provoke hostilities by riding up to the gate and discharging their pistols at the defenders. There was a return of fire, one of the troopers fell dead – and no excursion from the gates. Dundee heard the firing and formed his troop into battle formation, massed in the centre with flankers, and rode down to the walls. He was disappointed to learn the truth of the incident.

Phillip records that 'in grave anger and disappointment' he led his men off in the direction of Glamis, in the growing darkness. A dozen soldiers seized their opportunity and came out from the defences, attempting to harass his rearguard, but these were rapidly put to flight.

The Jacobites rode on to Glen Ogilvie where they spent the night. The unknown cavalry officer who wrote the *Memoir Of Dundee* several years after Killiecrankie claimed that Dundee 'tarried two nights with his wife at Dudhope', but this contradicts the account of James Phillip, and seems to be wrong on both counts.[152]

Next morning they were early in the saddle for a return to the Highlands. They had wasted a day on the fruitless detour to Dundee, and now had two days in which to cover over a hundred miles, if they were to be in time for the rendezvous in Lochaber on the 18th. The journey is described by James Phillip in epic terms and compared with Hannibal's trek across the Alps. Their route cut across the Sidlaws to Coupar Angus, by Dunkeld, by Weem Castle near Aberfeldy, headquarters of the Clan Menzies, keeping to the rough country. They rode by the Castle of Comrie and by Garth, once the seat of the Wolf of Badenoch, and reached Loch Rannoch. They traversed the wide reach of its waters, and reached the 'road' to Inverness, little more than a sheep track. They travelled in open country by way of Tummel Bridge onto an even smaller track to Dalnacardoch, heading for the Great North Road to Inverness which crossed desolate Rannoch Moor.

While the cavaliers rested on the moorland, scouts were sent out to reconnoitre for Mackay. Dundee had expected him to move south to intercept him at this point and bar his return to the Highlands, but Mackay was unaware of recent events and remained stolidly at Inverness. The troopers set off again, unaware that they were about to experience an ordeal in the worst conditions they had yet encountered. The route cut across low-lying and boggy country much intersected by burns and lochans; 'By plain and rock and cliff, by sweltering bog and gully' they toiled on. The West Highland Railway line probably closely follows their route. 'Now many of the wearied horses sink into the marsh and are lost in its depth. Failing to raise them, the riders place the saddles on their own shoulders and pursue their way on foot. I myself [James Phillip], having lost my horse, have to tramp by rugged path and hill, by rock and river. At length, by stream, by marsh, and quaking bog, by forest blocked with uprooted trees, by precipice and mountain height, we reach Loch Treig and there fix our lofty camp . . . Though the glories of Spring were clothing the Lowlands . . . we have to tear our limbs from frozen couches, and our hair and beards are stiff with ice. We pursue our way through regions condemned to perpetual frost, and never before trodden by the foot of man or horse. By mountains rising above the airy flight of birds, and cliffs towering to the sky, by devious paths among the time-worn rocks, our march unlocks the iron bolts of nature . . . Here no smoke or sign of human dwelling appears, but only the lair of the wild beasts, and a chaos of mountain, wood and sky.' In the morning the 'steam of the horses' breath looked like golden fire lit up by the dawn sun',[153]

All through this march, Dundee showed his qualities of leadership, cajoling and encouraging his men, leading by inspiration. He made the journey to Lochaber seem a crusade, a joke, an escapade and, above all, an adventure. Walking beside each man in turn, the power of his personality worked upon him. He was, comments Phillip, 'undismayed by hunger, cold or tempest. In the midst of difficulties and hardships he maintains his martial bearing, his fiery vigour, his steady constancy of mind, his unswerving fidelity.'

Descending at last to Glen Spean, they forded the Cour which feeds into the Spean, and made their way to Glen Roy. The horses which had survived were let loose to forage for themselves in the sparse fields where thistles outnumbered the grasses. The soldiers had only black bran bread and water with which to satisfy their hunger, then they were billeted out in the rude and primitive dwellings of Lochiel's followers. Dundee's men, mainly members of the gentry, secretly abhorred this rough diet, and many complaints were kept secret from Dundee himself, who asked no more than the meanest of his party, and did not complain.

The harsh weather, lack of food and shelter and mental strain were to blame for an illness that now struck him and lingered for days. Separated from his wife, his child and his home, the war was taking its toll. His hair was prematurely streaked with grey, his cheeks had a sunken look, his eyes were heavily bagged, and his once-proud scarlet uniform was in tatters. The illness revealed itself in a debilitating lethargy, and although shrugged off was to return in the next few weeks.

They made the short journey up Glen Roy to Mucomir on 16th or 17th May, where they awaited the gathering of the clan chiefs and the army that King James would send from Ireland. Dundee expected this to disembark at Inverlochy, conveniently near to the gathering point, and safe from attack.

The chiefs began to arrive at the rendezvous. The fiery cross had been sent out around the Highlands. This was 'a spear, shining with gilded point . . . crossed by wooden javelins . . . covered with red wax'. The cross was raised aloft amidst flaming torches and screaming war music of the bagpipes, and sent to all the clans, the token of unity against the common foe. It was also known as the 'Cross of Shame' – since any clan that did not answer its call was in disgrace ever after.[154]

The first of the chiefs to arrive was Alistair Dubh Mac-Donell, eldest son of the mighty Glengarry who was now too old and frail for fighting. Black Alistair – as he was known – was 'a tall man, somewhat black',[155] and was accompanied by his son, Donald Gorm, and his brother Aeneas or Angus, and nearly 300 fighting men, James Phillip describes Glengarry's men in affectionate detail. The young men wore the *lenicroich* or Highland shirt woven from tartan material displaying a triple stripe, over their shoulders hung tartan plaids, and they wore caps of steel and leather. Young Glengarry himself sat astride his horse in armour breastplate, a gold-embroidered cloak with broad baldric and buckled clasp across his left breast, and in his hand a large claymore. To Phillip, Black Alistair was 'a splendid barbaric sight'. Other weapons carried by the clansmen included studded targes, a variety of swords and dirks of all sizes, javelins and spears, bows and arrows, a few blunderbusses, flintlock muskets and Lochaber axes.

Alistair MacDonald – known as MacIan – of Glencoe was of giant proportions, towering head and shoulders above his own men. He had a flowing white beard whose ends curled backwards, his hair was long and unkempt, his eyes were wild and he wore a rawhide shirt. With a claymore in his beefy grasp, he must have presented a truly awesome spectacle. He was over seventy years old, yet strong and active, 'much loved by his neighbours, and blameless in his conduct . . . a person of great integrity, honour, good nature and courage'.[156] He brought with him the teenage Robert Stewart of Appin who had been glad of the excuse to escape the drudgery of study at his college. John Stewart of Ardshiel was in command of the 150 fighting men of the clan with his tutor, the Laird of Ballachulish. Phillip describes the Appin men wearing fur bonnets and carrying a banner which was 'blue charged with yellow figures'. Young Robert Stewart, he notes, is so young that the yellow down does not yet cover his cheeks.

The Laird of Morar arrived, commanding all Clan Ranald men on the mainland, about 200 all told. Kindly old Lochiel, the greatest of the chiefs, arrived: 'Stiff in brazen armour . . . gorgeous with gold lace, a two-edged sword by his side, and in his helmet, blood-red plumes.' There were numerous relations of Lochiel; his son-in-law, Alexander Drummond of Balhaldie, had been with Dundee since their meeting at Dunblane. Lochiel's eldest son, John, and his cousin, John Cameron of Glendessary, had charge of the closely related Lennox clan and the proscribed McGregors. Drummond of Balhaldie was to change his name back to McGregor after the death of Dundee, and declare himself chieftain of the Clan Gregor. The McNabs, an independent clan settled in the heart of Campbell country, but usually opposed to their policies, the Macaulays from Ardincaple, the McGibbons from Lennox and the Cowals from Perthshire made up the army which Glendessary seems to have had under his 'ruddy banner'.

Ranald MacDonald of Keppoch brought 200 men – which meant that Clan MacIntosh did not come. The MacIntoshes, under Cluny MacPherson, had received letters of fire and sword against Keppoch only the previous year and, assisted by Government troops, had tried to drive the MacDonalds from Lochaber. At the battle of Mulroy – only a few miles away – their advance had been halted by the ferocity of the MacDonalds. The two clans were bitter enemies and refused to fight side by side. It was probably as well for the unity of the Highland army that the MacIntoshes stayed away.

Sir Alexander MacLean of Duart, the 'commisar of Argyle', and Sir John MacLean of Otter were unable to reach the rendezvous in time and sent a note requesting a delay. They were allowed six days, but the nineteen-year-old Sir John, a 'pleasant and fastidious' youth with a great love of literature and languages, almost immediately fell ill, and Sir Alexander had to travel west to defend Kintyre against some men-of-war and a frigate that had appeared off the coast to harass his kinsmen.

MacNeil of Barra, whose warcry was 'Victory or Death', arrived, and the barefooted MacLeods of Raasay, carrying bows and arrows and axes. Their chief wore a brass-hilted sword, and the shields of his men were oblong in shape. William Fraser of Foyers had been entrusted with the leadership of the Lovats, and his kinsman Fraser of Culduthil came with him. John Grant of Glenmoriston – Iain a Chragain – brought 150 Grants, MacNaughten of Dunderaw arrived with 150 men from his castle on the shores of Loch Fyne. Alexander McAlester of Loup, described as a grim-faced man with auburn hair, brought all the MacLachlans from Morvern and Ardgour. Some of the Lamonts came with their honorary chief, Dougal of Craignish. They had been forced by law to adopt the name of Campbell, but welcomed the chance to assert their independence.

Some Lowland gentry arrived at the rendezvous: James Galloway Lord Dunkeld, a gentleman who had served as a mercenary abroad, particularly in Hungary (his son was later to become a General in the French army); Sir Alexander Innes of Coxton near Elgin; James Edmonstone of Newton of Doune on the banks of the Ardoch Water; Charles and James Kinnaird, brothers to Lord Kinnaird; and William Clelland of Faskin, who had served in the South-West with Dundee. Volunteers arrived from all points of the compass, though some, the clansmen in particular, were not exactly volunteers. It was well known for chiefs to threaten death and destruction of the homes of any vassals who might refuse to serve as soldiers. Many clans, however, had sent only a token number for Dundee's service, promising more in due course. It is simply not true that the entire Highland clans assembled willingly to fight for King James, and many of the virtues ascribed to the clansmen by historians are a product not of reality but of a wistful romanticism generated by Sir Walter Scott, James MacPherson, Byron and others. The total of the soldiers assembled for Dundee's inspection at Mucomir did not exceed 2000 greatly disappointing for him, and less than a third of those who would eventually join him, although most of these were to arrive too late for the battle, and in time only to hear the news of Dundee's death.

Dundee's own troop of cavalry amounted to almost ninety; his original troop from Edinburgh and the Gordon bonnet-lairds, friends and kinsmen, including his brother, his cousins Graham of Duntrune and James Haliburton of Pitcur, and his son's godfather, William Graham of Balquhaple. With the party also rode 'Scott, blind of an eye', according to James Phillip, whom Sir Walter was proudly to claim as an ancestor. He could equally be one of the author's! And indeed there were two 'Andrew Scotts' – one of whom had served in the Royal Scots under Captain Bruce; the other subsequently became a Colonel in the French army. A 'Walter Scott' was seized in May 1689 and examined before the Forfeiture Commission after Killiecrankie. There is no conclusive proof which of these, if any, was 'blind of an eye'. A young man of the name Johnstone, who figures later, and a fashionable Edinburgh advocate and intellectual, Gilbert Ramsay, also rode with the troop.

Dundee roused his sentries at dawn and just before noon made a speech to the assembled army. Then the pipes struck up the wild war music, and the army began its march north-east from Glen Roy.

Young Glengarry led the first line with a troop of thirty horse followed in order by the other chiefs and their clans with William Fraser of Foyers bringing up the rear. They marched around the side of Carn Liath and forded the Spey at Garva Bridge. As they passed through Badenoch, all who would not join them were burnt out. Dundee was unable to escape the consequences of the clan system, a system based on envy and bitter rivalry in an area of scant resources. He had been unable to attract the adherents of Clan MacIntosh, or their titular chief, Cluny MacPherson, because the Mac-Donalds of Keppoch were with him. He had to keep a close watch on the Camerons of Lochiel who were quite likely to fall on the Grants of Glenmoriston, and vice versa. Similarly, many of the Badenoch men were wary of joining him because they suspected that the Atholl men would ravage their territory if they left it unprotected. Some, to save their houses and possessions, joined with Dundee, while others fled to the hills.

The highly subjective account by the author of *Memoirs of Lochiel* – Lochiel's grandson – relates that 'it was Dundee's usewall custome to steall out privatly and visite his out-guards and sentrys in person, in order to keep them to exact duty; and though he never punished delinquents, yet he used such artfull methods, as soon made them very observant of his orders, by which means he was never catched napping. One night, in one of these salleys, he chanced to meet two fellows, each with a mutton on his back, returning to the camp. Though the great wants they suffered rendered such pilfery in a manner necessary, yet he reprimanded them in very sharp words, and threatened them with death if they committed such cryms for the future. One of the fellows, mistakeing Dundee, who was not much distinguished by his dress, for one of his troopers, was so provoked with his threatnings, that he satt down upon his knees, putt his gun to his eye, and would have infallibly shot him dead, had not his comrade cryed to him to "Hold!" for "it was the General." The poor fellow was so struck with the horrour of his crime, that he dropt down dead upon the sport.'[157] An unlikely tale indeed!

Dundee had some success when they returned to the green fields of the MacPhersons. Recrossing the Spey at Laggan, he marched past the village of Balnagowan, where he was able to persuade Cluny MacPherson and his clan to come out, albeit somewhat unwillingly, to join him from the nearby castle at Raitts. Not a trace of it remains, the castle having been razed to the ground by the Duke of Cumberland and then replaced in the nineteenth century by Cluny Castle.

The next day, 29th May, being the anniversary of Charles II's birthday, and also of the Restoration, a date joyfully regarded by most Scotsmen because it had signified the end of General Monck's invasion and Cromwell's hated occupation, required some kind of celebration. Dundee was aware of the Highlanders' love of ceremony, and addressed his assembled army from a grassy knoll in the middle of the camp, remarking the auspiciousness of the occasion. He arranged for a bonfire to be built, and the pipers played around it. Dundee and his officers and the chiefs drank a toast to the King. 'And with uncovered head he [Dundee] stood before the whole throng, and quaffed his goblet at a mighty draught.' The Highlanders expected festivities and dancing to follow, but Dundee cut the ceremony short and urged them instead to use the remainder of the day to attack Ruthven Castle, held for William by Captain Forbes and sixty or seventy Grants. It was the only garrison castle in the Highlands held for William, and its capture would be a fitting gesture with which to mark the date.[158]

Ruthven Castle stood on a grassy, man-made knoll overlooking the village of Kingussie, protected both to the north and the east by a bend of the River Spey, and joined at that point by the swiftly flowing Allt Mór which runs down from the great rock mass of Creag Dubh, the 'Black Rock of Clan Chattan', an outcrop of the Monadhliath, the Grey Hills. The castle stood at a crossing point of four tracks, and has played a part in several dramatic episodes: besieged by Argyle, held in turn by the great Montrose and General Monck, and used latterly as a prison. The castle no longer exists, and the ruins to be seen on the site are those of the later Hanoverian barracks destroyed by the Jacobites in 1745.

As he marched towards the castle, Dundee sent a messenger ahead to demand its immediate surrender. This was refused by Forbes. The siege then began, and the Highlanders surrounded the castle with a show of strength, pipes playing and bugles blowing, but Forbes still refused to surrender.

The MacDonalds of Keppoch were appointed by Dundee to collect brushwood and improvise scaling ladders. They filled in the ditch around the castle with 'piles of wood and beams' under intense fire from the ramparts, and they prepared with eager relish to smoke out the defenders.

Seeing the enthusiasm of the MacDonalds, Captain Forbes now realised the seriousness of his position. Having earlier sent his brother, Captain John Forbes, to acquaint Mackay with the situation, and believing he would shortly be relieved, he requested a parley to gain time, and offered terms: if the castle was not relieved within three days, he would surrender. Much to Keppoch's disgust, Dundee accepted these terms, and both sides prepared to wait for the three days. Dundee felt that capturing the castle intact, with its weapons and supplies, would be more beneficial than destroying it. He was, temporarily at least, in a relatively strong position.

In the *Account of the Proceedings of the Scottish Parliament,* it is noted: 'The Viscount of Dundee is in the West Highlands, like an Incendiary, to inflame that cold countrey; yet he finds small encouragement, the Natives there, according to their old custom, flock to him in great Numbers, not to serve him, but to serve themselves, by stealing his Baggage, and such other Booty as they can lay hold on; then they forsake him and his weary troops, which are not able to follow them. Their horses are so jaded with constant travel, and fainted for want of food, that they are altogether useless. Most expect, that the Viscount and his men will haste to Ireland for Self-Preservation.' The report ends with the smug assertion that 'Dundee, and the other Highlanders, his Confederates, will prove but a Morning Mist, that will soon vanish. This needs not to be doubted, we having often had the proof of it.'[159] Complacency, based on lack of real information, had already taken firm root at the Convention.

6

Dark John of the Battles

General Hugh Mackay of Scourie remained at Inverness all through May, until the 26th, occupying his time writing letters to clans he considered might still be persuaded even at this late stage to declare for King William III, and trying to patch together his scanty information on Dundee's movements.

On 21st May he was still corresponding with Cluny MacPherson:

> Sir – I cannot believe you so much an enemy to your eternall and temporal happynesse, as to joyne with a compnie of papists . . . My advyce then is that you order your following to draw to a head, and . . . send all their good[s] movable out of the way, I mean their cattell . . . what little harme you can suffer in the King's and Kingdom's service shall be richly repaired besydes the honour and satisfaction of conscience you shall gaine in hazarding freely and cheerfully all things for the maintenance of a cause . . . you shall be pleased to give me speedy notice of your resolution, that I may take measures accordingly . . .
>
> MACKAY.[160]

He monitored the painfully slow northward progress of his reinforcements under Colonel Ramsay, and the raising of strong new forces: 'It's lyk we may be shortly in a good posture, for we have now 7000 strangers, and 8000 new leavies within the Kingdom . . .' the Lord Advocate, Sir James

Steuart, had written in a private report to Lord Melville. His own men were quite exhausted after two months in the inhospitable North and their marches across wild Highland terrain, and he did not want to put them through further hardship until he was quite certain he would not be drawn into fruitless and debilitating manoeuvres.

There had been considerable criticism of Mackay's leadership and tactics, it being widely known that he had failed to raise the Highlands for William, or to isolate Dundee from his support. The truth was that Mackay had not used his time wisely: Dundee had had ample time in which to rally his supporters, to partly train them, to weld them into some sort of fighting force and to acquire weapons, supplies and money. Mackay had been unable to assure even those subjects loyal to William of protection, and consequently there was widespread fear of an unchecked Highland army indulging in the depredations previously visited upon the country by the armies of Montrose.

Nor was there any better news from Ireland. A Doctor of Divinity, by the name of Mockwall, who had escaped from that country, gave an account at the Convention on the 18th of the 'lamentable sufferings of the Protestants there, not so much by the King's army, as by the rabble, who follow the camp, who plunder and strip all they come near'.[162] On the 25th, news came of the siege of Londonderry, where it was said so many of the Royalists were killed that it was known as 'King James' Slaughterhouse'. The siege continued.

The great Scottish lords were even now facing both ways at once. Atholl wrote to Melville on the 21st: 'I write . . . that his Majesty [might] know, that the physicians thought it necessair for my wife and me to goe to the bathes for our health, being troubled by violent paines . . . soe I intend to begin my journey tomorrow. I hope your Lop will be pleased to vindicatt me to the King, if my journey is misconstrued by any of my countrymen. I have left my eldest son to manage my interest for the King's service; who I do not doubt but will doe it effectually, he being young, and I old and crasy, and not fitt for fatigue.'[163]

Lord John Murray had been complaining to Hamilton about the imputation that he was a traitor because Dundee had twice passed through Atholl with impunity – and about Colonel Ramsay's passage where goods received had not been paid for. Hamilton was unsympathetic. 'Wher armys comes such things will fall out,' he said, adding: 'it is impossible to avoide our troops comeing there . . . be the consequence what it will, and I wish you may take such courses as nether your father, yourself, nor your countrymen may be blamed, but neutrality will not long be alloued of.'[164]

In a letter to Melville from Holyrood House, Hamilton details the troop movements: 'The last we had from Major-General McKay, he was at Invernesse; Colonel Ramsay is gone to him with 600 of the best men from these old regiments . . . Sir John Lauder is come here, and his regiment lves in Kelso. Sir James Leslie's regiment is gone to Forfar, Berkeley's regiment of dragoons to Couper in Angus, and Heasting's regiment of foot at St Johnstoune [Perth] to wait McKay's orders; Marques of Atholl went from this to England on Thursday, and same day the Earl of Mar dyed at his house in Allowa very sudingly.'[165]

The Earl of Balcarres' condition was deteriorating, and Viscount Tarbat took it upon himself to enter a plea on his behalf to the Duke of Hamilton.

My Lord, you cannot imagine how much Balcarres usage is talkt of. He is a dying, and they would only give him the change of goeing out of the Tolbooth to a close hole in the towne under guard and centry, and 5000 pounds bail, besides the change beeing of no use, and noewayes advantagious to his health. He lyes still in the stinking prison; if what he proposes were dangerous, besides hurtful to the King, no discreet man would urge it; but if he give bail in ordinar summes to remove and remaine out of the Kingdome, and not return to any of the three dominions without the Kings allowance, and haveing his estats to losse to the [King] as goods, what danger can there be to give him these tearms, and all his crim being that another hath writt to him [King James, from Ireland], why might they not to your lordship, and I wonder they did not to me; it would be generous in yow

to vindicat our hard dealing by so secure a changing of the
condition . . .[166]

Viscount Tarbat seems to have consciously chosen the role of
intermediary, offering to negotiate with the clans for William
in the name of common sense and moderation, trading on
his reputation as a latent Jacobite. Now he was attempting a
similar act on behalf of the appointed leader of King James'
civic affairs. By this course, he believed he would be immune
from prosecution whichever side won, though he was wrong
because shortly afterwards he was imprisoned on the recommendation of General Mackay on the grounds that he had
not used his influence to assist the Government. Bitterly,
Tarbat was then to deny that he had ever had any influence
in the Highlands.

The Duke of Queensberry had sworn an oath of allegiance
to the new Government, and his brother, Major-General
James Douglas, who had led the Scots army to Salisbury,
was made an Earl for his information on the Dragoon Plot –
which had led to the arrest of the Earl of Dunmore and the
Earl of Airlie and others. Thus was his fifth, and final, change
of heart also his most profitable! The Earls of Panmure,
Southesk and Viscount Stormont had absented themselves
from the Convention, and Stormont had been declared a fugitive for failing to account satisfactorily for giving Viscount
Dundee a meal at his Castle. Most of the Bishops remained
loyal to King James, and came under a great deal of pressure. The Earls of Balcarres, Perth and Hume were prisoners.
Sir George MacKenzie of Rosehaugh was still at Oxford
University, and the Earls of Breadalbane, Errol and Aberdeen,
and the Earl Marischal and the Duke of Lauderdale were also
keeping themselves out of the way. The new Administration
was on very shaky ground. It was without doubt the least
stable Government for a century – and in this crisis a new
factor began to emerge: the dominance and importance of
England in Scottish affairs. Since the Union of the Crowns
in 1603, Scotland had at best been a statelet, devoid of real
independence, always liable to be dragged into European
conflict and religious turmoil at the heels of her powerful

neighbour. With Scotland so deeply divided, it finally became clear that only those politicians with the support of the English interest could hope to prevail. Most Whigs had long seen England as their natural ally, and now looked to her for direct military aid to subdue the 'uncivilised' Highlanders. The Tories harked back to the time when a Scottish King had attained the throne of England, and instead of Scotland becoming the dominant – or even an equal – partner, she had become little more than the tail of the donkey. Many Tories resented the growing English influence in their country, and the handing down of power at secondhand from the Royal Court in Whitehall. There is a sense in which the events of 1689, and the three Jacobite Risings which followed – doomed though perhaps they were – represent a last-ditch attempt to resist the pernicious influence of English power and one strand at least of their support was proto-nationalist. Even if perhaps Scotland was not a nation in any accepted modern sense of the word, being a feudal state ruled by a tiny minority, whose 'national' identity excluded the vast majority of the population.

Viscount Dundee may have been unaware of this aspect of the struggle to restore his King, but there is little doubt of the different attitudes of William and James to Scotland. To James, Scotland was the hereditary kingdom of his line, with an independent parliament; to William, Scotland was merely the northernmost part of his Kingdom. Certainly the struggle was not merely between the adherents of two claimaints to the throne of Scotland, nor was it merely a religious or dynastic struggle, and when the battle was lost, the Union of Parliaments followed with almost indecent haste. The events of 1689 were undoubtedly the entrée to the feast that was the Union of Parliaments for, after Killiecrankie the Whigs were to huddle closer to William of Orange, and the process of English domination was to accelerate.

Lord Belhaven, later to be one of the strongest opponents of the Act of Union, was at this time a newly-appointed Commissioner, and although he was to lead a troop of horse against Dundee at Killiecrankie, had strong reservations about the proceedings of the Government, which he expressed in a letter to Lord Melville on the 20th:

> . . . to my sad regraite, I see self-interest is heavier in the ballance than the interest of either religion or country, and greide and invie predomins over love and humilitie . . . make me recide from this principle, viz. to venter lyfe and fortune for his Majestic our deliverer, the Protestant religion, and the trew interest of our poor country, which at this tyme is in so much danger to be ruined by self-seeking interested men.[167]

That Mackay had remained so long at Inverness, given Dundee's marauding raids on Dunkeld, Perth, Dundee and now Ruthven Castle, was partly due to the failure of Colonel Ramsay's force to meet him within the timescale that Mackay had envisaged. He had ordered Ramsay north on 2nd May, more than three weeks previously.

Colonel George Ramsay, second son of the 2nd Earl of Dalhousie, was described by a contemporary as 'a gentleman with a great deal of fire, and very brave'. This was to prove inaccurate on both points. The Committee of the Estates issued an order on 6th May to Collectors of Customs to expedite Ramsay's baggage without searching it – so that he could make an early departure, but he was further delayed by the sudden appearance in the Firth of Forth of a number of ships – widely believed to be a French invasion fleet. After considerable panic, the ships were discovered to be nothing more than a number of Dutch herring boats. Ramsay finally began his march north on the 20th, crossing the Forth to Burntisland, and marching through Fife to Perth, which he reached on the 22nd. Hamilton wrote to Mackay on the 24th, his letter assuming the rendezvous had been accomplished.

But the two armies had not met up. Viscount Dundee had intercepted one of General Mackay's letters and learned of Ramsay's move north. The garrisoning of Ruthven Castle, he discovered, had been done specifically to facilitate the rendezvous. His army was between Ramsay and Mackay – so too were the fierce Atholl men, over whom their titular leader, Lord John Murray, had little control. Patrick Stewart of Ballechin, the factor of the estate, was orchestrating their actions in support of King James. It was he who had intercepted Mackay's letter, and imprisoned the messenger for three days while Dundee was informed of its contents, and it was he who now began to spread misinformation to Mackay and Ramsay.

Colonel Ramsay encountered no problems until he reached the Atholl district, when he began immediately to suffer hindrances and open hostility:

> In his march he discovered a great Body of Men upon the top of a hill, upon which he made a Halt, and sent to know who they were, and for whom, and who commanded them; and discovering that they were about 1000 men well posted on advantagious Ground; he sent to speak with the Commander Stewart of Bellaghan; who returned, That he would wait upon him by and by; but Colonel Ramsay observing one in Dundee's Livery with Bellaghan; when they met, he enquired for whom they were, and the reason why in Arms? Bellaghan answered, That they were Athol's men, and in Arms only to defend their own Country from violence in this loose time, both Dundee and Major General Mackay's Forces being so near; then Colonel Ramsay enquired whose Footman that was, who he observed in Dundee's Livery? Bellaghan replied That he was Dundee's Footman; whereupon the Colonel demanded the Footman, as belonging to a Traytor; but Bellaghan refused to deliver him, saying, That the Footman was his prisoner already, being seized before by him; then the Colonel charged Bellaghan to be answerable for the Footman; so seeing Bellaghan's Men numerous, and on advantageous Ground, he left them, and went forward on his way, six miles further; where being advertised that Dundee and his Forces were approaching, lest he might be set upon by Bellaghan's men behind him, and Dundee's men before him; the Collonel thought it most advisable to go to St Johnston, until Major General Mackay should joyn him, and so fight them both.[168]

He believed he was on the point of being attacked; that his position was desperate. So he blew up his own ammunition, left the baggage and made a hasty retreat the way he had come. Worse, he had, earlier in the morning confidently written to Mackay from Loch Garry informing him he would be in Ruthven Castle that evening, but shortly after the letter was sent, he was already returning to Perth.

The letter reached Mackay in Inverness, and he set out the next day (the 26th) for Ruthven Castle with a force of 100 English Horse (of Lord Colchester's Regiment), 140 dragoons, 200 Dutch foot and 200 of Reay's and Balnagowan's Highlanders – 640 men in all. He left a garrison of 300 men at Inverness, with orders to Lord Strathnaver to reinforce them from neighbouring loyal clans.

Just before he reached Ruthven Castle, he had a communication from Captain Forbes informing him of Ramsay's ignominious retreat, and the proximity of Dundee's forces. This must have startled Mackay, who believed the Jacobite army amounted to well over 3000. He did not dare risk a battle until he had Ramsay's reinforcements with him. Nor could he go as far south as Perth. He had to remain close enough to be able to join Ramsay, and yet prevent Dundee from rejoining his friends in the Gordon lands. He turned about and marched all day and all night eastwards to Castle Grant, leaving Ruthven Castle to its fate. From Castle Grant, he wrote a letter to Inverness ordering them not to surrender should they be attacked, and assuring them he would return to assist them in that event. He had a strong intuition that the counties of Moray, Banff, Aberdeen, the Mearns, Angus and Perth were likely to declare for James, and so he had no option but to remain in their midst.

Then Mackay showed considerable initiative. He doubled back and marched with as much secrecy as he could maintain to within a single mile of Dundee's position. He halted to rest his men from 4 p.m. to 10 a.m. the next day. Down on the level ground his cavalry had an advantage over the Highland infantry. In Alvie Parish, where he now was, begins a stretch of pleasant open country with thousands of silver birches and everywhere a faint, soft perfume. The Strath opens out, and the horizon is lower. There is a small church, very old, on a knoll above Loch Alvie, largely rebuilt (most recently by Sir Basil Spence), and it was round this kirk that Mackay camped, holding a very good defensive position. At his front lay a wooden bridge made of massive timbers and the tiny Loch Beag surrounded by low-lying marshy ground; at his rear was Loch Alvie; a burn protected his right flank and birchwoods, his left. He saw for himself that Dundee's army was camped in a wood protected by a marsh, where his cavalry would be useless.

But Mackay let the opportunity slip. The next morning he discovered Dundee had gone. He allowed his men to rest until 4 p.m., before retiring about four miles, when he wrote to the Government 'of his bad circumstances', complaining of the treachery of the Marquis of Atholl that had caused the precipitate retreat of Ramsay, and blaming Tarbat for supplying him with false information about the willingness of some clans, particularly the MacKenzies, to join him. As a result of this letter, the scheming Tarbat was arrested, but released due to the efforts of his cousin Lord Melville. Mackay sent an express to Colonel John Berkeley at Forfar, and Sir James Leslie at Coupar Angus, requesting them to join him with their forces.

Dundee had heard vague rumours of Mackay's advance – though he had had no idea that Mackay had come within a mile of him – and sent out two parties of scouts. His brother was in charge of one party, and the Laird of Loyal of the other. His information was that Mackay had been reinforced by a large force of Whig Highlanders: Munros, Strathnavers, Grants, Rosses of Balnagowan and the men of Lord Reay – when, in reality, most of these were still in Inverness. Even had he been outnumbered, Dundee was intent on provoking an encounter.

One of the scouts, Captain Alexander Bruce, with a dozen troopers, had gone in the direction of Kirk of Alvie, where they found General Mackay behind his defences. Bruce dismounted, and from a rock above the camp began to harangue the officers of Colonel Livingstone's Dragoons, with whom he had formerly served as a Captain-Lieutenant, adjuring them to come back to their rightful King. A few shots were exchanged, and Bruce galloped off to inform Dundee of

Mackay's position, and to confirm that his numbers were much smaller than had been reported.

Meanwhile, Captain Forbes, realising that Ruthven Castle was not now going to be relieved, duly surrendered it on 1st June, and the garrison were treated by their captors with the utmost courtesy. Forbes was allowed to ride through Dundee's camp to freedom, much to Keppoch's disgust. Keppoch's men were, however, allowed the consolation prize of utterly destroying the Castle, which Dundee could not afford to garrison for himself. No trace of the Castle remains today: the site, and presumably the stones too, were re-used to build a barracks for the Hanoverian troops – which in turn was destroyed by Jacobites just before Culloden.

Releasing Captain Forbes and his men proved to be a big mistake. Dundee had rather rashly given his word – and kept it to the letter, but Forbes' release had a disastrous result, as will be seen.

Forbes and his men made their way straight to General Mackay, and on the way, they met, close to Mackay's position, two troopers of the Scots Dragoons who claimed they were scouting for the General. Forbes told them what had happened at Ruthven and advised them to turn back as they would be running the risk of capture by the Highlanders. The troopers ignored his advice and continued on their way. This struck Forbes as being rather foolhardy, and he mentioned it to the General on his arrival at the camp. Mackay was instantly suspicious.

The two troopers were messengers from Colonel William Livingstone to Dundee. Now aware of the true numbers of Mackay's force, Dundee assembled his eager men and they set off rapidly towards Loch Alvie.

Mackay listened to Forbes' account of the siege of Ruthven. No doubt the Captain exaggerated the numbers of the enemy to make his own actions seem more justifiable. Mackay believed that his opponent had at least 3000 clansmen plus eighty or 100 horse, and he realised he must retreat immediately to avoid being annihilated. He had also begun to have deep suspicions about the Scots Dragoons, after Forbes' comments. 'One of these troopers, whose name was Provensall, further informed his Lordship [Dundee], that he and his comrade belonged to that regiment of Scots Dragoons, which was formerly commanded by the Earl of Dunmore; and that they had orders from their officers to assure him that they were all ready to live and dye with him in that service; that before they left England, all the souldiers of that regiment intended to have quitted and dispersed, as his Lordship's own troop had done; but having assurances from their officers, and, particularly, from Captain Murray, in whom they had great confidence, that the designe of keeping them together was truely for King James his service, they made a sham kind of complyance, but resolved to keep their oath of alledgiance, and never to serve King William.'[169]

By the time Dundee reached Loch Alvie, the General had gone. Now Dundee began a four-day headlong pursuit of Mackay via Kinakyle and Rothiemurchus Forest (now part of Glen More Forest Park) to Abernethy Forests. These pine forests are now separate, but in earlier days were one: the great Caledonian Forest. They spread across a great part of the Cairngorms like a dark green sea. Kinakyle was then an outcrop of birch trees which met the edge of the pine forests at Inverdruie. These are the refuge of the osprey and the capercaille. The pursuit followed the bends of the River Spey to Coulnakyle, a fording place about a mile from the modern-day Nethy Bridge Hotel, and continued south of Grantown-on-Spey, by the Haughs of Cromdale. The armies trailed each other around the Haughs as far as Ballindalloch Castle – the home of Grant of Ballindalloch, who was riding with Dundee – and the junction with the River Avon, with Dundee and the Highlanders close behind Mackay. They went along the banks of the Avon (probably following the route of the present-day B9009 road) to the junction with the River Livet near the ruined tower of Drumin. Once into Glen Livet, they came to the Burn of Tervie and travelled the long way around the deceptively gentle slopes of Ben Rinnes (2759 feet), an isolated, snow-capped giant. It was here that Dundee's army came close enough to see 'the hostile force passing into concealment behind a hill'. This was probably Meikle Conval (1867 feet) just short of Dufftown. The time was approximately 4 p.m., but it was 11 p.m. before they came close enough for battle. 'The Highlanders came up so closs with them at the foot of Glen Livet, that they raised a great shout, and threw off their plaids in order to attack them.'[170] The Highlanders poured across the Dullan Water, hard on the heels of their own cavalry. It looked as if battle would shortly commence.

Mackay sent his nephew and a hundred or so dragoons to observe Dundee's army from the top of the hill, in full view of the Jacobites.

Seeing this, and expecting that Mackay was now about to engage him, Dundee restrained the clans to allow the stragglers to catch up and arranged his army into its regiments. He put on his armour breastplate and helmet, and sent out a sortie of troopers around the back of the hill to cut off Major Mackay and his scouts. Mackay's nephew was so intent on observing Dundee's army that this move very nearly succeeded.

By this time, the sun had set and Mackay decided that the retreat should continue. He turned to the officers who were with him: ''tis long enough stayd here, 'tis better to stop, then gallop off.'[171] He recalled his nephew, who narrowly escaped the encircling movement of the Jacobite cavalry. On his return to the main army, Major Mackay nearly gave battle to a rear-party of Colchester's regiment, which, in the gathering dusk, he took to be Dundee's advance guard.

Mackay had ordered Sir Thomas Livingstone's Dragoons to retreat as fast as they could – they had reached the Bogie Water. The General did not want them anywhere near the field of battle in case they should defect. He did not catch up with them until four the next morning. His exhausted men had been force-marched through the night by the Fiddich, through to Mortlach, to the Deveron above Edinglassie. They were hotly pursued, so closely that their rearguard constantly fought off attacks by Fraser of Foyers and his clansmen, who were in Dundee's vanguard. The clans hurled imprecations and taunts at the dragoons, but this had no effect other than that of encouraging the retreat still further.

'Still rise the shouts of men, still comes the panting of pursuing horses; the air resounds with clamour . . . Here, at the double, comes a regiment of foot, there the iron hoof of the Cavalry cuts the quivering turf at the gallop,' recalled Phillip of Amerlieclose.[172]

At the Bogie Water, Mackay, seeing that the Highlanders were some way behind, called a halt. The horses were fed and the soldiers ate what little provisions were to be had. He heard that Berkeley and Leslie would join him later that day, and after allowing his men only two hours' rest, marched them a further three miles 'towards his succours, putting a very ill pass betwixt him and Dundee'.[173] He still believed he was being pursued, hence his further retreat to the foot of Suie Hill, on the edge of Whitehaugh Forest, two or three miles south of Clatt. Suie Hill is on the north-east corner of a small range known as the Correen Hills.

Dundee's army had in fact given up the chase, and halted for the night at Edinglassie on the Deveron, three miles from Strathbogie Castle, where they took on the pleasant task of consuming Mackay's provisions. Dundee could not risk coming too close to Mackay in the flat lands around Huntly where Mackay's more numerous cavalry would have the advantage.

Both armies were low on provisions after the four-day non-stop pursuit. Mackay had sent out foraging parties at Balveny, but had had to leave without them. He sent some men to Castle Forbes at Keig, four miles away, to see if any bread and oats could be obtained. His army was more than exhausted: morale was on the verge of collapse. It was only the arrival of reinforcements and the disorganisation of the Highlanders that saved them. The reinforcements arrived at Suie Hill; firstly, Colonel John Berkeley's Dragoons arrived at noon, and Colonel Sir James Leslie arrived at 6 p.m. after a rapid march from Forfarshire. At 10 p.m. the reinforced army set off the way they had come with enough light in the gloaming to enable the 200 Dutch Fusiliers to take their place at the head of the lines. Now that Mackay again out-numbered Dundee, he hoped to cover the eight miles quickly and surprise the Highland army at Edinglassie House, where he assumed it to be. Edinglassie House was the home of George Gordon of Edinglassie, a prominent Orange sup-porter.

Dundee had sent his Highlanders out into the surrounding countryside to forage for food, and had himself fallen ill. Confined to his tent with fever, he was unable to lead or control his men. The arduous conditions he had endured and continual mental and physical pressure had at last taken their toll. During his illness, with Mackay only a few miles away, his army all but fell apart. The clans began to quarrel among themselves and seeing Dundee too ill to rebuke them, they reverted to their ancient habit of plundering and ravaging the surrounding countryside: 'thinking themselves masters [they] grew very disorderly, and plundered without distinction wherever they came.'[174]

Here was proof that the Highland army needed Dundee's personal charisma to keep it together in good order. But he had endured more than the other officers. He had suffered the added anxieties of leadership of such an assorted com-mand. 'If anything good was brought to him to eat, he sent it to a faint or sick soldier. If a soldier was weary, he offered to carry his arms. He kept those who were with him from sinking under their fatigue, not so much by exhortation as by preventing them from attending to their sufferings. For this reason he walked on foot with the men, now by the side of one clan, and anon by that of another. He amused them with jokes, he flattered them with his knowledge of their genealogies, he animated them by a recital of the deeds of their ancestors and of the verses of their bards. It was one of his maxims that no General should fight with an irregular army unless he was acquainted with every man he commanded.'[175]

Dundee often wrote in his letters of the privations and suf-ferings endured by the officers and men serving with him, yet made no mention of the fact that he was party to these same privations. As he languished in sickness, he was unaware of the great danger he was in. He may have believed that Mackay would continue to retreat – certainly he was in no position to make an objective assessment of the situation.

Luckily for the Jacobite cause, the secret sympathisers in the Scots Dragoons once again managed to warn him of Mackay's attack, and from his sickbed he made hasty arrangements to re-assemble his army. He sent out the whole of his cavalry staff to rally his men in the hope of making a fight of it, but it soon became obvious that retreat was the only possible option.

Mackay heard of the precipitate and disorderly retreat and was confirmed in his suspicions of treachery within his ranks. An advance guard led by his nephew and Captain Forbes captured two dragoons, a servant, a small number of Highlanders lying hidden in a wood and a boy whose master was the same Captain Bruce who, at Kirk of Alvie, had harangued the Scots Dragoons about their disloyalty.

'The servant and the boy being examined, confessed that the serjant mentioned above, who had been commanded out with 12 dragoons to get news of the ennemy, had been in Dundee's camp, had spoke with the Lord Dundee apart, and that immediately thereafter the said Dundee had ordered the march.'[116] The dragoons were questioned and confessed to their part in the plot. An investigation was held and William Livingstone, Captain Creighton, two other Captains, Lieutenant Murray, Sergeant Provensal and several others were put under arrest.

In a later court martial held at Coulnakyle on 8th June, it was discovered that the dragoon messengers were John Connel and George Lenn. Connel gave the impression that he had been unwilling to carry messages to Dundee, although he had done so on several previous occasions, on one of which he had been paid £1 2d by Captain James Murray. He had refused to defect to Dundee, although both Murray and Livingstone had suggested this would be the safest option after handing over the message to Dundee. Lenn exhibited no such ambivalence. Sergeant Provensal also was supposed to have said that 'he hoped to see Major-General Mackay's head carried up the streets of Edinburgh, and set up as Argyle's was'.[177]

These prisoners were sent under an armed guard of 300 men to Edinburgh along with a letter to the Duke of Hamilton with Mackay's opinion that these officers 'by their own confession deserve death', and should be tortured. He singled out Captain James Murray as particularly deserving of this. 'If torture be just in any case,' he wrote, 'it is in this. And since the Law allows it, why should it not be used in a matter so essential to the service, and of such a pernicious consequence if it had taken intended effect.'[178]

No such treatment had been accorded to Dundee's prisoners, the Lairds of Blair and Pollock. It is possible that the Scots Dragoon defectors were discovered thanks to the efforts of these lairds in bribing a messenger to inform Mackay of the visit of Sergeant Provensal to Dundee's camp on 1st June.

Mackay marched to Edinglassie by Rhynie, Cabrach, the Deveron Water and Baldornie, keeping to the high ground, and when he arrived, at midnight on the 6th, he found the house sacked, with no sign of the Jacobites.

Besides the destruction of Edinglassie House, also destroyed were John Gordon of Cairnborrow's, George Calder of Aswanlie's and Alexander Gordon of Baldorney's – even though the last was a sympathetic Catholic. In the journal of Major General Mackay's march, there is a letter from an unnamed gentleman to a friend, dated at Alford, 9th June. 'It appeared', he writes, 'that much of the Duke of Gordon's land had been ravished by the Highlanders as Artlach and other places on its borders had been plundered. Dundee's forces appeared very impressive, the 2000 foot and 120 horse swollen by the baggage horse and stolen cattle.'[179]

Dundee's scouts had been close enough to see Mackay's approach, and the Highland army marched five miles to Auchindown Castle, on the banks of the Fiddich, south-east of Dufftown, and next morning, the 7th, faced the prospect of retreat the way they had come, backing away from Mackay's enlarged force through Glen Livet, back to the Haughs. Since this was a retreat, a dishonourable act in the eyes of the clans, Dundee's army began to thin out, some of the Gordon gentry riding off to their own homes. Several were seized by Grant of Grant, the Master of Forbes and Gordon of Edinglassie and perfunctorily hanged on the nearest trees.

While Dundee's army was camped at Cromdale in the shelter of a few houses, James Phillip relates that the sentries shouted out in the middle of the night. Dundee quickly formed his men, and with trumpets sounding they prepared for an attack. The attacking force, however, turned out to be a flock of sheep! Phillip narrates that Dundee laughed out loud when the situation became clear, but praised the sentries for their diligence, and his entire army for their discipline and eagerness to fight. Phillip describes the camp, the troops sleeping under improvised tents made of branches spread over with plaids.

They moved off again next morning, but as Dundee was still unwell, barely covered six miles to the woods of Abernethy. Mackay was ten miles off, but sent on an advance party of 300 English dragoons under Sir Thomas Livingstone and Grant of Grant, which came upon a party of MacLeans of Lochbuie at Knockbrecht Hill early on the Monday morning, 10th June. In the dark, the MacLeans had assumed the horsemen were Dundee's troopers, not realising the proximity of Mackay's army. Highlanders had a fear of cavalry – the big English horses – and, realising their mistake, fled to the high ground where they proceeded to rain down heavy boulders on the English. The dragoons were led by a young officer, Captain Anthony Ovington, who taunted the MacLeans as robbers and brigands, but this did not provoke the clansmen to come down and fight.

Rashly, the dragoons now dismounted – whereupon they became mere mortals. Captain Ovington led his men up the hill in orderly lines. A gallant figure in his scarlet uniform with rich gold lace and a fur-lined jacket hanging over his left shoulder, he believed that the MacLeans were too cowardly to fight, and it was a shock to him when 'the MacLeans . . . fell down upon them with sword in hand, cutt severalls of them to pieces before they could recover their saddles, killed the commanding officer, made several prissoners, and seized more of their horses, and haveing given them the chace for a good way, they early nixt morning entered Dundee's camp mostly mounted on the enemy's horses in a triumphant manner'.[180]

Captain Ovington, ascending the hill, received a bullet in his mouth which came out his back, and he died with a surprised expression still on his face. In MacPherson's *Original Papers* the senior officer is described as 'Captain Waine' and the total dead are put at seventeen, but Mackay's *Memoirs* claim, not surprisingly, that the MacLeans numbered 500, and that only Ovington and six dragoons were actually killed.

Dundee had heard the sounds of musket fire and sent out a scouting party to meet Hector MacLean and his party and bring them safely to his camp.

Mackay also heard the sound of firing and assumed that Livingstone and Major Mackay had engaged Dundee's main force. He crossed the river, but soon met Sir Thomas on his way back, and was informed of the situation. The combined army returned to Coulnakyle on the Nethy. Mackay used the next twelve hours to send out foraging parties to replenish his dwindling stocks.

Colonel Ramsay had been all this time at Perth, but now, reinforced by about a hundred dragoons and three hundred infantry, felt brave enough to attempt to join Mackay. Taking a large amount of supplies with him, after an uneventful march he met his commander near Aviemore on 11th June, the same day that Dundee's diminishing force fell back to Ruthven.

In order to disguise the fact that he was in retreat, Dundee told the clans that a great Gathering was arranged, and this was given some credence by the arrival of Sir Alexander MacLean with 200 men belonging to MacDonald of Largie and Gullusky. Sir Alexander had been engaged in a considerable struggle with a much larger force of Campbells around Kintyre and Gigha, which had included a twelve-hour engagement with the English fleet, and so vigorously had he defended his territory that the Campbells had fled at Kilmichael of Invereny near Glasrie. Sir Alexander and his men were flushed with success and enthusiasm.

Dundee received further reinforcements: over the sea from Skye came Sir Donald MacLean of Sleat, fashionably dressed in red coat and Highland trews, with 'five hundred fiery youths', according to James Phillip (700, according to Balhaldie). From the island of South Uist came sixteen-year-old Allan MacDonald, 12th Chief of the Clan Ranald, with his tutor, Donald MacDonald of Benbecula. This romantic youth was destined to go into exile in 1692, and such was his charm and poise that he won a beautiful lady, daughter of the Governor of Tangier, at the exiled Stuarts' Court in St Germain. They later set up a household in South Uist that was said to rival St Germain itself, attracting nobles, poets and scholars from all over Europe. Clan Ranald would throw it all away – with his life – at Sheriffmuir in 1715.

Dundee had another problem. He was facing an acute shortage of provisions, and the position was such that his army could no longer carry on; he was forced to dismiss the clans on the basis of a twenty-four-hour alert, keeping only Sir Alexander MacLean's party as a personal guard. With this small number he travelled to Keppoch and on to Strone, a distance of forty-five miles, arriving on 14th June. Strone is hidden behind the mountains of Glen Roy on the edge of Loch Lochy, two miles from Spean Bridge, and is not to be confused with the Strone on the west side of Loch Ness that overlooks Urquhart Bay.

Dundee's withdrawal to Strone had so clearly been a retreat to Mackay, who was also aware of the disintegration of his army, that he no longer considered his presence in the north absolutely necessary. He redeployed his forces. He sent Berkeley's regiment to Strathbogie where there was enough grass for their large English horses for a period of weeks, Ramsay with the Scottish-Dutch regiments went to Elgin, and Mackay himself took Livingstone's Dragoons, Leslie's foot, 300 of Leven and Hastings' regiments and 200 Highlanders to Inver-

ness where he was to remain for two weeks 'to see if the
ennemy would undertake anything further'. Mackay 'saw
no way to subdue the Highlanders, considering their country
was full of mountains, bogs, woods and difficult passes with
inaccessible retiring places, where it was impossible to hunt
them out, as well as to subsist a forthnight in such barren
and desert countries, but by placing a formidable garrison at
Inverlochy, with other smaller ones in their places'. He was
also extremely weary of this sort of war: 'it is certainly more
fit for a man of fewer years, and more accustomed with the
manner of the country . . .' The Highlanders, he wrote, 'are
absolutely the best untrained men in Scotland, and can be
equal'd to our new levies though they were better armed than
they are'.[181] A wiser Mackay, then, who now contemplated
a return south.

Melville had written to Lord High Commissioner Hamilton
on 4th June: 'His Majesty was pleased to tell me that he
thought it was of greater concern to the country in this present
juncture that the Generall Major should march southward
with his troopes towards Edinburgh and Glasgow. . . rather
than goe in pursuit of Dundie through the Highlands . . .
which does also expose the south and west countrys to great
danger in case of any invasion, the forces being from thence
at so great a distance . . .'[182]

Others were to be more blunt and accuse Mackay of 'wearing out the troops'. The fear of invasion was taken up by
Hamilton in his reply of 8th June: 'if they should be able to
land ane considerable force wee should be in an ill condition,
considering how disaffected all the north is, and if we should
absolutely, with all his forces, recall Mackay befor he disipats
or beats Dundie, all that countrey generally, lowlands as well
as Highlands, wold be in arms with him.' The Convention,
he assured Melville, 'thought it not fitt absolutely to recall
him [Mackay], but leave it much to himself, and desired him
to send any of the English horse that is with him to the west
countrey, where they can be best provided with horsemeat,
and most of our ouen new leveyed horse wee intend should
go there also, and some regiments of our foot lays there and

about Stirling, the rest being in St Johnstoun [Perth], Dundie, and about this place [Edinburgh].'[183]

In the meantime, almost forgotten because of events in the Highlands and in Ireland, the siege of Edinburgh Castle continued without much success. So much so that Melville, on the 13th, was instructed by the King to write to Brigadier Balfour to 'forbear his throwing of bombs and shooting much against the Castle until General Major Mackay comes north, that ammunition may be spared in the mean tyme, His Majesty being informed that the shooting and throwing of bombs . . . hes not that effect to the prejudice of the garrisone as could be wished'.[184]

Mackay wrote to Hamilton on the 13th from 'the head of Strathspey'. He had learned 'with wonder the apprehension of an invasion from Ireland, as the fleet should have prevented such'. He intended to come south as soon as he could, and in the meantime was sending on the dragoons. He had 'followed the rebels to the head of Badenoch and found them separated, but they can soon come together again. Viscount Dundee is said to be sick of a flux'.[185]

Following heavy fighting on the night of the 13th, the Duke of Gordon at last surrendered the Castle after negotiations with Sir John Lanier, the terms being ratified by the Convention the same day.

Following hard on the heels of the Castle's surrender, the news of Dundee's illness was received in Edinburgh with great jubilation. Sir John Dalrymple declared to Melville: 'God be thanked the Castle is delivered, and Dundys people dissipat, so the King's affairs heir are abow their mischeif.'[186]

The jubilation was somewhat premature. The Highland army had dispersed to their homes in good spirits. They had enthusiastically pursued Mackay about the countryside and had not yet been defeated. They were still eager for war, and regretted only that Dundee's illness had prevented them from finishing Mackay off altogether. Unaware in the main of Mackay's reinforcements, they believed that the withdrawal to Strone had been purely to effect a massive Gathering of the Clans. The King's messenger, Captain Hay, took the following, perhaps rather optimistic report from Dundee's camp to the King in Ireland, where it was received on 7th July:

> My Lord Dundee hath continued in Lochaber, guarded by only 200, commanded by Sir Alexander MacLean; but being in the heart of Glengairy and Locheil's lands, he thinks himself secure enough, though he had not, as he has, the Captain of Clan Ranald with 600 men within ten miles of him, and MacLean, Sir Donald, and McLeod, marching towards him; so that he can march with near 4,000 or refresh in safety till such time as the state of Affairs of Ireland may allow the King to send forces to his relief.[187]

Time was indeed on Dundee's side. There was growing anxiety in the Lowlands about invasion. On 12th June it was noted that there had been a large-scale distribution of leaflets in the churches. These leaflets stated that King James had been misguided by 'evil advice', and if the people would restore him to the throne, he would banish 'all obnoxious persons' from his Court – a clear reference to Catholics. On the 14th, a hearse with mourners on horseback that was slowly travelling into the Highlands was apprehended, and the coffin was found to be laden with guineas intended for the Jacobites. The Bishop of Galloway's daughter and granddaughter were arrested for conveying information to the Duke of Gordon and Viscount Tarbat. Two sons of the Marquis of Atholl, Lord Dunmore and Lord Edward Murray, and his son-in-law, Lord Lovat, were arrested, but another son, Lord William Murray, passed rapidly through Edinburgh and evaded capture. A fourth son, Lord James Murray, was already with Dundee. A 'penny post man' was seized in Holborn with thirty of King James' declarations in his pocket, which he was carrying to several gentlemen, and about the same time 'various people in different parts of England were taken carrying King James' commissions and letters of instruction'.[188]

The process of lobbying and canvassing continued unabated. Conscious of governmental suspicion of his family, Lord John Murray, the eldest son and heir of the Marquis of Atholl, attempted to bring the Atholl men under his authority.

A postscript in one of the Duke of Hamilton's despatches to Melville (4th June) reads: 'I had almost forgot to tell your L[ordshi]p that I had this day a letter from my son-in-law the Lord Murray, telling me that he hade got all his fathers vassals and men in Atholl, to ingadge not to joyne with Dundie.'[189] This was rather an optimistic claim in view of Mackay's denunciation in his long report to Hamilton on 27th June, three weeks later: 'What Athole's excuse may be (after his solemn protestations to me of his resolution to venture person and all for the Protestant religion, and the maintenance of the Government under King William and Queen Mary) I know not, notwithstanding wee saw that no countrey in Scotland favour'd the rebells more than his lordships did, not only by giving free passage to the lord Dundie, and treating him and those of his party kindly, but also by seizing my posts and leters, and sending them to the ennemy to take his measures thereby.'[190]

Murray wrote to Melville on the 11th to plead for mitigation: 'My Lord . . . I may say I have done a great deal to hinder not only the Atholl men, but many others from joining with Dundee; which had I not so much concerned my self in, its well known to all that country, that his party had been in 4 or 5 dayes more considerable than they are; and since my pains have proven so succesful, I hope no Information will have weight to occasion any trouble to my father, who went to England for his health, and to be as much as possible out of the noise of the world now in his old age.'[191] Murray then pleads for the release of his younger brother, a prisoner in Newgate gaol for his part in the dragoon plot.

The Marquis wrote to his son from Bath. Although he had absented himself from the political situation, he wanted to be certain that there would be no retribution for his actions: 'I am in peane I have not heard from my deare sonne sins I came from Scotland, nor indede from any. It was no small trubel and gret surprise to me to heare that the Atholl menne, by Beleachen's conduct, had caried themselves so ill in his Majestic's servis, and to refuse to declare themselves for King William . . . If thos things be troue Balachen was mad or grown sensless. You know vari well he had positive orders from me to intersepe Dundie if he came that way . . . if he had bene studing a way to wronge me he had done it, and has betraied his trust to me, for my enemies gives it out as if I had come a way a purpos to lett them joyne with Dundie and myselfe to pretend other wayes to the Kinge as if I knowe nothing of it'. He then assured his son and heir how false this is and 'how unlyk it wold be to the former actions of my life.'[192] As we have seen, it was, in fact, very much in keeping with Atholl's *modus vivendi*. In accord with the size of his estate – one of the wealthiest in the country – Atholl was often addressed as 'Most High Prince', and the family were playing a dangerous double game in the hope of keeping their estates intact whatever the political outcome.

Balcarres was another whose support for James had fallen by the wayside. Dundee's principal ally had been released from Edinburgh Tolbooth to his home on £4000 bail 'not to stirr out of it', but complained that his health was so ruined that he could not recover without full liberty. He promised, if this were granted, to 'live absolutely abstract, and doe nothing to the prejudice of his Government'. He had been asked to write, as a condition of his release, to Dundee and procure the release of the Lairds of Blair and Pollock – or he would go back to prison. 'I have never meddled with Lo Dundie since ever he weant from Edinburgh, nor intends nothing but a privat leife . . . intreat the King for me, that I be not reacned [reckoned] for another man's affair that I have no medling with, nor intends.'[193] Three months of captivity had broken Balcarres's spirits. Perhaps now he regretted his failure to join Dundee on the ride from Edinburgh?

Towards the end of June, a party of Camerons made an unofficial raid into Grant territory to punish those who had hanged their kinsmen at Edinglassie. Although neither Dundee nor Locheil had sanctioned the raid, Grant was clearly an enemy, the cattle stolen were desperately needed, and the raid was condoned.

Unfortunately, a young MacDonald who was staying with the Grants refused to leave them when they were attacked and was killed. Glengarry heard of the incident and went 'in a great rage to Lord Dundee, and demanded satisfaction on Locheil and the Camerons' for the death of his kinsman.[194]

Dundee listened patiently while young Glengarry raged, then asked him 'what manner of satisfaction he wanted. For', he said, 'I believe it would puzzle the ablest judges to fix upon it, even upon the supposition that they were in the wrong.' He added: 'if there was any injury done, it was to him, as General of the King's troop, in so far as they had acted without commission.' Glengarry still insisted on punishment. 'Dundee replyed, that had they been troops regularly payed and disciplined, undoubtedly they would have been lyable to such a punishment as the council of war should have inflicted on them – but as they lived upon themselves and were unaquainted with military laws, all that he can pretend to doe was to save the country in general from ravages and depredations of that nature. But, in the present case, the provocation they had was great, they resented a common quarrell, and had distributed the booty, which came season-ably enough to supply their urgent necessitys. Besides, they had troubled non but the King's open and declared enemys, and though it was irregularly done, yet he thought it good policy to conive att it. But, on the other hand he could not conceive the offence they had done Glengarry. They had, it was true, killed a fellow of his Clan, who was one of the enemy's party, and would not separate from them.'

'If such an incident', continued Dundee gravely, 'is just ground for raising disturbance in our small army, we shall not dare to engage the King's enemys, least there may chance to be some of your name and following among them who may happen to be killed.'

Glengarry blustered that 'since he could not have it from the General he would take revenge att his own hand'. Someone pointed out that he was outnumbered by Locheil. Glengarry roared back 'that the courage of his men would make up that defect'. Locheil replied quietly that he would be 'well-pleased to be out-done by Glengarry when they fought the common enemy together'. Honour seemed to be satisfied, for that evening Glengarry dined with Dundee, Locheil and the others as usual, and the incident was never referred to again. Glengarry had merely been humouring the vanity of his clansmen – an injury to the least one of them was an injury also to him.

MacPherson's *Original Papers* report that Hay the messenger arrived at Dundee's camp with expresses from King James 'which gave great joy to his Majesty's army here. My Lord Dundee is now drawing his forces together again, and resolves to march from this in a few days.'[195]

Dundee immediately wrote a long letter to John McLeod of McLeod, written at Moy in Lochaber on 23rd June. Moy, near the weir on the banks of the River Lochy, is a mile southwest of Mucomir and the loch, and is not to be confused with Moy Hall, ten miles south of Inverness, the seat of the Clan McIntosh, where Dundee had faced down Keppoch's plundeering clansmen on 1st May. The reason for the letter was that the McLeods, with the exception of the Raasay McLeods, were conspicuously neutral:

> . . . Mr Hay, who came hither yesterday from Irland, gives account that above three weeks ago, he was at the siege [of Derry], and then hors flesh was sold for sixpence, and for cannon bullets they were shooting lumps of brick wrapped in pewter plates. It is not certainly rendert . . . Some of the French fleet hath been seen amongst the islands, and hath taken the two Glasgow frigots. The King, being thus master by sea and land, hath nothing to do but bring over his army, which many people fancy is landed alraidy in the west. He will have litle to oppose him him there, and probably will march towards England; so that we who are in the graitest readiness will have ado to join him . . . He counts for great services . . . He promises not only to me, but to all that will join such marks of favour, as affer ages shall see what honour and advantage there is, in being loyall . . . I hope we will be masters of the north, as the King's army will be of the south.[196]

Major-General Mackay was under pressure from the Convention to return south to Edinburgh. The Commissioners were anxious about invasion and wanted Mackay's protection. They were rather less interested in the position in the remote Highlands. But Mackay at Elgin had received a short letter from David Ross of Balnagowan written on the 25th, which left him in no doubt that the situation in the Highlands was far from safe: '. . . from certain hands it is confirmed that the morn being Thursday, ther is ane generall randevoze of thes underwritten to hold at Invergerrie.' The letter goes on to list the clans: '. . . and from ther randevoze they doe intend to march northward and to force all the name of Freazer and the McKenzies to joyne with them, which as your Excellencie knowes, will not be ane unpleasant fora to them (and it's feared they wait such ane pretence) wherfor . . . I thought it my dewty to give your Excellencie this accompt by this express, and . . . I doe humbly, with all imaginable submission to your Excellencie, earnestly intreat that you doe not withdrawe your personall presence at this tyme from this poor countrie . . .'[197]

Ross was not alone in fearing Mackay's withdrawal from the north. Only recently the castles of Inverary and Braemar had been razed to the ground by the men of Mar so that they could not be used by Mackay's forces. Mackay had hoped that the Highlands would be well garrisoned, so that even after his departure they would be safe. But nothing he had advised in this way had been done. In fact, Mackay was heartily fed up with the Government who had sought to criticise him at every step, without either giving him supplies or suggestions as to his movements.

He felt it necessary to include an apology for his delay in returning to Edinburgh, in a comprehensive report to Hamilton written on the 27th, the day he left Elgin. In this letter, he makes various excuses for the situation; the small number of troops given him, that his plan had, in any case, never been that of a full scale military campaign against Dundee, but merely a pre-emptive move to prevent him from holding a general rendezvous. He complained that Dundee was always better informed that himself. He listed 'Ramsay's unsaisonable contremarch, which cannot, nevertheless, be much blamed in him . . .' and claimed that apprehensions of invasion in the west meant he must abandon the Highland campaign. He left some troops in the north:

I resolved to leave Colonel Levingstoun and Colonel Leslie
with their regiments, and the detachments of Levin and Hastings, in the north, which make a 1000 men in all, and to goe
south with the eight hondert foot detached out of our thrie
regiments, and Berckleys dragoons. Besydes the 1000 men at
Invernesse, I left a garison at Braan and Cultayland of a 100
men each, of my Lord Reays and Balnagowan's men, under a
Captain and Lieutenant each honder . . .[198]

Mackay wished to cajole the Convention and Privy Council
into funding larger garrisons in the north, and also that
'a body of eighteen hundert foot, and a hundred and fiftie
hors . . . be commanded to Argyll . . . which will keep those
Highlanders at home . . . and help to oppose a landing in any
place in Scotland where wee may have greatest apprehension,
and the ennemy greatest appearance of effectuating it'. He
wanted to provoke a second front on the west coast, which,
as will be seen later, was a shrewd move – had the Council
put it properly into effect.

General Mackay made a great many recommendations
in his report. Horses were to be stationed at Burntisland,
Dundee, Montrose, Aberdeen and Inverness for 'the quick
passage of expresses'. A Committee should be appointed
for provisioning the regular forces. He advocates torture of
the Dragoon plotters and urges their replacement by 'well-
affected officers'. Then he turns to the question of his own
movements: '. . . if the Rebels move down again, as the letters
which I send here (Ross of Balnagowan's letter and a letter
from Col. Livingstone) inclosed seem to import, I cannot,
without exposing the north, leave it, notwithstanding that I
believe I might be of some use there . . . If your Grace desyres
I be south, let the forces mentioned be quickly despatched to
the west Highlands; and then, when I am there, I shall help
to take measures for the further settlement of the peace of
the kingdom . . .'

As an experienced General, Mackay was aware that the
situation was far from being as secure as he presented it.
To paint a realistic picture, or one worse than the reality,
in the hope of forcing the Government to act on his recommendations, would have been to point to his own ineffectual

proceedings. Nevertheless, he sought to allay the apprehensions of the Lowland Whigs by the use of diplomacy and, while assuring the Council that matters were properly in hand, sought to play up the dangers of an invasion. Mackay's claim is not of success – he claimed only that he had created time for the levies to be raised and trained. Considering his brief – to capture Dundee and prevent a rising – he had failed. It comes as a surprise then to learn that he was at the same time writing to William of Orange asking that he be allowed 'to winter in Holland'.[199]

Viscount Dundee wrote a lengthy report to Melfort in Dublin on the same day that Mackay was writing his. Like many of Dundee's letters it contains elements of sarcasm, frankness, humour and, above all, a sparkling enthusiasm and optimism. The letter, written from Moy, on 27th June, cannot be bettered as a first-hand account: 'I was not a little surprised to find by yours that my name has been made use of for carrying on designs against you,' he begins, and indeed, a large part of the letter, the first few hundred words, are pre-occupied with trying to placate the ego of Melfort. Breadalbane had been corresponding regularly with Melfort through his messenger, Thomas Carleton, to whom Dundee seems to have taken exception: 'I had never seen the man in the face before, nor heard of him. He was not two hours in my company; and when he gave me an account of his pretended business to Ireland, I disliked most of it, as I signified to you by McSwyne [Dennis McSwyne, Dundee's own messenger to the Royal Court]; nor did I give him so much as a line with him that I remember. I leave you to judge if it be probable, that I would intrust myself so far to any, in such circumstances,' Dundee complained, insisting that he had been misrepresented. He then explained that: 'all my endeavours to lay you aside were only to yourself. I thought myself bound in duty to the King, and friendship to you, not to dissemble to you the circumstances you stand in with the generality of this country, and many in the neighbouring.' And dissemble he certainly does not: 'Your merit and rising fortune has raised envy; your favour with the King is crime enough with his enemies, and I am feared even with his ambitious friends.' He proceeds to plainly state Melfort's shortcomings. 'But I must tell you that, besides these generals, there are many pretend to have received disobligations from you, and others, no doubt, with design on your employment; yet the most universal pretext is the great hand you had in carrying on matters of religion, as they say, to the ruin of king and country. I must tell you I heard a great resentment against you for advising the giving the bulls for the bishops, and I am feared they themselves believe it. You know what the Church of England is in England; and both there and here, they generally say, that the king of himself is not disposed to push matters of religion, or force people to do things they scrupled in conscience; but that you, to gain favour with these of that religion, had proved and prevailed with him, contrary to his inclination, to do what he did, which has given his enemies occasion to destroy him and the monarchy. This being, as I assure you it is, however unjust, the general opinion of these nations, I thought, in prudence, for your own sake as well as the King's, you would have thought it best to seem to be out of business for a time, that the King's business might go on the smoother, and all pretext be taken away for rebellion; and this only in case the King find difficulty in his affairs.'

This was certainly telling it straight, but perhaps Dundee believed that an appeal to reason might yet convince Melfort to do the honourable thing: 'But I think you may come over; and when you have seen the state of affairs on the place, and spoke with everybody, you may think what will be best for you to do.' After this lengthy explanation was over, Dundee was finally able to turn to more practical matters. He had been surprised to learn from Drummond of Balhaldie that the Queen had sent him £2000 sterling, which he looks forward to receiving. It is interesting to note in passing that after a prison term in Edinburgh Tolbooth in December 1689, David Drummond was destined to become the Treasurer of the Bank of Scotland and a leading financial backer of Mar's Jacobite Rising in 1715.

'When we came first out,' Dundee reminds Melfort, 'I had but fifty pounds of powder; more I could not get; all the great towns and sea-ports were in rebellion, and had seized the powder, and would sell none. But I had one advantage, the Highlanders will not fire above once, and then take to the broad-sword'. Dundee expresses considerable surprise that 'in three months I never heard from you' and then offers a concise report of the political situation:

The Advocate is gone to England, a very honest man, firm beyond belief; and Athol is gone too, who did not know what to do. Earl Hume, who is very frank, is taken prisoner to Edinburgh, but will be let out on security, Earl Bredalbin keeps close in a strong house he has, and pretends the gout. Earl Errol stays at home; so does Aberdeen. Earl Marshal is at Edinburgh, but does not meddle. Earl Lauderdale is right, and at home. The bishops, I know not where they are. They are now the kirk invisible . . . The poor ministers are sorely oppressed over all. They generally stand right. Duke Queensberry was present at the Cross, when their new mock King was proclaimed, and, I hear, voted for him, though not for the throne vacant . . . He has come down to Edinburgh, and is gone up again. He is the old man, and has abused me strangely, for he swore to me to make amends. Tarbat is a great villain. Besides what he has done at Edinburgh, he has endeavoured to seduce Lochiel by offers of money, which is under his hand. He is now gone up to secure his faction, which is melting, the two Dalrymples and others, against Skelmurly, Polwart, Cardross, Ross, and others, now joined with that worthy prince, Duke Hamilton. M. Douglas is now a great knave, as well as beast, as is Glencairne; Morton; and Eglinton: and even Cassills is gone astray, misled by Gibby [Bishop Burnett]. Panmure keeps right, and at home; so does Strathmore, Southesk, and Kinnaird. Old Airly is at Edinburgh, under caution; so is Balcarras and Dunmore. Stormont is declared fugitive for not appearing. All these will break out, and many more, when the King lands, or any from him. Most of the gentry on this side the Forth, and many on the other, will do so too. But they suffer mightily in the meantime; and will be forced to submit, if there be not relief sent very soon.

Dundee then turns his attentions to the matter of invasion: 'I would first have a good party sent over to Inverlochy, about

5000 or 6000, as you have conveniency of boats; of which as many horse as conveniently can. About 600 or 800 would do well; but rather more . . . Inverlochie is safe landing,' he reasons, and 'far from the enemy, and one may chuse from thence, to go to Murray by Inverness, or to Angus by Athol, or to Perth by Glencoe, and all tolerable ways. The only ill is', he considers, 'the passage is long by sea and inconvenient, because of the island; but in this season that is not to be feared. So soon as the boats return, let them ferry over as many more foot as they think fit to the Point of Kintyre.' Dundee clearly planned to march towards Kintyre himself, to meet the royal army at the neck of Tarbert. He had been spreading misinformation: 'I have done all I can to make them believe the King will land altogether in the west, on purpose to draw their troops from the north, that we may the easier raise the country, if the landing be here. I have said so, and written it to every body; and particularly I sent some proclamation to my Lady Errol, and wrote to her to that purpose, which was intercepted and carried to Edinburgh, and my lady taken prisoner. I believe it has taken the effect I designed; for the forces are marched out of Kintyre.' Dundee discusses various suggested landing places, including Elie (in Fife) and Galloway and Kirkcudbright and their respective advantages. He believed, because of the rumours of invasions and their various suspected locations, that Kintyre was now the best site: 'Nobody expects any landing here now, because it is thought you will alter the design, it having been discovered; and to friends and all I give out I do not expect any. So I am extremely of opinion, this would be an extreme proper place, unless you be so strong that you need not care where to land. The truth is, I do not admire their mettle. The landing of troops will confound them terribly.' Dundee concludes the letter with the information that the government was anxious about a rumour that eighty ships bearing 15,000 men had set sail from Brest but that they did not know whether this force was sent to Ireland or to invade England or Scotland. The breathless tone of the report, if you discard the timewasting diplomacy to assuage Melfort's ego, points to Dundee's belief that the tide was turning in favour of the Stuarts.[200] The letter was followed by another, written the next day (the 28th), for he had managed to recall Mr Hay and both were taken to Melfort at the same time. The second letter introduces a theme that was to recur in his correspondence until three days before Killiecrankie: the seige of Londonderry. In this second letter, Dundee is 'glad to hear by your Lordship's that the King's affairs prosper so well, and that Derry will soon be ours'. Although there was to be an offer of surrender by the Castle Governor on 11th July, which provoked speculation of final Stuart victory in Ireland, false reports that the city had fallen continued to inspire or deflate support on either side. 'I have so often written over all that Derry was ours, that now, say what I like, they hardly believe, and when I talk of relief out of Ireland they laugh at it,' Dundee claimed, 'though, I believe, ere long, they will find it earnest, and then our enemy's confusion will be great. As to the places of landing, I am still of the same mind.' And then again, Dundee has to return to the niggling theme of explaining his attitude regarding Melfort's position:

> As to yourself, I have told you freely my opinion, and am still of the same mind. You desire I may tell you your faults. I use to see none in my friends; and for to tell you what others find, when I do not believe them, were to lose time. But I must tell you, many of them who complained of you have carried themselves so, that what they say deserves not much to be noticed. However, they have poisoned the generality with prejudice against you; and England will, I am afraid, be uneasier to you than Scotland. It is the unjustest thing in the world, that not being popular must be an argument to be laid aside by the King. I do really think it were hard for the King to do it; but glorious for you, if once you be convinced that the necessity of the King's affairs requires it, to do it of yourself, and beg it of him; but this only, as I said in my last, in case of great difficulties, and in the way I advised, which I think the King will not refuse you . . . I wonder you could have the least thought that I would concert with anybody against you, having parted so good friends . . . many did tell me that there would be no living if you returned; so, when no

arguments for you could prevail, I have, may be, to smooth
them, said that, if all were well, you would be prevailed with
not to meddle any more . . . If you will allow, I will say, that,
though you come to see the King once landed, you design not
to stay, unless you think that you may embolden your enemys.
I give my humble service to my Lady, and am, My Lord,

Your most humble and faithful servant,

DUNDIE.

These letters, in places sarcastic ('that not being popular . . .'
and 'having parted such good friends') and in other sections
critical, for, earlier in the letter, he refers to Melfort as: 'one
whose family, education and inclination is so cavalier' reveal
Dundee's patience beginning to wear ever so slightly thin. In
the circumstances, it is revealing that Melfort should have
taken up so much of his time with trivia, with tittle-tattle
and gossip, to which Dundee was forced to respond in like
manner. Instead of earnestly addressing himself to Dundee's
pleas for weapons, ammunition and supplies, Melfort seems
to have been more preoccupied with remarks made indirectly
to Dundee about him, while Dundee, facing the combined
armies of Mackay, Ramsay and Argyll with less than twenty
pounds of ammunition, had to expend valuable time assuring
Melfort that there was no plot against him . . . that he had
said nothing derogatory about Melfort, nor heard anything
derogatory about him.[201]

While Dundee was writing to chiefs such as Iain Macnach-
tan of Dunderawe summoning the non-Campbell clans of
Argyll to build a more solid confederation, Melfort was writing letters to all and sundry in Scotland, expressing his hopes
of vengeance upon his enemies: 'We deal too leniently with
our enemies,' he said, 'when we were in power, and possessed means of crushing them . . . but we will reduce them
to hewers of wood and drawers of water.' These letters were
sent without great precaution to ensure they reached only the
proper hands, and were easily intercepted, as was perhaps
Melfort's intention, and read at the Convention, where they
provoked great indignation. Balcarres later commented on
the letters: 'What the Earl of Melfort's design was in using

these expressions to one he then knew was in the hands of your enemies, I will not determine . . . nothing could be more to the prejudice of your affairs, and to my particular hurt.' And the only immediate result of Melfort's activities was that poor Balcarres was re-arrested and confined to the dungeon of Edinburgh Castle.[202]

7

Final Manoeuvres

With General Mackay gone south, the campaign, by early July, had come to a temporary halt. Both armies had experienced retreat and the optimism of advance, and both had retired to re-organise. The past three months had been a kind of prelude to the major engagement that had become inevitable since Dundee's cavaliers hoisted the Royal Standard on Dundee Law. From opposite ends of the country they were preparing for that decisive battle; it was fated that within the month they would meet in a glen that was in the almost exact centre of Scotland.

At Edinburgh, Mackay suffered the delays of Parliamentary proceedings, while at Strone on the shores of Loch Lochy, Viscount Dundee patiently awaited his Irish reinforcements, and appointed a further Clan rendezvous for 29th July.

Ireland was very much on everyone's minds. The campaign there was in stalemate and few troops could be spared to send to Scotland. Dundee, who had written, 'I know not what the matter is' in his report to Melfort, expressed optimism on the same day in his letter to McNaughton of Dunderawe: 'all goes there to our wish only Darie has been obstinat but it is over befor nou.'[203] He wrote on the 15th to Lord Strathnaver who had dared to issue him a warning: 'they . . . made you, I doubt not, believe that Darie was relieved three weeks ago. By printed accounts, and I can assure you, it never was relieved, and now is taken.' On the 20th, one week before Killiecrankie, he wrote the second last in a series of letters to the prevaricating Cluny MacPherson: 'Derry is certainly taken by storm last week . . .' Even as late as the 23rd he was assuring Lord John Murray, Atholl's eldest son, whom he still hoped to convert: 'I upon my word of honour, I can assure yow Derry was taken this day, eight dayes; they gote their lives.'

The Siege of Londonderry became probably the most celebrated in British history, and an excellent account appears in Patrick MacRory's *The Siege of Derry* (1981). Governor Lundy had offered a capitulation on 11th July, thence creating rumours in Scotland that the town had actually been taken, but the citizens and garrison continued to defend their city and forced Lundy to abdicate. Lundy avoided a lynch mob by escaping in female clothing. As the song goes:

> When James and all his rebel band
> Came up to Bishop's Gate,
> They nobly stood upon the walls
> And forced him to retreat.[204]

Melfort must have been aware that every day spent in front of Derry's walls was a day lost in Scotland, but he was angry with Dundee for daring to suggest that he should resign. And had such an early return to Scotland been contemplated, Melfort's influence would necessarily be at an end. Certainly, most of James' advisers were 'for making it a blockade and so going on to Scotland with the rest of the army'. Had they prevailed over the King's caution, the entire course of the war would have been changed. It was in Scotland, not Ireland, that the main scenario was evolving. James preferred to regard Londonderry as a useful training-ground for his heterogeneous armies: one of the classic blunders of British history. Had he transferred his army to Scotland, simultaneously landing his large French army in the west of England to create a second front, the course of history could have been very different. But we will never know exactly how much influence Melfort exerted on the King, or how much he succeeded in misrepresenting Dundee's position to the King. Gilbert Burnet's *History of His Own Time* informs us that Dundee had 'sent several messengers over to Ireland, pressing King James to come . . . but at the same time he desired, that he would not bring the Lord Melfort over with him . . . or employ him more in Scotch business . . . It may be easily supposed, that all this went against the grain with King James; and that the Lord Melfort disparaged all the Earl [sic] of Dundee's undertakings . . . So the Earl of Dundee was furnished with some small store of arms and ammunition, and had kind promises, encouraging him, and all that joined with him'.[205]

The King's father had sacrificed Strafford to the London mob, and his brother had left Montrose to his fate, now James seemed to succumb to the family trait: Dundee was on his own. With only 'some small store of arms and ammunition and . . . kind promises', he was doomed.

He continued, nevertheless, to write letters exhorting some of the more wayward clans to gather. A common feature of these letters is his woefully optimistic exaggeration of his own forces and of James' proceedings in Ireland. There are hopeful references to large contingents landing from Ireland, when no such landings had, or ever would, take place. It is almost as if he was over-compensating for others' lack of faith. Whatever his personal feelings might have been, his letters remain skilful, diplomatic, at times urbanely polite, at others darkly threatening, and most are leavened with traces of irony or sarcasm. Every single letter contains the irrepressible spontaneity and vitality that was Dundee's unique trademark.

Balcarres was afterwards to remark of him: 'Your Majesty's friends, who knew him best, were in doubts if his civil or military capacities were most eminent. None of this nation knew so well the different interests, tempers, and the inclinations of the men most capable to serve you. None had more the ability to insinuate and persuade. He was extremely affable; and, although a good manager of his private fortune, yet had no reserve when your service and his own reputation, required him to be liberal, which gained him the hearts of all who followed him, and brought him into such reputation, that, had he survived that day, in all probability he had given such a turn to your affairs, that the Prince of Orange could neither have gone nor sent into Ireland; so your Majesty had been entirely master of that Kingdom, and in condition to have landed with what forces you pleased in Scotland, which, of all things, your friends most desired.'[206]

The Convention of the Estates was meeting at Edinburgh, and was once again subject to divisions and power struggles. There were disagreements among the Commissioners, between the Commissioners and the military – even among the military themselves. Consider this interesting exchange of letters between Hamilton and Melville on and July Hamilton enclosed Mackay's letter 'Which he [Mackay] desired might be forwarded to your Lordship by a flying packet, *but I thought this way would come soon enough for all it contained* [emphasis added]. By our intelligence, we believe his is not true; for we have accounts this day that Dundee is still in Lochaber . . . However, we are, on Mackay's desire, sending the Earles of Argyle, Glencairne and Eglinton, with their regiments, and his troop, and my Lord Angus regiment, and Gruibets troop, and two troops of the new dragoons to Argyleshire; and from that, if Dundee and the Glencamerons goe north, to fall in to their country.'

Melville replied, with a trace of unction: 'I am very glad you think the hazard is not great from the V. Dundee and the Irish'.[207, 208] Eglinton complained bitterly to Melville on the 4th: 'I ame commanded by the Counsel to march with ane partie of horse and foot near 3,000 to the highlands, to ingadge my lord Dundie if possible. The Earls of Argil and Glencairne comand the foot and I the horse; but I find, I being but ane independent captaine in ther absence, must obey the meanest feild officer.'[209]

Hamilton wrote further, in confident style, to Melville on the 6th: 'If we are free of the fears of invasione, I think we have forces in abundance to discuss Dundie, and secure the peace of the Highlands, tho the English troops were recalled'. Hamilton clearly regarded others, and perhaps especially Melville, as being too apprehensive and cautious. He informed Secretary Melville that 'We expect Major Generall Mackay here nixt week . . .'[210]

The Convention was split into two: the old guard of Tarbat, Sir John and Sir James Dalrymple and others like Lauderdale and Breadalbane were opposed to the clique that included the new power-brokers Sir James Montgomerie of Skelmorlie, the Earl of Glencairne, Lords Polwarth, Cardross and Ross, and, of course, Hamilton. There were those like the Earl of Crawford who believed that 'the conforme preachers have everywhere debauched the people, and render'd them disaffected to the civil Government; nor have one of six read the proclamation, or pray'd for our King and Queen, nor observ'd the thanksgiving'. 'It is evident', he declares, 'that the number of our King's friends is small in this nation, except those who are of the Presbyterian way.'[211] Crawford believed that the blame for this lay squarely with the Convention, and wrote secretly to Melville on the 16th: 'Our Church Government will probably be tabled tomorrow. All do expect the Commissioner [Hamilton] will oppose any settlement that may lean towards Presbyterie.'

'I have this day assurances from a good hand, that the Earl of Tweeddale is makeing a strong partie for your lordships post, that the English clergy are active for him, and that he is under some promises to serve that interest what he can, if by their means he shall prevale, that our Commissioner and the Episcopall partie in our Parliament are strong agents for him.'

Then, in a somewhat lower, and more sinister, tone: 'The Commissioners' temper is such in the Parliament and Council, that his interest in both is much fallen, in so farr that there is also great a wearying of him by all ranks, as ever was of any in trust in this nation. The frequent adjournments, discouraging language, peremptorness in all Judicatories, examination of suspect persons by himself without other witnesses, ready dismissing of them, hath putt the nation in a great fright. Read and burn this, from, My Dear Lord etc. . . .'[212]

Worse was to follow. The rascally Sir James Stewart of Goodtrees, previously Melfort's assistant, who was now a dedicated supporter of William of Orange, wrote to his friend,

William Denham of Westshield in London, on the 11th: 'Yow have heard of the plott discovered Sunday last, by a letter to Duke Hamilton, and that the Parliament allowed to Councell to torture, as they should sic cause. In all appearance there was a designe to murder some persones; for Wilsone, ane Irishman, confesses that ther was a bond, signed by fourteen, containing ane oath of secrecy, and a promise to obey implicitly Wilson's orders; which, tho he says was only about ther intentions of going to Dundie, yet no doubt ther was more under it. Ther are many taken in to custodie, and it is confessed, that ther was advice given at Oxenfoord two or three hours before the partie cam ther, of ther coming hither to search for the Lord Balantyne; and the advice was given to Earle Lauderdale and Lord [John] Maitland [his brother, 1st Duke of Lauderdale], who wer ther for the tyme; and the informer added that the advice was given by one in the Government, which brings Sir John Maitland under suspicion, and the rather because he was absent . . .' The discovery of this plot, Goodtrees boasts, 'does greatly brack King James' party'.[213] The mighty Lauderdale, upon the evidence of spies, was jailed in the Tolbooth. The Earl of Breadalbane, who was discovered to be in daily correspondence with Viscount Dundee, was also arrested.

The Lord Balantyne (or Bellenden) referred to in the letter was a notorious Jacobite fugitive. He had made frequent visits to Balcarres in the Castle dungeons and was instrumental in dissuading that Lord from negotiating for the release of the Lairds of Blair and Pollock. Challenged by a sentry at the Pleasance Gate in the name of 'William and Mary', Bellenden offered him 'King James' Pass', produced a pistol, and shot him dead. A price of 2000 merks had been advertised for his capture.

A proclamation had also now been issued at the Convention for Dundee's capture 'Dead or Alive' – with an offer of 18,000 Scots merks (about £1000 sterling) to any person or persons 'who shall apprehend the said John, Viscount of Dundee, and shall deliver him . . .' In a letter Sir John Dalrymple declares gleefully, 'We have by proclamation put

£20,000 sterling on Dundee's head.' Since £1 sterling was worth £12 Scots, this would have been a fantastic sum, far greater than that offered for the capture of Montrose, and is almost certainly an error, since there is no record of any sum other than the 18,000 merks.[214]

Sir James Stewart wrote again to William Denham two days later: 'It's reported this afternoon that ther are fifteen hundred Irishes landed in Kintyre.'[215]

On the same day, Hamilton was transmitting 'by a flying packet . . . ane account of three French ships being on our coast, with men from Ireland'. In the same letter he mentions that Mackay had arrived in Edinburgh the previous evening (the 12th).[216] Correspondence he had received from the Earl of Argyll was sent with the flying packet to Melville. Argyll's letter, written from a position of some strength at the head of a 3000-strong army at Dumbarton opined that the main Irish invasion was to land in England. He further believed that King James' Scots advisers, the Earls of Seaforth and Buchan, knew 'the considerable force we have raised and modelled, so it is not to be conjectured they can propose by this small handfull of men or *anie rabble Dundee can offare of Highlanders* [emphasis added] to run us all down. Their designe', he concluded, 'is certainlie to make a diversion whilst about the same tyme they invade Ingland . . .' He suspected that any landing at Inverlochy would be of minor significance – a diversion from the main force. He had intercepted various letters. Two of these, dated 10th and 11th July, from Captain Will Campbell and Captain David Cairnes, were accounts of the capture of their vessels in an encounter with three French frigates. Cairnes' boat escaped, but ran aground at Mull. His account was written from Campbeltown. The French ships sailed under English flags, deceiving the Scots frigates, and they had seized a third vessel containing fifty tons of provisions from Chester. The French sailed to Islay, abandoning the Scots' vessels. A letter from Dugald Campbell of Glensaddell, written also from Campbeltown, corroborated the account, and another, from Inverary two days later, described the French landing at Carsaig in Argyll and drinking with the countrymen at an alehouse, where 'they gave account they wer of the forces sent out of Ireland'.[217]

Sir William Lockhart summed up the Scottish situation in a letter to Melville that predates the Act of Union in its analysis: 'On[e] of them [the factions in Parliament] said to my selfe, that tyranie was alyk wherever it was, and we wer lyk to have as much tyranie under King William, as we had under King James.'

'The King, as King of Scotland, had nothing but trouble. He nather nor ever wold gett sixpence out of it, all its reveneu being all wyse consumed on it selfe; that already it had cost him fortie or fiftie thousand pound to protect them. What if the King, for this disobedience and disrespect, should withdraw his forces – or by sending the M. General into Ireland, what a sad caise we should be in?'[218]

There, in a nutshell, was the Whig dilemma, and the paradox of their position in Scotland. That many of them recognised this is not in doubt. Scottish Whigs rapidly began to integrate into the English nobility and acquire English estates. They had been doing this in fact since 1603 if not earlier, but well before the Act of Union in 1707 there was a substantial majority of Scots nobles with a vested interest in unification. This was largely a side-effect of the Jacobite Rebellions.

Greed and self-interest were to the fore. Lockhart, in a later letter to Melville, was to pity the Earl of Leven, who 'pour man, hath gon to serve the King in his person, whyll Annandale and Ross, who pretend to regiments, wold chuse rather to stay and lead a faction in Parliament, than serve the King in the felds . . . Ther desyr in this besyds ther trouble in Parliament, is to goe for London with the rest'.[219]

Mackay had requested the two Lords to join his army, but they managed to persuade the Convention that their role as Commissioners was more important. Lockhart disparagingly comments: 'I shall not say how consistent it was with ther honour.' In that same session of Parliament, it is noted that the population of Ayrshire 'are become very unruly'. The rumour was that they intended shortly to march in arms upon the Parliament 'to quicken' the proceedings.

There are fourteen letters written by Dundee in the period between 10th July and 22nd July still in existence. After that date, there are only two texts, both disputed and the subject of controversy; the speech to the troops at Killiecrankie and, on the back of the page, a letter to the King from the battlefield itself. It is therefore worth examining these final letters, in order to try to interpret Dundee's attitude and state of mind.

He wrote on the 10th to two heritors of the Marquis of Atholl – Leonard Robertson of Straloch and John Robertson of Bleatoun – requesting them to come to Blair Atholl and join Pitcur and the rest of the loyal gentry. It was a circular letter, intended for widespread dissemination. 'You need not have the least apprehension,' he asserts. Then comes an obvious threat. 'I will bring such a body of men to your immediat assistance as will confound all the enemies dares appear. Som are marcht already,' he declares. 'I will be with you, or meet you [i.e. whether you like it or not!] with 4000 Highlanders, Islanders, and Lochaber only besyds all that will joyn us from Badenoch, Atholl, Mar and other loyall contries . . . So you have a glorious occasion, and no great danger . . . I will . . . see you rewarded.' This is an extraordinary letter with its appeal firstly to patriotism, vanity and daring ('glorious occasion'), secondly, pandering to the spirit of caution ('no great danger'), and thirdly, a direct appeal to greed. The postscript has a further characteristic touch – menace – but with a light, imperceptible irony, barely revealing the mailed fist beneath the suede glove. 'I am resolved that whoever refuses . . . to joyn the King's Standard, at my call, who have his Majestie's commission and authoritie to make war, I will hold them as traitors, and treat as enemies, but I need not suspect any of you,' he adds, reassuringly. And then, the final clincher: '. . . I designed not to have stirred for som tyme, had I not heard that Major-General Mackay was to fall upon your countrey and Mar.' In other words, Dundee is offering to protect, not punish them, because he knows that, despite their present inaction they are patriotic Jacobites – of course they are!

He had received a curious letter from John Gordon, Lord Strathnaver, dated from Inverness, 3rd July, which in effect called upon him to surrender: 'I . . . wish that you would follow the Duke of Gordon's example, and I am persuaded it will be found for the best course.' The final line of the letter claims that 'the contents of this letter wer written by my Lord Strathnaver upon my desyer and bie my orders' and the signature was that of Sir Thomas Livingstone, Mackay's commander in the north.[220]

This letter was intended as a warning, and as a taunt. Both gentlemen felt that Dundee, albeit a traitor, was a Lowlander – one of them – and deserving of more consideration than the barbaric savages in whose power they assumed him to be. To this letter Dundee replied in nonchalant and sarcastic style on the 15th:

Your Lordships, dated the 3rd, I received the 13th, and would have returned an answer before now, had I not been called suddenly to Enverlochie, to give orders anent the forces, arms and ammunition sent from Ireland. My Lord, I am extremely sensible of the obligation I have to you, for offering your obligations for me and giving me advice in the desperate estate you thought our affairs were in. I am persuaded it flows from your sincere goodness, and concern for me and mine, and in return, I assure your lordship I have no less concern for you, and was thinking of making the like address to you, but delayed till things should appear more clear to you. I am sorry your Lordship should be so far abused, as to think that there is any shadow of appearance of stability, in this new structure of government these men have framed to themselves; they made you, I doubt not, believe that Darie was relieved three weeks ago. By printed accounts, and I can assure you, it never was relieved, and now is taken. They told you, the English fleet and Dutch were masters of the sea. I know for certain the French is and in the Channel, in testimony whereof they have defeated our Scots fleet. For, as they came alongst, they fell on the two frigats, killed the captains, and seised the ships, and brought the men prisoners to Mull. They tell you Shomberg [William of Orange's General] is going to Irland to carry the war thither. I assure you the King has landed a considerable body of forces there, and will land himself amongst our friends in the west, whom I am sorry for, very soon. So, my Lord, having given you a clear and true prospect of affairs, which I am afraid among your folks you are not used with, I leave you to judge if I or you, your family or myn, be most in danger. However, I acknowledge francly, I am no less obliged to your Lordship, seeing you made me an offer of assistance in a tyme when you thought I needed it. Wherein I can serve your Lordship or family, at any time you think conveneint [sic], you may freely employ me: for, as far as my duty will allow me in the circumstances we stand, I will study your well, as becomes, My Lord Your most humble servant,

DUNDIE.

Perhaps a superior, reading this reply, would have been led to wonder from the tone of it, whether Strathnaver really had made an offer of assistance to Dundee.

Two letters, sent on the 14th and 18th and an undated letter which was probably written several days later, were addressed to Cluny MacPherson. He was to write three more letters to Cluny, dated 20th, 22nd and the 26th (which letter is the final undisputed letter he is known to have written). Dundee was to expend a considerable amount of effort on persuading, cajoling and finally, threatening, MacPherson to join him. He did not wish to leave a gap in Badenoch, a chink in the armour of the clan Confederation, through which Mackay could threaten his rear. Cluny and 200 MacPhersons had of course joined him briefly in the pursuit of Mackay from Edinglassie, which made his prevarication now all the more irritating. The first letter informs him that 'tis high time to draw to armes', the second employs more direct instruction: 'I expect you will have all your contrey in armes on Monday . . . Nobody offers to sit my sumonds so I expect that you will not . . . lait me have your positive answer in wryt not by proxie . . .' The third is a proclamation so that 'You will see thereby hou you ought to walk'.[221]

The Irish reinforcements had at last arrived at Duart in Mull on 12th July under the command of Colonel Alexander

Cannon, a Lowland Scots officer of little experience, and certainly none of the Highlanders' brand of guerilla warfare. There are conflicting accounts of their numbers. Balhaldie's account is 'three hundred new-raised, naked, undisciplined Irishmen'.[222] Yet Colonel Cannon embarked at Carrickfergus on the 10th 'with a regiment of Irish 500 strong, in three frigates, commanded by Monsieur De Quesne'. This was the occasion of the naval engagement mentioned previously, and De Quesne, after capturing the Scots frigates, 'safely landed the forces he had on board'.[223] While Balhaldie may have wished to underline the inadequacy of the reinforcements, and the betrayal of Dundee by the King, equally James (in his autobiography, *The Life of James II*) may have wished retrospectively to increase their numbers to exonerate himself.

In a letter to 'Our Right Trusty and Well-Beloved Cosen and Councellor, John, Viscounte of Dundee', dated from Court in Dublin Castle, 7th July – which did not arrive until much later – James states: '. . . we have sent ane regiment to your assistance, and all the Scots officers, excepting Buchan and Walcob [Wauchope], whom we could not dispense till the siege of Derry was over, which is now near done, and so soon as that is over, we shall send them to you with all speed . . .'[224]

Whether Dundee actually rode to meet Cannon is in doubt, but Colonel Cannon was shortly to lend his assistance to Dundee's attempts to persuade Cluny MacPherson, writing to him from Strone between the 14th and 18th; by the 14th he was with Dundee in Lochaber. His letter is wooden, straightforward – with none of the wit or vitality of the Viscount's epistles: 'Therefor I hope that as you have still evidenced your loyalty at all tyms, so now you will be pleased to continue, which no man that knows you will dout of, and send to joyne me at Balwither al the fensable men you can, I am sur the measurs that is taken at this tym in al appearance will answer the expectation.' The letter has a formal remoteness. It is hardly a passionate or inspiring summons.[225]

Whether or not the parliaments were 'all by the ears', as Dundee had claimed in his letter of the 18th to Cluny, the actions of the Government at this time are summarised by Hamilton: 'We have not yet heard of Dundee's motions, since he has had that assistance from Ireland my last told you of. Argyle is gone to that Shire with about 3000 men . . . Major General Mackay goes next week to Atholl with about 5000 men . . . The rest of our troops is all drawing together about Stirling, except two battalions of the troops came with Mackay, that stays in this town to guard it and the Castle. And . . . we have ordered Sir Charles Grahame to command Stirling.'[226]

Dundee now faced the prospect of being attacked on two fronts, and worse, the prospect of being isolated from a further landing of troops by the movements of the Government-backed Campbells, led by the Earl of Argyll. Strategically, he had to move into the centre of the country, yet remain near enough to join with any landing force and consolidate his army. He had estimated that the main Irish force would land before the 29th, which was the date appointed for the clans to join him in strength. He proposed to use the intervening time in exactly the way that he had done two months earlier: recruiting drives into areas that had not yet declared for him – and a rapid move into the vacuum that Mackay's absence had created. This meant the adjacent, crucial areas of Atholl and Mar; rich, fertile and with numerous fighting men; neither as yet fully committed to either side. Dundee had sent messengers to many of the gentry in both regions, and believed that the majority, despite the posturings of their titular leaders, would join him. This was confirmed by the hasty move of Lord John Murray from Edinburgh – and his vain attempts to organise his heritors and vassals to remain neutral if they could not support William. Aware that this might prove unpopular with them, Lord Murray refrained from publicly announcing his support for William, and appointed a rendezvous of all Atholl men at Blair, giving the impression that this was for consultations to take place. When he arrived in the district, he received a letter from Patrick Stewart of Ballechin, his factor, written on the 17th from Blair Castle: demanding that he declare for James ' . . .

but if your Losp be off ane other mynd, as God forbid, it is
to no purpose your Losp cum to this cuntrie, for it will bring
all the armies heir, and maik it the seait off the wair till it
be reuin'd . . .'[227] Murray still did not quite comprehend the
situation, and continued to his family seat of Blair Castle,
where to his shock and outrage, he was refused entry by
Ballechin, blunderbuss in hand. After a great deal of verbal
skirmishing, the son and heir of the Marquis of Atholl was
forced to deploy his men in a blockade around his own Castle.
He held the rendezvous of his father's subjects as arranged,
and wrote to his father-in-law, the Duke of Hamilton, requesting artillery and a trained gunnery officer. The request was
passed to Mackay, who, thoroughly disgusted with Murray,
informed him that as he would be in the area shortly, he
should do nothing until he arrived, but keep up the blockade –
if that was within his capabilities! He 'desired no more of
my Lord Murray than to keep his men from joining against
him, being resolved to take the country of Athole on his way
to Lochaber'.[228]

The somewhat diminished Lord Murray received a long
letter from Dundee on the 19th:

> My Lord, I was very glad to hear that yow had appoynted a
> randezvous of the Atholl men at Blair, knowing as I doe from
> your Lordships oune mouth your principles, and consider-
> ing your educatione and the loyaltie of your people, I am
> persuaded your appearance is in obedience to his Majesties
> commands by the letter I sent yow, which is the reason why I
> give yow the trouble of this line, desiring that wee may meet,
> and concert what is fittest to be done for the good of our
> country, and service of our lawfull King . . . by declairing
> openly for the liberty of your country, and the lawfull right of
> your undoubted sovereigne, you may acquyre to yourself and
> family great honours and rewairds . . . yow are wiser then
> to thinke, tho yow were of other principles, that the Atholl
> men can be, contrary to their inclinatione, ever induced to
> fight against their King . . .

Dundee attempts to draw Murray into the government of
King James' affairs with a ragbag of offers and hints and talk
of indemnities and rights to be given to prebyterians. Dundee

addresses the subject of Melfort's unpopularity. He wishes to assure 'many persons of quality' who are 'apprehensive of my Lord Melfort's ministry' that 'he [Melfort] is resolved to leave him [the King] against his will, if he sees that his presence is any way prejudiciall, and with joy, he says, in good earnest, he would resigne his office of Secretarie for Scotland to any honest man, and bids me give him advyce'. This was untrue, as we have seen, Melfort had no intentions of resigning under any circumstances, nor was he ever likely to accept Dundee's advice on the subject but Dundee could almost hear Lord Murray's heavy breathing as he read this, could well imagine that noble Lord's hands beginning to shake. Could it be . . . was it possible . . . that he himself . . . could be . . . Melfort's successor if James were restored? After all his father had been titular head of the Jacobite party at the Convention. But – as Murray read on – 'as I writt now to your Lordship: so I have done to all others I can reach with letters . . .' Murray's dream would fade as he scanned the rest of the letter, desperately trying to find some hope in it for himself: 'Now is the time these things ought to be treatted; for, if once the King enter on the head of a royall and alreddy victorious army . . . there will be no more place for treating, but for fighting. The Parliaments of England and Scotland are by the ears,' he concludes 'and both nations in a flame. Use the time.'[229]

Murray did not reply to the letter; instead he sent it directly to Lord Melville, Secretary of State at Whitehall. Quite possibly, Murray's personal sympathies were more with King James than he cared to reveal, but he had no alternative than to remain on King William's side – after all, one brother was already with Dundee, and two others were imprisoned – someone had to keep the estates intact. His fears would diminish when General Mackay's army arrived. Dundee was simply a fugitive with a rabble army. While he was ruminating on this, a further letter arrived from Dundee: 'Ballechin hes obeyed the order I gave to possess that Castle of Blair for the King. I hope, since it was in obedience to the King's authority, you will not blame him. Your Lordship or any declairs. for the King, will not need to fear; soe, for God's cause, doe now what you ought.'[230]

Dundee had indeed sent a royal commission to Ballechin on the 21st, which offered him the commission the King had sent to the Marquis of Atholl to on the following grounds; 'being disappointed of yt assistance by the said Marquess . . . Wee by vertue of his Majestic's authority, takeing to our consideration your constant loyalty, and tryed couradge and conduct, wt your forwardness in this occasione for his Majestie's service, do appoint you Patrick Steuart of Ballechin to command es Colonell all men of Atholl, Vassalls, Tennants, and neighbours . . . to receave your orders and obey you in every thing.'[231]

Ballechin was a dour, level-headed old laird who had loyally served the Murray family for years as a factor. Lord Murray, at the blockade, was to receive a letter from his wife, Lady Katherine: 'I could not forbear lafing when your brother Will [with Dundee] told me of Balaquen's giving it out yt he is to be Marques of Atholl.'[211] Such an idea, of the loyal servant aspiring to such honour by his own diligence, was plainly beyond her imagination, although Dundee had recognised Ballechin's abilities, he himself having risen from similar humble beginnings.

MacPherson's *Original Papers – Affairs of Scotland* informs us that Sir Alexander MacLean with his regiment of 400 clansmen was then at Cromar (presumably attacking Craigievar Castle, the seat of the Master of Forbes, who was now isolated from Mackay's army). Dundee requested Sir Alexander to break off his activities and march south to relieve Blair Castle. He was unable to do this himself because he had to remain for the rendezvous of the clans.

Dundee wrote to Breadalbane on the 20th. This is the only letter which survives from what was apparently a frequent correspondence. It is clear that the gout-stricken Earl was up to his neck in Jacobite intrigue and as we have already seen, was in constant correspondence with the royal court. His most recent activities involved an attempt to persuade Argyll to change sides. Dundee agrees this is a good idea but seems to also envisage the replacement of Argyll by Breadalbane: 'If Argyl wer out of the way Bredalben would be in all those contreys and have the wholl name to follou him.' And this attempt to persuade Breadalbane to renounce Argyll was related to the fact that the Macleans, who were in dispute with him were strong allies of Dundee. In the event, Argyll was to betray Breadalbane by informing Hamilton of his correspondence with James in Ireland and what Dundee refers to as 'your great work' came to nothing.

Dundee wrote on the same day again to Cluny MacPherson in no uncertain terms, on the 20th: 'It is nou no mor time to look on wher all your nighboors ar ingadged. I asseur you it will prove your uter ruin if you doe, so you will doe well to drawe to armes or be looked on as rebelles.' Presumably Cluny had tried to lie his way out of his situation, because Dundee does not mince his words in the postscript: 'That McKintosh is a lying rogue. The Duke of Gordon gave him no commission to forbid you to ryse.'

He wrote again on the 22nd ordering Cluny to provide provisions for his army when they come into Badinoch. 'I am unwilling that they should go loose in your countrey (to seek provisions as they did last) for fear of ruining it.' He wants provisions for 1500 men for two days, claiming that the rest of our men are provided although, of course, he had no other men. He ends with his strongest threat yet: 'I pray yow force me not, to do things to yow, against my inclination.'

The evidence of this letter, which proves that Dundee intended to march a week earlier than the rendezvous date, contradicts MacPherson's account.

General Mackay, fuming at the delays of an inefficient bureaucracy, and the miserliness of the Convention, finally set off from Edinburgh on 22nd July. This again contradicts MacPherson, who declares that Mackay had reached Blair Atholl on the 17th, but that the blockade had already been raised by Sir Alexander MacLean. The weight of evidence suggests that MacPherson is inaccurate on this and most subsequent points: Murray wrote to Mackay on the 22nd or

23rd and Mackay replied from Perth on the 25th. Mackay's army at this time consisted of 'about 4000 foot and 4 troops of horse and dragoons'. He had sent orders for four more troops of horse, and two of dragoons, to follow. It was a formidable army. General Mackay also had three small leather cannonades with him, which he hoped to use at the siege of Blair Castle. These were nicknamed 'Sandy's Stoups' after their inventor, General Alexander Hamilton, and were made from a combination of tin, leather and cordage – the idea being that they were easier to transport across rough country. Mackay believed that by capturing Blair Castle he would force Dundee back to the West Highlands where he would be surrounded by Argyll's army from the South-West, and his own from the North-East. Mackay marched to Stirling and then to Perth, which he claimed in his *Memoirs* to have reached 'about the 22nd or 23rd of July'. His own letters reveal, however, that he did not reach Perth until the 25th.[233, 234] He received a panicky note from Murray, informing him that Dundee was on the move South, and that if he reached Blair first, the Atholl men were likely to join him, to the number of 1500.

Murray had received yet another letter from the Viscount, written on the 23rd. This was remarkably civil and sympathetic in the circumstances. 'Tho ther be no body in the nation so much in my debt as your Lordship: having writen tyce to yow without any return; yet, being concerned that yow should have [no] ground of offence that might in the least alienat your inclinations from the King's service, or discourage yow from joyning with us his faithful servants . . . If, after all I have said in my former letters and this, I gette no return, my Lord, I must acknowledge I will be very sorry for your saike . . .'[235]

Dundee by this time had marched with his full army – no more than 1800 men at most – into Badenoch by the shore of Loch Laggan to Cluny Castle, from where no doubt the letter to Murray was written. He waited there for a day, and receiving no answer, wrote a final letter to him on the 25th, which he entrusted to Major William Graham of Balquhaple

and Gilbert Ramsay, the Edinburgh Advocate, to act as
messengers:

> My Lord – I have written often to your Lop and not only
> desired yow to declare for the King, but endeavoured by
> reason to convince yow that now is the proper time, which
> the state of affairs may easily show yow., to all which I have
> never had any return from yow, by word nor writ, tho I can
> tell yow there is none of the nation has used me so, and I
> have tryed all that have not already joyned Major Generall
> Mackay, on this side Tay, who have any command of men;
> yet, that I may leave nothing untryed that may free me from
> blame of what may fall out, I have sent these gentlemen to
> wait on your Lo: and receive your positive answer; for you
> know, my Lord, what it is to be in arms without the King's
> authoritie. You may have the honour of the whole turn of
> the King's affairs; for, I assure yow, in all human probability,
> turn it will. Ther is nobody that is more a weelwisher of your
> father and family, nore desires more to continue as I am, my
> Lord, Your most humble servant,
>
> DUNDIE.[236]

Lord Murray received two letters from Ballechin from Blair
Castle on the 5th. The second confirms that 'my Lord Dundie
will be heir with his quholl armie this night'.

Murray, it must be supposed, was in rather a panicky state,
and refused to see the two officers. Graham and Ramsay
made it known to the assembled Atholl men what their
message contained. According to Balcarres, the Atholl men
'without further ceremony run to the River of Tumble, which
was near them, filled their bonnets with water, and drank
King James his health with many loud huzzas and aclama-
tions, and so deserted him in a full body'.[237] This story was
repeated by others to give the impression that 1500 Atholl
men, pipes playing, had marched off in a patriotic fervour
to join Dundee – which is nonsense. Possibly a small number
did as suggested, but more likely the entire story is fictitious.
No Atholl men, with the honourable exception of a handful
under Lord William Murray, Pitcur, Ballechin and his son,
joined Dundee in arms.

Major Graham and Gilbert Ramsay galloped back to their

leader and informed him of Murray's conduct, and the inclination of the Atholl men. Dundee realised that Lord Murray was not now likely to defect, and was in fact probably actively co-operating with Mackay. Learning that Mackay was at Perth, he realised he would have to defend Blair Castle or Ballechin would be overwhelmed. He had been pre-empted in his actions by Mackay's move North. The Clans were not to be together for a further three days. He had less than half Mackay's force. It has been claimed that Dundee signed a bond in favour of Cluny MacPherson that day for 659 merks, which, Professor Terry claims, was 'to purchase an extension of his irresolute attitude'.[238] This is clearly an error. The bond mentioned was signed at Breackachie on the 26th – but of April, not July – during his first stay at the farm, and was simply payment for goods received then. He left Badenoch on the morning of the 26th, and halted three miles from Blair Castle, presumably in the vicinity of Pitagowan and the modern-day Clan Donnachaidh Museum.

Lord Murray fled south by the Pass of Killiecrankie to Moulin, taking a number of the Atholl men with him. He claimed in a despatch to Melville that he 'did send about ane hundred of my men to secure the pass of Killiecrankie'.[239] He sent a messenger to General Mackay requesting him to avoid marching through Atholl. This extraordinary request, almost countermanding the dispatch, borders on treason or temporary insanity. The messenger returned to him at 5 p.m. the same night: 'My Lord. The General Major cum heir at twell o'clock. I delivared your Lops letter to him, and delt with him that [h]is armie might not march the Atholl road; he told me that it was a thing impossible that he could pas by Blair Castell untill it wer in the Kinges hands or your Lops.'

Mackay had plainly lost patience, as had Dundee, with the pathetic posturings of Lord Murray, and the messenger further notes: 'Mackay declairs if the castell is not in yor hands or he coms, that he will get it, cost what it will; he also declairs that if yor Lop wer no ther on the head of your men, or in the least he wer oposed, he wod burn it from ye on[e] end to ye uther.'[240] Mackay mitigated this threat somewhat in his own note that day to Murray, as he set out from Perth: 'If the Castell of Blair did surrender I might haply take my march another way.'[241]

The Castle had not surrendered. In fact, hearing of Lord Murray's retreat, Dundee relieved Ballechin before nightfall on the 26th. Once ensconced in its spacious premises, he wrote what was to be his final letter. A final attempt to persuade Cluny MacPherson: 'Sir – My Lord Murray is retyred doun the countrey. All the Atholl men have left them saive Stratherel, Achintully, and Baron Read, Straloch, and they will not byd my doun coming to morou. The rest of the heritors will be here to morou. They will joyn us, and I supose to morou you will have ane answer so if you have a mynd to preserve yourself and to serve the King be in armes to morou that when the letter comes you may be here in a day. All the world will be with us blissed be God'.[242]

Whether or not this letter – clearly a final summons – had the desired effect, the MacPhersons of Cluny did assemble and march to join Dundee, although they arrived too late for the battle itself (but not too late to be attainted with the rest of the clans).

Blair Castle is today well worth a visit. Some parts of the building date from the thirteenth century – Cumming's or Comyn's Tower, for example – and it is an excellent museum of Highland weaponry and relics. The Statistical Account described Blair as 'one of the most splendid hunting châteaux in Europe'.[243]

Lord Murray's letter to Mackay reporting that he had stationed a hundred men at the Pass of Killiecrankie, also expressed doubts that they would remain there long. Accordingly, Mackay sent Lieutenant-Colonel George Lauder on the 27th with '200 choice fusiliers of the whole army to keep the said passe till I should cum up'.[244] Murray was unsure of his men's loyalty, and it seems fair to conclude that a large number had indeed defected – not to Dundee – but to their own homes, and to the hills in the hope of picking off stragglers from the armies. When Lauder arrived at the Pass, he found no-one there, least of all Murray's men. Mackay heard about midnight, at Dunkeld, that Dundee had reached Blair.

Viscount Dundee had been informed by a correspondent, a Mr Buchanan from Edinburgh, that Captain Creighton was to be hanged. The Dragoon plotters were then in the Tolbooth, in separate cells where they had lain for weeks, unable to communicate with each other. Dundee dashed off a hasty letter to the Duke of Hamilton, President of the Council, informing his Grace 'That if they hanged Captain Creighton, or if they touched a hair of his tail, he would cut the Laird of Blair, and the Laird of Pollock joint by joint, and would send their limbs in hampers to the Council'. Blair was of course Hamilton's son-in-law, and doubtless this threat played some part in effecting a stay of execution for the Captain. The only evidence for this disputed letter, however, is the unreliable *Memoirs* of Creighton himself, and the letter does not appear elsewhere.

Thus, on the eve of 26th July, the two armies slept, seventeen miles apart, and there could be few who doubted that battle would soon be joined.

8

'If any of us shall fall . . .'

The next day, the fateful 27th, seems to have been clear and sunny, a perfect summer's day, and in the lee of the hills and forests, perhaps became quite warm as the redcoats began their march from Dunkeld to Pitlochry. The air was fresh with ozone and scented with pine, and for half the march they were accompanied by the sparkling waters of the Tay, until, before Logierait, they encountered the River Garry which pours down the Strath from Lochs Tummel and Faskally. They must have set off early, for 'About ten of the cloack I arryved at the said passe and met with my Lord Murray', Mackay wrote in his autobiography, *A Short Relation of What Passed*. Murray told him that most of his men were gone to save their cattle from the Highlanders, but 'with all that he thought he should get them keep'd from joyning Dundee so long as he should stay upon their head, but that by no means they wold joyn mee.'[246] At Pitlochry he rested his men for two hours and learned from Lauder that the Pass was open; there was no sign of the Jacobites. He ordered a resumption at noon, and the regiments began to march towards the foot of the snow-capped Ben Vrackie that dominates Strathgarry.

Mackay waited at the entrance of the Pass and sent on 200 of the Earl of Leven's regiment under command of a lieutenant to assist Lauder's men in guarding the head of the Pass. When he was convinced that it was safe, he ordered the army to enter it. Three regiments of infantry led the column: Brigadier Bartold Balfour and Colonel Ramsay and their Scoto-Dutch regiments, followed by Viscount Kenmure's regiment of irregular levies. Lord Belhaven's troop of cavalry came next, then the Earl of Leven's infantry. Mackay's regiment, like Balfour's and Ramsay's drawn from the Scots Brigade in Holland, was commanded by Mackay's brother, Lieutenant-Colonel James Mackay.

Just two miles north of the village of Pitlochry, the gorge dropped away sharply, and the steep sides, thickly covered with pine trees, concealed the rocky defile beneath. The River Garry thundered down among the rocks in full spate, leaving stagnant black deeps or swirling whirlpools in its wake, or bright foaming waterfalls trapping the sunlight through the trees and reflecting the colours of the rainbow. The beauty of this wild place would not have appealed to the soldiers. For them, the Pass simply meant hard physical work, hauling themselves and their equipment between rocks and around sudden twists and bends, concentrating only on keeping their feet, close as they were to the edge of the precipice.

The baggage horses, nearly 1500 in number, trailed behind, escorted by the Earl of Annandale's horsemen. Most of the baggage was to remain on the haugh on the left bank of the river at the foot of the Pass. Colonel Ferdinand Hastings' regiment was initially left behind to guard the equipment, but shortly was ordered up with the rest. Mackay felt his superior numbers would cause the Highland army to flee before him, and anticipated a brief siege of Blair Castle, then a short chase which, if it did not lead to Dundee's capture, would certainly drive him into the remote North-West. He was in confident mood.

By contrast, the spirit among Dundee's principal officers in Blair Castle was one of caution. News had come through late on the 26th that Mackay was already in the Pass of Killiecrankie. What the scouts had seen of course was Lauder's 200 men guarding the Pass. Upon receiving this information, Dundee held a full Council of War in the banqueting room of the Castle. He sat at the head of the large pine table and watched his officers seat themselves around it. Lairds and Gentlemen of the loyal shires: Haliburton of Pitcur, Sir William Wallace of Craigie, his brother David, Fendraught, Charters, Major William Graham, Lord William Murray, James Middleton, Lord Dunkeld, Captain Alexander Bruce. Some had been with him since his service in the South-Western shires, most were old friends, but seated on the other side of the table were the important clan chiefs who had brought men with them: Black Alistair of Glengarry, Sir John MacLean of Duart, Lord Dunfermline, Donald MacDonald of Sleat, Sir Alexander MacLean of Otter, the fiery Keppoch, MacDonald of Largie, the stately Ewan Cameron of Lochiel – who had arrived hastily that very evening with 240 men – young Clanranald with his tutor, Grant of Glenmoriston, Drummond of Balhaldie, the dauntless veteran Gordon of Glenbucket, and Alasdair MacDonald, known as 'McIan' or 'old Glencoe' who was described as being built like a haystack. There was Colonel Alexander Cannon and Colonel Purcell who had brought the Irish battalion from Carrickfergus. And yet, for all these men of rank and ability, the total strength of the army at their command was a paltry 2000. Many of the clans had hung back to see how things would go, many had sent a small number, promising more later, and worst of all, there was no word from Dublin of the Irish army that James had promised.

The Lowland officers advised caution. The clansmen were tired and hungry; Mackay's army outnumbered them heavily; it was too risky to fight and jeopardise the cause until reinforcements arrived. They advocated a few carefully selected skirmishes to boost the morale of the clans until the Irish army arrived with the King once the siege of Derry was over. Drummond of Balhaldie agreed: 'It is next to madness for us to seek an engagement with Mackay. We are here assembled for the purpose of awaiting our friends. It is not fit that we should meet him now until they have come up with us.'

Lord Dunfermline spoke of the intelligence they had received about Mackay's movements. His troops were seasoned, well-trained and well-fed. (This was not entirely accurate: apart from the three battalions of the veteran Scots Brigade, which had been depleted of much of their best soldiers, the majority of Mackay's men were irregular levies.) Mackay was a veteran soldier and 'our Highlanders are few in number and in need of food and rest. We cannot hope to get the better of "him from Scourie" until our supplies and our men are come down.'

There was a clamour of agreement around the table, and the Viscount noted that it mostly came from the professional soldiers and Lowland gentry. Nevertheless, it was the majority view, and 'occassioned a general silence'. He caught a few whispered words of Gaelic, and a couple of dark, meaningful glances among the clan Chiefs. 'But, att last, Alexander MacDonald of Glengarry . . . took the opportunity of declaring his sentiments.'[247] He slowly rose to his feet with an air of injured pride. Described as 'brave, loyall, and wonderfully sagacious and long-sighted', it was said that 'he loved not to deviate from the customes of his predecessors'. He thought he had detected in the advice of the Lowlanders some slur on his clansmen: 'Gentlemen, you have said that our clansmen are hungry and tired, but our men are Highlanders and are well-used to such hardships. We come from a warrior race; the children of Fionn, descendants of the Lords of the Isles, whose great deeds have been often done on empty stomachs. Our men have the great tales of our ancestors, the legends our bards have retold, to drive them on. They shall not fail us should we fight, Gentlemen, that I can promise you. What matter numbers when we have such men as these?' Glengarry sat down, his eyes fierce with pride.

'Aye. We must fight!' cried Clanranald with the impetuosity of youth. 'Before yon Mackay reaches us. For then you would have us run before him like dogs'.

'Our men weary of retreat . . .' Alexander Maclean began, faltering, his eyes switching to the silent figure of Dundee, who, all this while had been observing old Lochiel. Sprawled in the corner, Sir Ewan Cameron was unconcernedly twirling his moustaches, his plaid wrapped round him. He had not yet spoken in the debate.

McIan of Glencoe, sixty years old, a veritable giant of a man, demanded an immediate march against Mackay to trap him in the Pass. There were yells of agreement from the chiefs, and contradictory claims from the officers that Mackay must already be through the Pass.

James Haliburton of Pitcur stood up amid the confusion. 'My Lord, we could argue this the whole day. You are our leader, and by your word we will either fight or stay our hand. What say you?'

Dundee gestured for silence. 'I have listened to your counsel, but I will not give my judgement until I have heard from one who has not only done great things himself, but has had so much experience that he cannot miss to make a right judgement of the matter, and therefore yours, Lochiel, shall determine mine!'

All heads turned to Lochiel, who raised his hand in a deprecatory gesture and smiled warmly. 'Tush, my Lord, you make the tale ever bigger in the telling. It is not advice from me you are needing as full well you know. You are our leader here, although as you have commanded my opinion, I shall give it in a word – to fight. Our men are in heart; they are so far from being afraid of their enemy, that they are eager and keen to engage them, least they escape their hands, as they have so often done. Though we have few men, they are good, and I can venture to assure your Lordship that not one of them will faill yow.'

Lochiel's advice and the quiet thoughtful tone of his voice gave way to sudden tumult. Viscount Dundee sat through it, smiling broadly. Lochiel was right. They must attack before Mackay reached Blair Castle. They had no time – no provisions – for further defensive manoeuvres. Retreat was simply not possible. There had been too much retreat already.

Sir Ewan Cameron of Lochiel was a living legend among Highlanders and Lowlanders alike. He had led the revolt against Cromwell's invasion, and never had been conquered. He was reputed to have killed the last wolf in Scotland, and, in another desperate encounter with English troops, momentarily disarmed, had torn out an assailant's throat with his teeth, and later jested that it was 'the sweetest bite he ever tasted!' Like Dundee, Lochiel's loyalty to the Stuarts was beyond question. They had first met at Court in Holyrood during James' visit to Scotland as Duke of York, when, as Colonel Graham, Dundee had watched the dignified Lochiel being knighted for his services and loyalty.

After a pause, Lochiel had continued: 'If your Lordship thinks proper to delay fighting, and wait the arrivall of our men, my opinion is, that we immediately retreat again to the mountains and meet them; for I will not promise upon the event, if we are not the aggressors. But be assured, my Lord, that if once we are fairly engaged, we will either lose our army, or carry a compleat victory. Our men love allways to be in action. Your Lordship never heard them complain either of hunger or fatigue while they were in chase of their enemy, which att all times were equall to us in number. Employ them in hasty and desperat enterprizes, and you will oblige them, and I have observed, that when I fought under the greatest disadvantage of numbers, I had still the compleatest victories. Let us take this occasion to show our zeall and courage in the cause of our King and countrey, and that we dare to attack ane army of Fanaticks and Rebells att the odds of near two to ane. Their great superiority in numbers will give a necessary reputation to our victory, and not only fright them from meddling with a people conducted by such a General, and animated by such a cause, but it will incorage the whole Kingdome to declare in our favours.'

This speech was calculated to appeal to the spirit of daring in all the men in the room, the mere mention of the word 'retreat' being enough to have the chieftains grinding their teeth, while the prospect of battle whatever the odds was guaranteed to make their hearts beat faster.

'Ane advice so hardy and resolute could not miss to please the generous Dundee,' claimed the author of *Locheil's Memoirs*. 'His looks seemed to brighten with ane air of delight and satisfaction all the while Lochiell was a-speaking. He told his council that they had heard his sentiments from the mouth of a person who had formed his judgement upon infallible proofs drawn from a long experience, and ane intimate acquaintance with the persons, and subject he spoke of. Not ane in the company offered to contradict their General; it was unanimously agreed to prepare for battle.'

Before the Council broke up, Lochiel begged to be heard for a few words: 'My Lord, I have just now declared in presence of this honourable company, that I was resolved to give ane implicite obedience to all your Lordship's commands; but, I humbly beg leave, in name of these gentlemen to give the word of command for this ane time. It is the voice of your councill, and their orders are, that you doe not personally engage.'

Lochiel and the others felt so strongly about the danger to Dundee that they declared heatedly that they would not fight if he were to risk his person. Later commentators, aware of Lochiel's reputed powers of the 'second-sight', have read much into this, but at the least it is an affirmation of the importance of Dundee's personality to the cause of King James.

His reply is also recorded: 'Gentlemen – as I am absolutely convinced, and have repeated proofs of your zeale for the King's service, and of your affection to me, as his General and your friend, so I am fully sensible that my engageing personally this day may be of some loss if I shall chance to be killed; but I beg leave of you, however, to allow me ane shear-darg [one day's work at the harvest] to the King, my master, that I may have ane opportunity of convincing the brave Clans that I can hazard my life in that service as freely as the meanest of them. Ye know their temper, Gentlemen, and if they doe not think I have personal courage enough, they will not esteem me hereafter, nor obey my commands with cheerfulness. Allow me this single favour and I here promise, upon my honour, never again to risk my person while I have that of commanding you.'

Thus, early next morning the Highland army set off to meet Mackay. They left the road and marched across country behind the Hill of Lude, around the edge of tiny Loch Moraig, and from there followed the Clune burn down to the lower slopes of Craig Eallaich. General Mackay, having arrived at

the Head of the Pass, observed 'some partys of them began
to discover themselves betwixt us and Blair; whereupon the
General, galloping to the ground from whence they were
discovered . . . ordered Brigadier Balfour to dispatch quickly
the distribution of his ammunition, and to put the men under
arms, while, having observed the motion of the ennemy, he
should chuse the field of battle'.

There has been much academic debate about the precise
site of the Battle of Killiecrankie, Mark Napier's account
of 1862 was taken up by the Ordnance Survey who marked
the site on the low ground beneath Urrard House, where
'Claverhouse's Stone' still stands, about four and a half feet
high in the middle of a field, entirely unmarked: no signposts
or plaques. Professor Terry's later work claimed a site almost
half a mile to the north-west, between Lettoch and Aldclune.
Lord Macaulay claimed the battle took place on the small hill
to the immediate north of Killiecrankie village – known as
Raon Ruari – and Michael Barrington slightly adapted Terry's site by moving it to the narrow plateau between the lower
slopes of Craig Eallaich and Urrard House. The final proof
is contained in the only first-hand account (in any detail) to
survive, which is that of General Mackay:

> Being come up to the advanced party he saw some small
> partys of the ennemy, the matter of a short mile, marching
> slowly along the foot of a hill . . . marching towards us. But . . .
> having discovered some bodies of them marching down an
> high hill within a quarter of a mile to the place where he
> stood, when the gross of their body appeared, fearing that
> they should take possession of an eminence just above the
> ground where our forces halted on, of a steep and difficult
> ascent, full of trees and shrubs, and within a carabin shot
> of the place whereon we stood, whereby they could undoubt-
> edly force us with their fire in confusion over the river, he
> galloped back in all haste to the forces, and having made
> every battalion form by a Quart de conversion [half-turn to
> the right] . . . upon the ground they stood, made them march
> each before his face up the hill, by which means he prevented
> that inconveniency, and got a ground fair enough to receive
> the ennemy, but not to attack them, there being, within a

> short musket shot to it, another eminence before our front,
> as we stood when we were up the lowest hill, near the river,
> whereof Dundee had already gott possession before we could
> be well up. and had his back to a very high hill.[248]

Mackay commented disparagingly that it was typical of Highlanders to ensure they had a safe method of retreat at their
backs before engaging in battle.

The 'high hill' is plainly Craig Eallaich, and after following the path General Mackay must have taken, it must be
concluded that Napier's and Macaulay's sites are logisti-
cally impossible, and Raon Ruari is too small, bearing in
mind the numbers of soldiers involved. It would have been
nonsensical to ascend it and it was almost certainly ignored.
Mackay's entire army had cleared the Pass successfully before
the Jacobites were even glimpsed by Lauder – who may have
been almost the length of Aldclune, and certainly as far as
Dalnasgadh – several hundred yards further west than Urrard.
Yet Professor Terry places the battle almost on the slopes of
Lude Hill: too far in the opposite direction. The longer one
spends walking in the vicinity, the more one is convinced that
the 'lowest hill near the river' was the steep, wooded ridge
that stretches south-west from Raon Ruari to the banks of
the Clune burn. Breasting this ridge, the slope on which the
Highland army was deployed comes into view – the lower
slopes of Craig Eallaich itself. Mackay's army formed along
the top of this ridge on either side of Urrard House, perhaps
a mile in total length. The new A9 road thus cuts straight
across the narrow plateau which divided the two armies, a
plateau barely two or three hundred feet wide, although, of
course, the construction of the road with its elevated section
makes the scenario less easily imaginable.

Within this flat plain, amid some rather boggy ground
(then as now), there is a modern cairn marking the battle.
On the slopes directly above, across the road, can be seen the
mass of stones which is the ruins of an old wellhouse. The
valley is dominated by Ben Vrackie to the east, and Craig an
Eironnach and Tulach Hill to the south and west respectively,
both heavily wooded.

'If any of us should fall . . .'

The armies prepared for battle. Mackay remarked, with the wisdom of hindsight: 'all our officers and soldiers were strangers to the Highlanders' way of fighting and embattailing, which mainly occasioned the consternation many of them were in.'

'Having got up the hill with five battalions and a troop of Horse . . . and seeing Dundee master of an eminence so near him, [Mackay] resolved to make the best of that ground, and rather receive the check there in good order, than to put his men out of breath and in disorder, by attacking the enemy against a hill. Betwixt the height which he had marched up from the river, and the foot of that whereon the enemy were placed, there was a convenience (livel ground) to embattail our men in one line, taking the former at our back, tho with a continued ascent from us to them. Having got upon the ground which he had remarked, he bagan to even his line, leaving a little distance betwixt every little battalion, having made two of each, because he was to fight three deep; only, in the midst of the line, he left a greater opening where he placed the two troops of horse (the other being come up just as he had taken his ground with Hastings' battalion).'

Mackay hoped to outflank the Highlanders on either side of their line. He had been surprised, on reaching the level ground, to see the main Highland army on a further slope above him, startlingly near to his own forces. He certainly believed he had made the best of the situation: 'Seeing mee ranged sooner than he [Dundee] thought, (having, as I beleeve, designed to cum down upon the same ground before I could get possession of it . . .)' It is not to be supposed, however, that Dundee and Lochiel, having decided to fight against such odds, and having arrived at the battlefield before Mackay, had not carefully planned their strategy.

The extract above clearly reveals Mackay's naivety as to Dundee's tactics. With the inbred superiority of the experienced professional in charge of regular forces – though Mackay's army on this occasion largely consisted of irregulars – he contemptuously under-estimated both the Highlanders' strength and their tactical sense. Mackay was out of touch with the Highlands and the Highlanders; he understood little of their ways. He was a foreigner in his own land.

He made a short, phlegmatic speech to some of the battalions nearest him: 'Honour, religion, country and fidelity to his Majesty King William requires that you behave yourselves manfully, but also the consideration of your own lives. You shall not escape if you turn your backs to the enemy because they are speedier of foot than ourselves, and the men of Atholl would be worse than the enemy if they were to find you.'[249]

To men already apprehensive, this speech with its superfluous reminder of the hostile nature of the countryside and its denizens, quite apart from the menace of the Highland army itself, was more likely to induce panic than to bolster their courage. Many of the men, used to the flat lands of Holland or the green downs and gentle hills of England, found the Scottish countryside positively intimidating: Mackay noticed that the Jacobites 'seemed to extend their order beyond our right wing' and so ordered his line to move to the right. Mackay did not want to be flanked at the head of the Pass because he was awaiting the rest of his army. This move, he noted 'brought the enemy, whatever its design might have been, to a stand, and so we lookt upon one another for at least two hours . . . wherein nothing past but som light skirmishing'.[250]

Seeing the movements Mackay had made, Dundee had altered the arrangements of his own men, spreading them out even further, leaving gaps between them in order to do so. On his right wing, he placed Sir John Maclean of Duart, then the 300 Irish caterans, then the men of Clanranald, then the MacDonalds under Young Glengarry. After that came a battalion made up of MacDonalds of Glencoe, Grants of Glenmoriston and Stewarts of Appin. In the midst of the line was the small troop of Horse, numbering now only about forty. To Dundee's exasperation, this was commanded, not by the vastly-experienced Dunfermline, but by Sir William Wallace of Craigie – brother-in-law to the Earl of Melfort – who had received a commission from him only the previous day; yet another example of Melfort's counter-productive meddling. On their left-hand side were the Camerons under Lochiel, the MacDonalds of Kintyre and the Macleans of Otter, and on the far left wing were the MacDonalds of the Isles.

Some Jacobite musketeers had moved forward to some buildings on Mackay's right flank from where they began to use Hastings' infantry battalion for target practice, and the mounted figure of General Mackay himself whenever he came into range. Several dragoons were killed before Mackay ordered a detachment to charge the snipers, several of whom reached the safety of their own ranks. Mackay had hoped that this might bring on a general engagement, but it did not. He 'resolved then to stand it out, tho' with great impatience . . . and to provoke them, he ordered the firing of the three little leather field-pieces, which . . . proved of little use, because the carriages being made too high to be more conveniently carried, broke with the third firing'. Balhaldie records the incident, possibly entirely fictitious, of a Grant clansman in Glengarry's battalion being struck on the targe by a cannonball, which knocked him over. He promptly regained his feet, unhurt – which, Balhaldie records, provoked a terrific roar of amazement and glee among the Highland ranks; for the clansmen, this was a good omen.

Viscount Dundee rode continuously along the front of his lines, doing his best to restrain the impatient clansmen. He had taken his officers' advice so far as to leave off his scarlet coat in favour of one of a 'sad colour' – grey/buff – beneath his armour breastplate. From Balhaldie's testimony it would appear, however, that he also exchanged his morion, or steel helmet, for a wide-brimmed plumed chapeau. He made a speech to his army, presumably in English, which less than a tenth of his audience would have understood:

Gentlemen,

You are come hither this day to fight, and that in the best of causes; for it is the battle of your King, your religion, and your country, against the foulest usurpation and rebellion; and having, therefore, so good a cause in your hands, I doubt not but it will inspire you with an equal courage to maintain it. For there is no proportion betwixt loyalty and treason; nor could be any betwixt the valour of good subjects and traitors. Remember that today begins the fate of your King, your religion, and your country. Behave yourselves, therefore, like true Scotchmen; and let us, by this action, redeem the credit of this nation, that is laid low by the treacheries and cowardice of some of our countrymen; in which, I ask nothing of you, that you shall not see me do before you; and if any of us shall fall upon this occasion, we shall have the honour of dying in our duty, and as becomes true men of valour and conscience: and such of us as shall live and win the battle, shall have the reward of a gracious King, and the praise of all good men. In God's name, then, let us go on, and let this be your word: King James and the Church of Scotland, which God long preserve.[251]

'Each clan,' Balhaldie tells us, 'whither small or great, had a regiment assigned them . . . the designe was to keep up the spirite of emulation in poynt of bravery; for, as the Highlanders putt the highest value upon the honour of their familys or Clans, and the renown and glory acquired by military actions, so the emulation between Clan and Clan inspires them with a certain generous contempt of danger, gives vigour to ther hands, and keenness to their courage'. Dundee was in fact so outnumbered that there were great gaps between his battalions, and a large space left in the centre. He 'could not possibly stretch his line so as to equall that of the enemy; and wanting men to fill up the voyd in the centre, Locheill, who was posted nixt the horse, was not onely obliged to fight Mackay's own regiment . . . but also had his flank exposed to the fire of Leven's battalion'.[252]

Lochiel commanded his men, 'posted in the centre, to make a great shout, which being seconded by those who stood on their right and left, ran quickly through the whole army, and was returned by some of the enemy, but the noise of the cannon and musquets, with the prodigious echoeing of the adjacent hills and rocks, in which there are several caverns and hollow places, made the Highlanders fancy that their shouts were much brisker and louder than that of the enemy, and Lochiell cryed out, "Gentlemen, take courage. The day is our own . . . they are all doomed to dye by our hands this very night!" '

By these words the clansmen were encouraged, and 'the sun being near its close' – it had been shining in their eyes – Dundee finally motioned with his sword for the attack. It was about half an hour before sunset. It must be left to the imagination to grasp the ferocity of the Highlanders' charge down the slope, shouting their Gaelic war-cries; the dying sun glinting along the edges of the blades, the rim of targes. To the redcoats in the growing darkness of the valley, they must have seemed more numerous and more terrible than their fears had led them to believe. They began to fire their flintlocks when the Jacobites were 100 paces from them, but still the clansmen came on, fired once at close range, threw down their guns, 'and fell in pell mell among the thickest of them with their broadswords'.

There is a brief first-hand description by one of Balfour's soldiers, Donald McBane, who committed his military experiences to print in *The Expert Swordsman's Companion*, published in 1728: 'The sun going down caused the Highlandmen to advance on us like madmen, without shoe or stocking, covering themselves from our fire with their targes. At last they cast away their muskets, drew their broadswords, and advanced furiously upon us, and were in the middle of us before we could fire three shots apiece, broke us, and obliged us to retreat. Some fled to the water, and some the other way. I fled to the baggage.'[253] McBane in fact leaped across the Garry where it is at its narrowest – between two large rocks – a prodigious feat commemorated with a plaque, and referred to ever since as 'The Soldier's Leap'.

According to the *Memoir of Dundee*, 'the first officer that left his post . . . was the Lord Leven; the glistening and clashing of the Highlandmen's swords and targes scared his horse so much, that he ran six miles before he could draw bridle'.[254] This contradicts Mackay's account of 'the diligence and firmity of the said Earle . . . who keept the feeld of battail . . .'[255]

Viscount Dundee was thundering down the hill in the centre of the attack at the head of the small force of cavalry, when Melfort's placeman, Sir William Wallace, 'either his courage failing him, or some unknown incident interposing . . . ordered the horse to wheele about to the left, which not only occasioned a halt, but putt them into confusion. Dundee, in the meantime, intent upon the action, and carryed on by the impetuosity of his courage, advanced towards the enemy's horse . . . without observing what passed behind, untill he was just entering into the smoak . . . The brave Earl of Dunfermline, and sixteen gentlemen more', ignoring the orders of Wallace, 'followed their Generall, and observed him . . . turn his horse towards the right, and raising himself upon his stirrops, make signes by waveing his hatt over his head for the rest to come up'.[256]

It was then that a fateful bullet found its way beneath the armour plate in Dundee's left side.

The MacDonalds poured down upon the left wing of the army – Ramsay's and Balfour's regiments – and caused these battalions to flee 'without any firing'.[257] Mackay saw this and ordered the two troops of horse to outflank the MacDonalds, but this resulted in confusion as the cavalry did not have 'the resolution to obey their orders and in a very short tym all did run except a parte of the Earl of Leven's regiment, which by the diligence and firmity of the said Earle . . . keept the feeld of battail . . . so that I found myself [Mackay] abandoned in the midst of the ennemys, I pearced throw them, being well-hors'd, and seeing som red coats in the feelds, I went to them . . . desyring the officers to doe their utmost to get as many rallied as they possibly could, but . . . receiving notice that none of the officers could persuade their men to stand, much less to return back . . . wee [retreated] in the best order wee could . . .' Notwithstanding Mackay's later protestations of an orderly retreat, it is clear that his army were routed and fled in considerable disorder. Brigadier Balfour and Mackay's brother, Lieutenant-Colonel James Mackay, were killed 'after their men abandoned them'.[258] Most chose to take their chances on the hills of Atholl and many were subsequently slaughtered by the Atholl men. A large flat horizontal stone several miles further which is embedded in the track is reputed to be Balfour's gravestone.

Mackay was joined 'two mile from the feeld of battaill' by Colonel Ramsay, who had managed to rally about 200 men, which made a total of about 600 or 700 men who marched back to Weems Castle and from there to Perth, via Stirling. 'The Highlanders had ane absolute and compleat victorey. The pursute was so warm that few of the enemy escaped.'[259]

THE BATTLE OF KILLIECRANKIE

Clavers, and his Highland-men, came down upon
    the raw, man,
Who being stout, gave mony a clout;
    The lads began to claw then,
Wi' sword and target in their han',
    Wi' which they were na slaw, man;
Wi' mony a fearful heavy sigh,
    The lads began to claw them.

O'er bush, o'er bank, o'er ditch, o'er stank,
    She flang amang them a', man,
The Butter-box got mony knocks,
    Their riggings paid for a', then.
They got their paiks wi' sudden straiks,
    Which to their grief they saw, man
Wi' clinkum clankum o'er their crouns,
    The lads began to fa', then.

Hur skipt about, her leapt about,
    And flang amang them a', man;
The English blades got broken heads,
    Their crowns were cleav'd in twa, then.
The dirk and door made their last hour,
    And prov'd their final fa', man;
They thought the devil had been there,
    That play'd them sic a paw, then.

Sir Evan Dhu,* and his men true,
    Came linking up the brink, man;
The Hogan Dutch they feared much,
    They bred a horrid stink, man.
The true Maclean,† and his fierce men,
    Came in amang them a', man;

Nane durst withstand his heavy hand.
A'fled and ran awa', then.

Oh fie for shame! ye're three for ane!
Hur nainsell's won the day, man;
King Shames' red-coats should be hung up, Because
they ran away, man.
Had bent their brows like Highland truws, And made
as lang a stay, man,
They'd saved their King, that sacred thing,
And Willie'd run awa' then.

[*Lochiel]
[†Maclean of Duart]

The only battalion that did not retreat was Hastings' English
Foot, who held their ground so that the Earl of Dunfermline
and a handful of horsemen who were heading some clansmen
had to fall back, 'and on their way discovered the body of
their noble General, who was just breathing out his last. The
fatal shott that occasioned his death, was about two-hands-
breadth within his armour, on the lower part of his left side . . .
Observeing still some small remains of life, they halted about
the body to carry it off.' As they were doing so, they were
subjected to a barrage of musket fire and Haliburton of
Pitcur was mortally wounded. The Earl of Dunfermline, 'who
had then his horse shott under him', retreated to the rear
and 'poured out a flood of tears' on the corpse of Viscount
Dundee. Reputedly, a person named Johnstone, who may
or may not have been his manservant, had been near him
when he received his mortal wound and caught him as he
sank down in the saddle.

'How goes the day?' Dundee asked him.

'Well for King James,' came the answer, 'but I am sorry
for your Lordship'.

'If it is well for him,' Dundee's voice came in a whisper, 'it
matters the less for me.' According to Johnstone, he never
spoke again. Later, the dead body of Dundee was stripped of
its armour, clothes and other personal possessions by some
Cameron clansmen, who may not have realised who he was.
When Dunfermline and the others found the body later, it

was nearly naked. They wrapped Dundee's corpse in two plaids and carried him to Blair Castle.[260]

Approximately 2000 redcoats perished at the battle or in the next two or three days. Five hundred prisoners were taken to Blair Castle by the Atholl men, including many officers. The standard of William of Orange had been captured by Sir Alexander Maclean. All the baggage, equipment and supplies were left on the field, with a great many discarded weapons. About 800 or 900 Highlanders had been killed, although two days later their army was greatly reinforced by 500 Camerons with Lochiel's son, John, and cousin Glendessary, 200 Stewarts of Appin, some MacGregors, 250 MacPhersons, the same number of MacDonalds of Lochaber and Glencoe, and about 1500 of the Atholl men. Frasers from the Braes of Mar, Farquharsons, Gordons of Strathdon and Glenlivet and many others arrived at Blair Castle to learn of the victory and of the death of their leader. Their numbers had swollen to over 5000, an army that would have gratified the dead Viscount.

The command was assumed by Colonel Alexander Cannon who sent a party of Robertsons to seize provisions at Perth, and these men were routed by Mackay and some thirty killed. That Cannon should have wasted his time with petty guerilla actions despite the overwhelming strength of his army, and the decisiveness of the victory, underlines his inherent caution. The disaster of the skirmish at Perth had a further dispiriting effect on the clans, and did not improve Cannon's chances of leadership which were finally destroyed, within the week, by the shambles of the siege of Dunkeld.

Dunkeld was defended by a regiment of Cameronians – dour, grim followers of the Covenanter Richard Cameron, from the South-West of Scotland. These men hated and feared 'Bluidy Clavers' and fought with fanatical zeal under the inspired leadership of the young Lieutenant-Colonel William Cleland, and repulsed the Highlanders with heavy losses. By a quirk of coincidence, Cleland had been one of the Covenant leaders at Drumclog responsible for Dundee's defeat, and now, like Dundee, died in the moment of victory at the siege of Dunkeld.

Defeat at Dunkeld more or less ended the Rebellion, and the claymores and broadswords were carried home to clachan and croft until nineteen years later they were to be drawn again.

There has been a great deal of controversy surrounding the death of Viscount Dundee, and much argument presented on all sides. There are three schools of thought. Firstly, that Dundee was 'shot dead on the head of his horse';[261] secondly, the account given earlier; that he survived a very short time, but died in agony on the battlefield; and lastly, that he 'survived not four hours', long enough for him to dictate a final letter, which was included in James MacPherson's *Original Papers,* MacPherson obtaining the letter from the Bodleian Library in Oxford.[262] The original had been destroyed, but the copy was found in the papers of Sir David Nairne, Melfort's Secretary at James' Royal Court. This was certainly the traditional belief until at least the middle of the nineteenth century, when it was first called into question, along with other documents which MacPherson was associated with (the 'Ossian' poems), and the authenticity of the letter disputed.

According to Dalrymple's *Memoirs of Great Britain And Ireland,* King James received news of the victory, but not until later of the death of Dundee – which seems to support the authenticity of the letter. Certain historians, principally Macaulay in his prestigious *History of England,* hearing that it was MacPherson who had first produced the final letter, instantly denounced it: 'I need not say it is as impudent a forgery as Fingal,' he declared.[263]

Much use has been made of the comparatively few sources available to protagonists from both sides. There is the letter of Thomas Stewart of Stenton, a property near Dunkeld, who was at Tulliemet on the day of the battle. He wrote, from hearsay, that 'my Lord Dundee was shot dead on the head of his horse'.[264] There is the testimony of Lieutenant Nisbet and James Osburne and others among Mackay's officers, who swore, in the Forfeiture Proceedings, that Dundee had recovered consciousness, but that the cause of death was 'a shot in his left eye'. They had viewed the corpse some weeks later, in the vault in Old Blair Church.

Balcarres' *Memoirs* and Balhaldie's *Memoirs of Lochiel* both give the impression that Dundee met an almost instantaneous death on the field. There is also the statement of a witness, James Malcolm, son of the Laird of Balbadie, who 'saw the late Viscount of Dundie lyeing dead of the wounds he received that day in the feight'.[265] There is a Gaelic poem attributed to Ian Lom, the bard of the MacDonalds, who was also present at the battle, in which 'neath the folds of thy clothing the bullet pierced thee'.[266] Lastly, there is the crucial letter of Lord James Murray of Dowally to his brother, Lord John Murray, written from Tulliemet the day after the battle. Lord James was in communication with both parties – his brother William was at the battle – and his letter about Dundee 'being killed' must make it highly unlikely that the Viscount was carried to Blair Castle alive, or that he dictated a letter at all, though undoubtedly the controversy will continue.

One of the most outlandish suggestions put forward concerning Dundee's death is that of the dour Calvinist, John Howie of Lochgoin, in 'God's Judgement on Persecutors', who claimed that 'his own waiting-servant, taking a resolution to rid the world of this truculent bloody monster, and knowing that he had proof of lead, shot him with a silver button he had before taken off his own coat for that purpose'.[267] Howie was just one of a generation of Presbyterian pamphleteen who were to blacken Dundee's name in defiance of all facts and evidence.

In Balcarres' *Memoirs* it is recorded that, next day, an officer passing over the field where Lord Dundee had been killed, found lying there a bundle of papers and commissions, which he used to carry about with him; 'those who had stript him thought them of so little concern, that they left them upon the ground. This gentleman showed them to several of your [the King's] friends. One of them did no small prejudice to your affairs, and would have done much more if it had not been carefully suppressed. This was a letter from the Earl of Melfort to the Viscount of Dundee, telling he had sent over to him your Majesty's declaration, which contained, not only an indemnity, but a toleration for all persuasions.'

Those who had hunted, and finally killed, Dundee were now to be pardoned by the King! Balcarres continues: 'This the Earl of Melfort knew would be extremely offensive to the Viscount of Dundee; therfore, to satisfy him, he writes 'That, notwithstanding of what was promised . . . yet he had couched the words so, that your Majesty could elude them when you pleased, nor would you think yourself obliged to stand to them'. As Balcarres comments: 'This not only dissatisfied the Viscount but most of your best friends, who thought an ingenuous and candid way of dealing had been more for your honour and service.'[268]

Viscount Dundee had died in vain. All his efforts had been undone by Melfort. And Melfort's influence, on the day before the battle to give command of the cavalry to Wallace instead of Dunfermline, was, almost certainly, the immediate cause of Dundee's death. Balhaldie believed that the sudden swerve of Wallace was due to a sudden loss of nerve, and that it fatally exposed Dundee at short-range to enemy fire.

Dundee's funeral took place on 30th July at Blair Castle, and his body was interred in a vault at Old Blair Church. The breastplate he wore on the day of the battle is preserved in Blair Castle, and sports a hole through the centre. This was added later, on the advice of a later Duke of Atholl, presumably to make it more authentic and warlike.

Besides the Viscount, James Haliburton of Pitcur died several days later, as recorded in one verse of a famous folk-song:

> The bauld Pitcur fell in a furr,
> And Clavers gat a clankie-o,
> Or I had fed an Athole gled,
> On the braes o'Killiecrankie-o.
> And ye had been waur I hae been
> Ye wadnae been sae cantie-o!

An' ye had seen waur I hae seen,
I' the braes o' Killiecrankie.

Other dead Jacobites included MacDonald of Largie, a young
man in his twenties, Gilbert Ramsay, the fashionable advocate, who had ridden to Lord Murray on the 25th with
Dundee's letter, a brother of Glengarry, and many relatives
of the MacDonald and Maclean chiefs. The next day 'the
Highlanders went and took a view of the field of battle, where
the dreadful effects of their fury appeared in many horrible
figures. The enemy lay in heaps almost in the order they were
posted; but so disfigured with wounds, and so hashed and
mangled, that evin the victors could not look upon the amazing proofs of their own ability and strength without surprise
and horror. Many had their heads divided into two halves by
one blow; others had their sculls cut off above the ears by a
back-stroke, like a night-cap. Their thick buff-belts were not
sufficient to defend their shoulders from such deep gashes as
almost disclosed their entrails. Several pikes, small swords,
and the like weapons, were cut quite through, and some that
had scull-caps had them so beat into their brains that they
[had] died upon the spot.'[269]

Following the defeat at Dunkeld, several of the Jacobite
leaders, including Lord Dunfermline, Lord Dunkeld, Colonel
Cannon, and Dundee's brother, David Graham, made their
escape to France. Viscount Dundee's child, James, tragically
died before the end of the year, whereupon David Graham
became the 3rd Viscount, appearing in the list of officers
subsisted in the service of King James at Dunkirk in June
1692, with the rank of Colonel.[270] Never having married,
David Graham is again consigned to the oblivion of history,
his entire life having been spent in the shadow of his eminent
brother. A namesake, David Graham of Duntrune, assumed
the title some years later, and the 5th Viscount, William
Graham, joined the 1715 Rising. His son, James, the 6th
Viscount, fought in 1745, and after Culloden he too escaped
to France to die in exile.

The Highland chiefs, loyal to Dundee's memory, and in
defiance of all the powers of the state, jointly signed a disdain-

ful letter to the new Government, assuring Mackay: 'we will all die with our swords in our hands before we fail in our loyalty and sworn allegiance to our Sovereign.'[271] The clans were to rise with undiminished ardour on three further occasions against the new 'British' Government, with the proud motto 'King James And No Union' inscribed on their sword handles.

Dundee's widow, Lady Jean Graham, was wooed and won by Colonel William Livingston, Viscount Kilsyth – the former head of the Dragoon Plot – and went abroad with him to Utrecht, where she gave birth to a son. Even here they did not escape a tragic destiny. Both she and her son were killed by the collapse of a roof, perhaps caused deliberately, in 1695. Livingston survived to fight alongside many of Dundee's former comrades, including William, the 5th Viscount Dundee, and many clansmen in the Rising of 1715.

I include the disputed final letter, on the grounds that, though forgery it may be – and Barrington is not alone in emphatically denying this – it is certainly 'in the style of Dundee'. Barrington declared that 'this deathbed letter embodies the concentrated essence of his life and principles and character,' but its authenticity cannot be believed.

Letter to King James after ye ffight

Sr.

It has pleased God to give yor fforces a great victory over ye Rebels, in wth 3,4ths of them are fallen under ye weight of our swords. I might say much of this Action iff I had not ye honor to comand in it; but of 5000 men wth was ye best computation I could make of ye Rebels it is certain there can not have escaped above 1200 men: wee have not lost full out 900. This absolut Victory made us Masters of ye ffield & ye Enemy's Baggage wch I gave to yor soldiers, who to doo them all right both officers & comon men, Highlands and Lowlands & Irish behaved themselves wth Equal Gallantry Wt ever I saw in ye hottest Batles fought abroad by disciplined armies, and this MacKay's old soldiers felt on this Occasion, I Can not now Sr be more particular but take leave to assure yor Matte ye kingsom is generally disposed for yor service and impatiently wait for yor Coming: and this success will bring

in ye rest of ye Nobility and Gentry having had all theyre
assurances for it except ye Notorious Rebels. Therefore Sr for
God's sake assist us tho it be wth such an other detachment of
your Irish fforces as you sent us before especialy of horse and
Dragoons & you will Crown our beginnings wth a Compleat
success & yorselfe wth an entire possession of yor Ancient
heriditary Kingdom of Scotland. My wounds forbid me to
enlarge to yor Matie. at this time, tho they tell me they are no
mortall. however Sr I beseech yor Matie, to belive whether I
live or dye I am entirely yors

DUNDIE[272]

And so ended the victor of Killiecrankie, the man who had
done his duty, and with him ended the cause of King James
VII and II. The news of his death filtered through rather
slowly. Dalrymple's letter to Melville on the 28th brought 'sad
and disturbing news . . . which makes a great consternation
heir . . . but some people already appear no so concerned as
the shoak requirs. I think the other syd of Tay is lost . . . The
Lord help us.' Mackay wrote to Hamilton from Stirling on
the 30th, announcing the certainty of Dundee's death, but
Hamilton had written two days before to Melville assuming
that it was Mackay who was dead.[273] William of Orange,
hearing of the defeat several days later, said 'he knew the
Lord Dundee so well, that he must have been either killed
or mortally wounded, otherwise, before that time, he would
have been master of Edinburgh'.[274]

An elegy, written in Latin within months of the battle by
Dr Archibald Pitcairn, and translated by John Dryden, 'the
greatest genius of his age', sums up the career of John Graham
of Claverhouse, 1st Viscount of Dundee:

O last and best of Scots, who didst maintain
Thy country's freedom from a foreign reigne,
New people fill the land now thow art gone,
New gods the temples, and new Kings the throne!
Scotland and thow didst in each other live,
Thow wouldst not her, nor could she thee survive.
Farewell, who dyeing didst support the State,
And couldst not fall but with thy country's fate.

EPILOGUE

The Legend

If we could rewind history so that Dundee galloped again against the redcoats, only this time, amid the smoke and confusion, a flintlock musket misfired, as they so often did, and a bullet missed its mark, or struck armour an inch higher . . . or if we could rewind to the previous day so that Dunfermline rather than Wallace was to lead the cavalry on the field . . . in short, if Dundee had survived to oversee his great victory – what then? When William of Orange heard of the battle several days later, he declared that 'he knew the Lord Dundee so well, that he must have been either killed or mortally wounded, otherwise, before that time, he would have been master of Edinburgh'. From what we have seen of his tactical skill, Dundee would certainly have moved rapidly southwards, increased by the new recruits who arrived on the 28th, to 5000, a real army for the first time. But the contention that he then could have captured Edinburgh is fanciful, quite apart from the question of the Williamite armies elsewhere in Scotland. His army was composed of Highlanders, irregulars, who would have less stomach for battle far from home. How would they have fared in an inevitable pitched battle in the south, fought on regular military tactics? Perhaps Culloden answers that question; then again, there was Prestonpans and the Highlanders got as far as Derby in 1745. But as later events confirmed, divisiveness and factionalism was a particularly serious problem for the Jacobite leadership – the main cause of the fiasco in 1715 – and of course, in 1689 there was still Melfort, spiteful, jealous Melfort to contend with, an *agent provocateur* as Balcarres regarded him, who preferred defeat with himself at the helm to victory if it were to mean that he would be dismissed.

It is not staking too great a claim to declare that with Claverhouse's death, King James' cause disintegrated, and with it, the possibilities of independent action by the Scottish Convention, restricted since the Union of Crowns in 1603, were constricted even further. The Whigs huddled closer to England, where power and influence was ever more obviously seen to be located. If the 'end of an auld sang' was heard in 1707, it was merely an echo of 'Killiecrankie'. And Sheriffmuir and Culloden were fainter repeats of the that refrain. When, in 1715, an anonymous Highland chief in the midst of the battle of Sheriffmuir sighed; 'O, for an hour of Dundee,'[275] he was not expressing nostalgia for the romantic legend of the 1st Jacobite leader; he was stating the practical reality. The lack of a strong leader who had the qualities of military experience, political judgement and personal charisma was the main cause of the failure of the three Risings after 1689. The dynastic ambitions of the Stuarts, who had reigned in Scotland since 1371, and for a thousand years before that, according to their contemporary supporters, were dashed not at Culloden, Sheriffmuir, even Boyne Water, but – paradoxically – in victory on the slopes of Killiecrankie. The failure of James, and later Stuarts, to regain the throne ended the collaboration of Scotland with France, thus enhancing the role of England. The duplicity of Melfort played its part even in this, when some letters of his from the Court at St Germain were, by mistake, put into the post for England, where they were read in astonishment. This incident so provoked the French King that Melfort was banished to Algiers, where he remained for many years, and thereafter the exiled Jacobites were to become less popular in France. The 'auld alliance' was replaced by a period of domination by England and English politics.

The Scottish Parliament acted quickly after the Forfeiture Proceedings to pass an Act wiping out Claverhouse's 'name, fame and honour'. His line was declared extinct and banned for all eternity, and the Graham shield and phoenix crest were 'riven furth and delett' from the newly-created *Book of Arms*.[276] This was to be expected, and many others were to share a similar fate, holding their titles *de jure* in exile, hoping that one day they would return to claim their rightful inheritance.

It is time now to reconsider the main areas of controversy covered in the book and come to a conclusion of sorts. The first of these concerns Claverhouse's final resting place. Early biographers repeated a story that his remains had been disinterred from Old Blair churchyard – which, according to Macaulay, had itself disappeared – and reburied in the churchyard at Old Deer in Aberdeenshire. This has proved to be entirely false. There is, however, a stained-glass window erected to his memory in the chancel of Old Deer – which is probably the source of the rumour.

Local history books in Dundee have repeated the myth that Claverhouse burnt the 'rotten row' or the Hilltown, which was part of his own Barony, in rage at his tenants' refusal to join him. It never happened, as can be easily proved by the fact that the military and militia commanders inside the city made no mention of this in their meticulous reports which are freely available in the Privy Council Registers. Similarly, it has been authoritatively stated that he was known to ride a black charger named 'Satan'.[277] There is no proof of this, and indeed testimony and information from letters that he rode 'a sorrel mare'. These fabrications are certainly dramatic, as is the story invented by Howie of Lochgoin of Dundee's death by silver bullet, and would be readily believed and repeated by a superstitious audience.

A more serious controversy surrounds the authenticity of the final speech to the troops and the letter to King James after the battle, both being produced from the Nairne Papers by James MacPherson. No-one seems to dispute that the documents – albeit copied – are of the appropriate period, though it has been suggested that they were part of a broadside written by London Jacobites after the battle in order perhaps to counter disastrous rumours of Dundee's death.

The widest area of debate attaches to the 'Bluidy Clavers' or 'Persecutor' myths of cruelty and savagery, widely repeated by nearly all those who have written of him, including Sir Walter Scott, who stated: 'He disgraced the virtues of a hero by the sanguinary persecution which he exercised . . .' He was 'cruel even to atrocity . . .', exhibited 'a disregard of his fellow subjects . . . the unscrupulous agent of the Privy Council . . . united the seemingly inconsistent qualities of courage and cruelty . . . the virtues and vices of a savage chief . . .' He was 'fierce, unbending . . .' with 'no emotions of compassion'. Lord Macaulay believed he was 'rapacious and profane, of violent temper and of obdurate heart, [and] has left a name, which, wherever the Scottish race is settled on the face of the globe, is mentioned with a peculiar energy of hatred'.[278]

Bruce Lenman, author of *The Jacobite Risings In Britain,* refers to his 'long record of high-handed police duties',[279] and there have been harsher criticisms, but it is worth considering again the precise details of these so-called atrocities. The testimony of Privy Councillors and Commissioners must be examined. Some, such as Queensberry and Lauderdale, had at various times reprimanded him for not being severe enough. MacKenzie's statement that he was 'more lenient than the civilians' is also pertinent, as is his concern for the prisoner, the Rev. Francis Irwin, ill with 'the gravelle', and his liberating of Edward Maxwell of Hill from Kirkcudbright Tolbooth. It will be remembered also that he had petitioned the Privy Council for authority to commute the death penalty for some Dundee thieves, and had spoken up for the wronged soldiers in Douglas's regiment. There is the evidence in his letters of his policy of sparing 'the little people' and giving the benefit of the doubt to those who would agree to keep the peace in the future. All of which is entirely consistent with the character of a man of justice and mercy – a kind and compassionate man – within the obvious constraints of his commission.

The sum total of victims of whom there is absolute proof is . . . *one!* This was John Brown of Priesthill, who, it will be remembered, was shot after a chase across the moors, when he refused to co-operate. In the circumstances, Claverhouse performed his duty. In fact he spared John Brown's nephew, when others would have executed both fugitives.

The large numbers of Covenanter victims of the 'Killing Time', apart from being a highly dubious set of statistics (produced by Covenant-supporting historians) and uncheckable, were for the whole of Scotland, and Claverhouse was merely one troop Captain. There were many others – not least Grierson of Lag – who had the good fortune to be less easily mythologised, and thus have escaped vilification. Dundee would not have been performing his commission if he had not been responsible for the death and capture of fugitives, many subsequently tortured by the Privy Council; but there is no evidence whatsoever for the myths of cruelty, atrocity and brutality.

The period of history from the end of the regime of Cromwell to the Rebellion in which Claverhouse played such a prominent part has been characterised as a period of civil wars and bloody struggle between religious factions. It was also a period of deep and grinding poverty in Scotland. Most of the people were oppressed in some way or other, and mostly for other than their religious convictions. Old peasant women thought to be witches were perhaps persecuted most of all, and it was an age in which quite extraordinary cruelty was perpetrated by those with any kind of authority at all. Officialdom was often motivated by the power of superstition, greed, envy, spite – or all of these. Few soldiers living in seventeenth-century Scotland could emerge from history with lilywhite, unstained hands. I believe, however, that John Graham was no worse – and in fact, a great deal better – in deed and aspiration than the majority of his peers. His career should also be put into the context of Scotland's two premier heroes; one murdered his rival in cold blood in a church, the other slaughtered a total stranger for a trivial insult – and yet such deeds are commemorated as our glorious history. History must not be sanitised in the service of modern prejudice.

Claverhouse has also been accused of being simply 'a very unimaginative soldier for whom the arrival of an order from a superior terminated all speculative thought, if indeed he ever indulged in such'.[280] This echoes J. H. Burton's criticism that he 'had not sufficient command of grammar to have put his thoughts into the clear emphatic shape in which they are preserved, if he had ever formed them in his mind'.[281] This is hard to accept. We have the considerable evidence of a hundred letters to disprove it. And surely declaring war on the might of William of Orange almost single-handedly was a bold and purely *speculative* move? When we examine the wit, humour, ambiguity and often sarcasm of his letters to Mentieth, Cluny, Lord Murray, Strathnaver and others, we must conclude that he had a highly-organised and witty mind. These surviving letters, perhaps only a tiny fraction which he wrote, reveal a man as comfortable with a pen as with a cutlass, and never dimwitted or less than precise in his thinking. These generalised attacks smack of the pettiness of Sir Walter Scott's widely-quoted remark – based on the evidence of only one letter – that Claverhouse spelt like a chambermaid. In the seventeenth century there was no orthography; all, whether Kings or chambermaids, spelt as they liked.

History is largely a matter of reputations, a few artefacts and splendid monuments. The legend of Graham of Claverhouse is memorialised by three marvellous buildings: Mains Castle, now a licensed private restaurant; Dudhope Castle, whose cannons lunge over the parapets at the modern city, provides a home for the Dundee Business School of Abertay University and Dundee College; Claypotts Castle, in the care of Historic Scotland, one of the best buildings of its type, is only open to the public by arrangement.

'Bonnie Dundee' is the most important historical figure associated with the city of Dundee, and it would be appropriate if the remaining artefacts, including the Jacobite mourning ring containing a lock of his hair, sundry weapons and armour and his original letters could be collected and presented to

Dundee Museums and Art Galleries for the establishment of a '17th-Century' or 'Bonnie Dundee' room or section. A new plaque at Old Blair Churchyard is also overdue. The plaque above the vault in the ruined chapel is historically inaccurate (his age given as forty-six instead of forty); and perhaps the rather inconspicuous cairn in the field above Urrard House at Killiecrankie which serves also as a modern memorial for quite a separate purpose could be rebuilt by permission of the owners, to commemorate exclusively this highly significant battle. On the credit side the Visitor Centre in the Pass of Killiecrankie, open from April to October and run by the National Trust for Scotland, is one of the most popular sites in Scotland, attracting thousands of tourists from all over the world, who come to view the spectacular beauty and wildlife of the area – and to learn a little of that ancient battle and the man known as 'Bonnie Dundee'.

References and Sources

Chapter One: Young Grahame

1. Suggested by Preface p. XCI in 'Memorialls; or, The Memorable Things That Fell Out Within This Island From 1638 to 1684' by Rev. Robert Law, edited by C. K. Sharpe, Constable, Edinburgh, 1818.

2. The Warrant of June 1642 is contained in 'The Privy Seal of Scotland' 2nd Series, Vol. 7, p. 262. His attendance at the General Assembly is contained in 'Records of the Commission of the General Assemblies of the Church of Scotland' 1650–2, edited by Revs. Mitchell and Christie (1909), SHS 58, p. 265.

3. The Papers of Sir John James Grahame of Fintry KCMG, HMC 55, pp. 209–210.

4. Acta Rectorum of St Andrews University, p. 471.

5. 'A Short Account of Scotland', by Rev. Thomas Morer (1702), p. 95.

6. 'Memoirs of Great Britain and Ireland', by Dalrymple of Cranstoun, London, 1790, Vol. 2, p. 73.

7. Roll of Eminent Burgesses of Dundee, edited by A. H. Millar, 1887, p. 166.

8. Register of the Privy Council of Scotland, 3rd Series, Vol 2, p. 598.

9. This poem appears in 'Fugitive Scottish Poetry; principally of the 17th Century', edited by David Laing, 1825.

10. 'The Grameid' – Latin epic poem by James Phillip of Amerlieclose near Arbroath; written in the Horatian epic style in 1691, translated and edited by Alex Murdoch, 1888. SHS Vol. 3, pp. 201–2.

11. 'Life of Mackay', by Mackay of Rockfield, Bannatyne Club 53, 1836, p. 7,

12, 'The Scots Brigade In Holland', SHS Vol. 1, Division 4, p. 582. The final line of the 1st Volume.

13. 'Memoirs of Sir Ewan Cameron of Lochiel', by his grandson, Drummond of Balhaldie, Bannatyne Club 1737, p. 275.

14. 'History of England', by Lord T. B. Macaulay, Everyman's Library, Dent, Vol. 3, p. 269; also 'House and Clans of Mackay', by Robert Mackay, p. 388; 'Scots Brigade in Holland', Vol. 1, pp. 470–1.

15. 'Privy Council Acta' (MS Register House), 3rd Series, Vol. 5, p. 370.

Chapter Two: The Good Policeman

16. State Papers of Charles 11, Vol. 397; 'An Account Of The Present Posture Of Affairs In The Shyres Of Ayre And Renfrew', Nov. 5, 1677.

17. 'John Grahame of Claverhouse', by Professor Charles Terry, London, 1905, pp. 36–7

18. This and subsequent letters to Linlithgow were printed in 'Letters of John Graham of Claverhouse', edited by Andrew Murray Scott, SHS 5th Series, Vol. 3, miscellany XI, pp. 142–156.

19. 'Six Saints of the Covenant' by Patrick Walker, Hodder & Stoughton, 1901, Vol. 2, p. 64.

20. 'Letters', pp. 146–7, 150, 157–68, 171, 176–7.

21. 'Privy Council Acta', 3rd Series, Vol. 6, p. 291.

22. 'History Of His Own Time', by Gilbert Burnet, Oxford, 1833, Vol. 2, p. 818. Also in 'Memorialls', by Rev. Robert Law, pp. 148–9.

23. 'Memorials And Letters Of Dundee', by Mark Napier, Edinburgh, 1862, Vol. 2, p. 185.

24. 'Memoirs Of Captain John Creighton, from his own materials, drawn up and digested by Dr J. S. Swift DS PD, first printed 1731. From 'Swift's Works', edited by John Hawkesworth, Vol. 13, pp. 179–80,

25. 'Concise History of Scotland', by Fitzroy MacLean, London, 1970, p. 137.

26. 'History of the Suffering of the Church of Scotland' by Rev. Robert Wodrow, 1721, edited by Rev. Robert Burns, Glasgow, 1838, Vol. 3, p. 69. Creighton's Memoirs pp. 179–80.

27. The song 'Drumclog' appears in 'Minstrelsy of the Scottish Border', edited by Sir Walter Scott, Vol. 3, no. 188.

28. 'Memoir Of The Lord Viscount Dundee, The Highland Clans and the Massacre of Glencoe with An Account of Dundee's Officers after they went to France, by an officer of the army', London, 1711. This fascinating document, only twenty-six pages in total length, is perhaps written anonymously because of the warmth of its pro-Jacobite sentiment. 'What is written of Scotland', it declares, 'is so much stained and tainted with an AntiMonarchical and National Pencil, that it is not to be credited . . . neither can there be any history wrote of Scotland for forty years past, but what must be obliged to me . . . and what these ignorant Party Scribblers write of King James' and King William's lives are so false and biased, that they lead men into gross mistakes and errors . . .' These comments appear in the Preface. Reference to the movements of Government forces appears on pp. 6–7.

29. Song 'Bothwell Bridge' in 'Minstrelsy of the Scottish Border', Vol. 3, no. 209.

30. 'History of Scotland', by Andrew Lang, Edinburgh, 1904, Vol. 3, p. 354.

31. Ibid., p. 360. Also Law's 'Memorials', pp. 186 93, 202.

32. 'The Rise And Influence Of Rationalism In Europe', by Lecky, London, Vol. 3, p. 41.

33. 'James II' by Peter Earle, London, 1972, p. 68.

34. Extracts from The Records of the Royal Burgh of Stirling, AD 1667–1752, p. 33.

35. From Tyler's poem of The Tempest 1681, 'Memorials Dundee–Napier', Vol. 1, p. 319. Also quoted in Terry, p. 99.

36. 'Sir George MacKenzie, King's Advocate – His life and Times', by Andrew Lang, London, 1909, p. 283.

37. The Lauderdale Papers, Vol. 3, p. 160.

38. 'Letters' pp. 168–232.

39. 'Sir George MacKenzie – Life and Times', Lang, p. 283.

40. Reg. Privy Council 3rd Series, Vol. 6, p. 148.

41. 'Memoirs of Sir James Dalrymple, 1st Viscount of Stair', by Aeneas J. Mackay, Edinburgh, 1873.

42, 'Law's Memorials', p. 258.

43. 'Memoirs of Dalrymple', p. 179.

44. 'History of His Own Time', Burnet, Vol. 2, p. 325.

45. 'Letters to the Earl of Aberdeen' 1681–4, Spalding Club, 1851, no. 22, p. 88.

46. 'Historical Notices', by Sir John Lauder of Fountainhall, Bannatyne Club, 1848, Vol. 2, p. 389.

47. Privy Council Acta 3rd Series, Vol. 8, p. 158.

48. Ibid., vol. 7, pp. 633–4.

49. 'Charters Of Dundee', edited by A. H. Millar, 1880, pp. 103–5.

50. Ibid., pp. 109–10.

51. 'Glamis Book Of Record', by Patrick, 1st Earl of Strathmore, HMC 9 (1890), p. 168.

52. Reg. Privy Council, Vol. 9, p. 165.

53. 'Letters' p. 225–7.

54. Reg. Privy Council, Vol. 9, pp. 355–74; see also Vol. 10, pp. 557–91.

55. Ibid., Vol. 9, p. 123.

56. 'Law's Memorials'.

57. 'History Vindicated in the Case of the Wigtown Martyrs', by Rev. A. Stewart, 2nd Edition, Edinburgh, 1869. This sets out to attack Napier's dismissal of the incident, and attempts to reinstate Wodrow's evidence. Stewart backs his case with (a) Tradition (b) Early pamphlets (c) Earlier histories; as with (b) largely written by Whig clergymen – and minutes of the Church Courts (the same) (d) the 'evidence' of gravestones. He does not attempt to prove that Claverhouse was involved in the incident – thus effectively proving that he was not.

58. 'Buccleuch MSS' HMC Report, p. 192, p. 47, pp. 60–105.

59. Privy Council Acta, Vol. 7, p. 279.

Chapter Three: The Revolution

60. 'Scottish Worthies', by Rev. B. Craven, Edinburgh, 1894, P.

61. Pepys Diaries, Vol. 8, p. 8.

62. 'James 11 – A Study In Kingship', by John Millar, London, 1978, p. 12.

63. These letters from 'Hamilton MSS' HMC 21, 11th Report, Appendix Part 6 (1881), p. 175.

64. 'Glencoe and the End of The Highland War', Paul Hopkins, John Donald, 1986, pp. 102–107.

65. 'Fountainhall's Notices', Vol. 1, p. 709.

66. Ibid., Vol. 2, p. 858.

67. Report on the MS of the Duke of Buccleuch and Queensberry, HMC 11, The Drumlanrig MS, Vol. 2, p. 97.

68. 'Fountainhall's Notices', Vol. 2, p. 407.

69. 'Hist. of Suffering Church Scotland' by Wodrow, Vol. 4, pp. 420–42 3.

70. 'Letters', Appendix, p. 263–4, see also 'My Ladie Dundee' by Katherine Parker, 1926, App. 5.

71. The King's letter appointing Claverhouse Provost of Dundee can be read in Burgess Roll, Dundee, p. 166.

72. 'Memoirs Touching The Revolution In Scotland', by Colin, Earl of Balcarres, Bannatyne Club, 1841, p. 4. These Memoirs were written at some considerable distance from events, perhaps 20 years later, and some detail is lost. A fine sense of indignation at the needless loss of Claverhouse and the betrayal by Melfort – remains. The volume is dedicated, and addressed, to the exiled King.

73. 'Fountainhall's Notices', Vol. 2, p. 860.

74. Reg. Privy Council Vol. 13, App. 15, XXIII.

75. 'Memoirs of Thomas Bruce, Earl of Ailesbury', edited by W. E. Buckley, Roxburghe Club, 1890, Vol. 1, pp. 220–1.

76. This letter occurs in Vol. 13, p. 295 of Reg. Privy Council.

77. 'Glencoe and Highland War', Hopkins, p. 123.

78. Balcarres Memoirs, p. 11.

79. Papers Queensberry & Buccleuch, HMC 15th Report, App. Part VIII. Note to Blathwayt in 'Letters' p. 233.

80. Charter of Viscount Dundee in the Warrant Book XIII, Scotland

81. Letter from the 'Chronicles of the Families of Atholl & Tullibardine Collected and Arranged by John, 7th Duke', Edinburgh, 1896, p. 271.

82. Balcarres' Memoirs, p. 17. Lord President, Sir George Lock-hart, in Catalogue of Hamilton MSS, HMC 55, 1897, p. 76. 'Lives of the MacKenzies', from William Fraser's Cromartie Book.

84. Creighton's 'Memoirs', pp. 219–20.

85. Reg. Privy Council Vol. 13, Introduction, p. XII.

86. Balcarres' 'Memoirs', p. 20.

87. MSS of Sir Hugh Le Fleming Esq. of Rydal Hall, HMC 12th Report, item 3382.

88. Ibid., item 3400.

89. Balcarres' 'Memoirs', biographical note, p. XVII.

90. 'Cartes Memorandum Book', reprinted in 'MacPherson's Original Papers, Containing the secret history of Great Britain from the Restoration to the accession of the house of Hanover', London, 1775.

91. 'Hist. Own Time', Burnet, p. 537.

Chapter Four; Shades of Montrose

92. 'Letters, p. 216–20.

93. Balcarres' 'Memoirs', p. 23.

94. Ibid., p. 25.

95. This, and subsequent extracts, are from 'Account on the Proceedings', a contemporary document, though somewhat inaccurate. See also Balcarres' 'Memoirs', pp. 25–6.

96, 'Characters of the Nobility of Scotland' by John Mackay, from 'Memoirs of the Secret Services of John Mackay Esq.', c. 1694, p. 120.

97. Balcarres' 'Memoirs', p. 26.

98. Ibid., p. 25.

99. 'The House of the Gordons' by J. M. Bulloch, New Spalding Club, 1903, Vol. 2, p. 593. See also 'Grahame of Claverhouse', by Michael Barrington, 1911, London, p.221.

100. Reg. Privy Council Vol. 13, p. 254.

101. Tyrconnel's letter is partially reprinted in Buccleuch MSS, HMC 45, Vol. 2, Part I (1674–1696), pp. 36–7.

102. Acta Parliamentorum (Acts of the Scottish Parliaments), AD 1689, William and Mary, p. 9.

103. Ibid.
104. Balcarres' 'Memoirs', p. 27.
105. 'The Melvilles And The Leslies', by William Fraser, Vol. 3, p. 235.
106. Acts Scot. Parl., p. 10.
107. Ailesbury's 'Memoirs', Vol. 1, p. 250.
108. Balcarres' 'Memoirs', p. 28.
109. Ibid., pp. 28–9.
110. Ibid., p. 29.
112. See margin notes on the Duke of Gordon's copy of Balcarres' Memoirs. In the same handwriting, necessarily 20 years after the incidents described, there is a denial that Gordon was already surrendering the Castle in February. The Duke's emendations blame Balcarres among others for the poor provisioning of the Castle.
113. Memoirs Great Britain and Ireland, Dalrymple, Vol. 1, Part 1, p, 287: 'I wheresoever the spirit of Montrose shall direct me'. This was presumably adapted by Sir Walter Scott in the song 'Bonnie Dundee'.
113. The song first appeared in 'Minstrelsy of the Scottish Border', Edinburgh, 1803.
114. Balcarres' 'Memoirs', p. 30.
115. 'Sir George Mackenzie – Life and Times', Andrew Lang, p. 301.
116. Reg. Privy Council, Vol. 13, Introduction p. LVI.
117. 'Letters', pp. 234–5.

Chapter Five: Rebellion

118. 'Life of Mackay', pp. 16–7.
119. 'Memoirs of the War Carried on in Scotland and Ireland, 1689–91', by Major-General Hugh Mackay, edited for the Bannatyne Club (45) by J. M. Hog and others (1833), p. 8.
120. 'Leven and Melville Papers', edited by H. L. Melville, Edinburgh, 1843.
121. 'Hist. Own Time', Burnet, Vol. 4, p. 47.
122. Leven and Melville Papers, pp. 3, 4, 6–7; letters 3, 4 & 7.

123. The letters to Dundee and Balcarres were printed in Buccleuch MSS, HMC 44, Vol. 1, Part 1, p. 38.

124. 'Chron. Fam. Atholl & Tullibardine', pp. 289–90.

125, Leven and Melville Papers Vol. 2, Part 1, p. 40.

126. Ibid., p. 42.

127. Buccleuch MSS, HMC 55, Vol. 2, Part 1, p. 46.

128. Ibid., p. 47.

129. Letter reproduced from 'The House of Forbes', Third Spalding Club, 193 7, no. 7, p. 213.

130. Mackay's 'Memoirs', p. 42.

131. 'Letters' p. 236.

132. Creighton's 'Memoirs', pp. 228–9.

133. Mackay's 'Memoirs', p. 12.

134. 'Grameid', p. 56.

135. 'Grahame of Claverhouse', Barrington, p. 252.

136. All the quotes in this paragraph are from Lochiel's 'Memoirs', p. 243.

137. Mackay's 'Memoirs', p. 15.

138. This booklet is included in Mackay's Memoirs, p. XVII.

139. 'Gleanings From The Charter Chest At Cluny Castle', edited by Provost MacPherson for the Gaelic Society of Inverness in 1889, p. 25.

140. The letter, reprinted in A. & H. Tayler's biography, 'John Grahame of Claverhouse' (1939), p. 244, was first printed in William Fraser's 'Cromartie Book'.

141. Mackay's 'Memoirs', p. 19.

142. Dundee Burgess Roll, p. 168. It is possible that the Roll is in error due to a transposition of the month – May for April – for by a strange coincidence Dundee had been present at a baptism in Mains Parish Church on 9th April – that of his own son. Another possibility is offered by the discrepancy between 'Old Style' and 'New Style' of dating – some ten days – which may have allowed Dundee to attend a baptism later in May during his visit to the town after the raid on Perth.

143. Creighton's 'Memoirs', p. 230.

144. MS of Duke of Roxburghe, Earl of Strathmore, Countess Dowager of Seafield, HMC 14, App. p. 17.

145. Grameid, p. 59. Evidence of Lieutenant James Colt at Forfeiture Proceedings; Proceedings of Parliament, July 14 AD 1690, Appendix, p. 54.

147. 'Short Account of Scot.', Morer, p. 99.

148. Evidence of Colt, Forfeiture Proceedings, see 146.

149. 'Chron, Fam. Atholl & Tullibardine', p. 277.

150. 'Grameid', p. 62 note.

151. All these quotes, Ibid., p. 64.

152. 'Memoir of Dundee', 1711, p. 18,

153. 'Grameid', p. 78.

154. Ibid., p. 111.

155. Lieutenant John Hay's Evidence at the Forfeiture Proceedings, recorded in Proceedings of Parl., July 14 AD 1690, App. pp. 59–60.

156. Lochiel's 'Memoirs', p. 321.

157. Ibid., p. 277.

158. Ibid., pp. 171–2.

159. Account of the Proceedings (June 1st to 4th), Number 26.

Chapter Six: Dark John of the Battles

160. 'Gleanings', pp. 29–30.

161. Leven and Melville Papers, pp. 23–4. There are some doubts about the authorship of this letter.

162. HMC 11th Report, Part VII (1888), no. 3510A, May 18th.

163. Leven and Melville, pp. 21–2.

164. The Atholl MSS, HMC 26, 12th Report, Part VIII, p. 162.

165. Leven and Melville, pp. 27–8.

166, MSS of the Duke of Hamilton. HMC 2 1, 11th Report, p. 11.

167. Leven and Melville, pp. 69–70.

168. Account of Proceedings (June 8th–11th), number 28.

169. Lochiel's 'Memoirs', p. 241.

170. Ibid., p. 242.

171. Mackay's 'Memoirs', p. 33.

172. 'Grameid', p. 186.

173. Mackay's 'Memoirs', p. 34.

174. Hay's Report contained in MacPherson's Original Papers, Vol. 1, p. 356.

175. 'Memoirs of Great Britain and Ireland', Dalrymple, Vol. 2, p. 74.

176. Mackay's 'Memoirs', p. 38.

177. Account of Proceedings, British Museum press mark 600 m.4(8).

178. Mackay's 'Memoirs', p. 240.

179. Journal of Major-General Mackay's March Against The Viscount Of Dundee – A letter from A Gentleman In The Major-General's Army To A Friend, dated Alford 9th June, 1689 – in 'Account of the Proceedings'.

180. Lochiel's 'Memoirs', pp. 244–5.

181. These extracts are from the Appendix, p. 230 in Mackay's 'Memoirs'.

182. MSS of Duke of Hamilton, HMC 2 1, 11th Report, the Appendix, part VI, p. 187, letter no. 201.

183. Mackay's 'Memoirs', p. 226; also Leven and Melville Papers, p. 51.

184. Leven & Melville, p. 57,

185. Mackay's 'Memoirs', pp. 226–7.

186. Leven & Melville, pp. 63–4.

187. James MacPherson's Original Papers, Vol. 1; Affairs of Scotland, p. 358; Hay's Report.

188. These extracts are taken from HMC 11th Report Appendix Part VII (1888), items 3529, 3535.

189. Leven & Melville, pp. 40–41.

190. Mackay's 'Memoirs', pp. 235–41

191. Leven & Melville, p. 54.

192. Chron. Fam, Atholl & Tullibardine, pp. 282–3.

193. Leven & Melville, pp. 92–3.

194. This incident is related fully in 'Memoirs of Lochiel', pp. 253–4.

195. MacPherson's Original Papers, Vol. I; Affairs of Scotland, p. 358.

196. 'Letters' p. 238–9.

197. Mackay's 'Memoirs', p. 237.

198. This report occurs in 'Affairs In Scotland' in Mackay's 'Memoirs', p. 235, no. 11.

199. This letter appears in 'Life of General Mackay', by Mackay of Rockfield, Appendix to pp. 157–8.

200. 'Letters' p. 240–6, 247–8.

201. 'Hist. Own Time', Burnet, p. 50; see also 'Claverhouse', by Gordon Daviot (1937), p. 310.

202. Balcarres' 'Memoirs', p. 37.

Chapter Seven: Final Manoeuvres

203. All the letters of Viscount Dundee used in this chapter are taken from 'Letters', pp. 246–262.

204. 'The Siege of Derry', by Patrick MacRory, London, 1981. The lyrics used are from 'Derry's Walls' folksong, included in the above book, p. 221.

205. 'Hist. Own Time', Burnet, p. 50,

206. Balcarres' 'Memoirs', p. 47.

207. Leven & Melville, pp. 134–5.

208. Ibid., pp. 135–6.

209. Ibid., pp. 138–9.

210. Ibid., pp. 143–4.

211. Ibid., pp. 139–40.

212. Ibid., pp. 171–2.

213. Ibid., pp. 164–5.

214. The proclamation offering £18,000 Scots appears in 'Memorials of Dundee', by Mark Napier, Vol. 3, Appendix, pp. 702–3; whereas Dalrymple's higher sum is contained in his letter, published in Leven & Melville Papers, p. 193.

215. Leven & Melville, pp. 167–169, postscript.

216. Ibid., p216, p. 170.

217. HMC 21, 11th Report, Appendix Part VI, p. 182, item 173.

218. Leven & Melville, pp. 159–61.

219. As n.218, p. 202.

220. The letter written to Dundee by Lord Strathnaver was found among 'The Nairne Papers' in the Bodleian Library, and first printed by James MacPherson in his 'Original Papers'. It is reproduced in Napier's biography, Vol. 3, p. 607.

221. 'Letters' pp. 250–2, 256, 260–1, 262.

222. 'Memoirs of Lochiel', by Balhaldie, p. 257.

223. 'Life of James 11', Peter Earle, London, 1972, p. 115.

224. Ibid.

225. Gleanings, p. 31.

226. Leven & Melville, p. 174.

227. Ballechin's letters to Lord John Murray are contained in Chron. Fam. Atholl & Tullibardine, pp. 286–7, 293–4

228. Mackay's 'Memoirs', p. 47.

229. 'Letters' p. 253–6.

230. Ibid., p. 256.

231. Ibid., p. 259–60.

232. Chron. Fam. Atholl & Tullibardine, pp. 289–290.

233. Mackay's 'Memoirs', p. 248.

234. Ibid., p. 48; letter from Stirling on 24th – 'I am this far towards the Highlands.'

235. 'Letters' p. 261.

236. Ibid., p. 261–2.

237. Balcarres' 'Memoirs', p. 44.

238. 'Claverhouse', by Terry, p. 331.

239. Leven & Melville, pp. 223–225.

240. Chron. Fam. Atholl & Tullibardine, pp. 295–6.

241. Ibid., p. 296.

242. 'Letters' p. 262.

243. 'The New Statistical Account of Scotland', 1845, Vol. 10, 'Perth', p. 569.

244. A Short Relation (Mackay's Memoirs), App. 263; also Chron. Fam. Atholl & Tullibardine, p. 299.

255. The only reference to this letter appears in Captain Creighton's 'Memoirs', p. 233. Professor Terry and Mark Napier

both deny the validity of this evidence but Gordon Daviot and Alison Southern believe the letter is characteristic of Dundee. My own view is that it is only as reliable as the rest of Creighton's 'Memoirs', which were based very loosely on facts. Creighton was hardly in a position to be aware of correspondence between Dundee and Hamilton, although he most assuredly did gain his freedom in due course, and possibly invented this letter to boost his own importance. His account has the Duke of Hamilton declare: 'I fear we dare not touch an hair of Creighton's, for ye all know Dundee too well to doubt whether he will be punctual to his word . . . let the fellow live a while longer.' (p. 234)

Chapter Eight: 'If any of us shall fall . . .'

246. 'A Short Relation' (Mackay's 'Memoirs'), App., pp. 263–4.

247. This, and subsequent, quoted from Lochiel's Memoirs, p. 259.

248. All the comments, despite being in third person, are by Mackay from 'Memoirs', pp. 49–55.

249. Short Relation (Mackay's 'Memoirs'), p. 262, no. 29.

250. Ibid.

251. 'Letters' Appendix, p. 264, also see Lochiel's Memoirs, p. 268: 'waveing his hatt over his head' implies, I think, that it would not have been a steel cap or morion – which would have been difficult to remove with one hand.

252. Ibid., p. 266.

253. 'The Expert Swordsman's Companion', by Donald McBane (1728).

254. 'Memorials of Dundee', Napier, Vol. 3, p. 328. See also Lochiel's Memoirs, p. 272, which corroborates that Leven fled 'though not attacked'.

255. Mackay's 'Memoirs', App., p. 255.

256. Lochiel's 'Memoirs', p. 268.

257. Mackay's 'Memoirs', App., p. 265.

258. Ibid., p. 59.

259. Lochiel's 'Memoirs', p. 268

260. Ibid., pp. 270–1.

261. From the letter by Stenton of Stenton reproduced in MSS of Duke of Atholl (HMC 12), App., Part VII, and also in Chron. Fam. Atholl & Tullibardine, p. 304.

262. 'Letters' Appendix, p264–5. The copy of the letter was discovered among the Nairn Papers in the Bodleian Library by MacPherson, and had Dundee's speech to the troops on the back. It was reproduced by Napier (Vol 3, pp. 652–3) and is generally acknowledged to be a contemporary document, although whether or not it is genuine must be the subject of considerable doubt.

263. 'Hist. Eng.', Macaulay, Vol. 3, pp, 362–3.

264. 'Claverhouse', by Terry, App. 11, p. 126.

265. Forfeiture Proceedings; Proceedings of Parl., July 14 AD 1690, App., p. 58.

266. 'Scottish Historical Review' Vol. III No. 9, October 1905, article: 'Killiecrankie described by an eye-witness'.

266. 'God's Judgement on Persecutors', by Rev. John Howie, p. XXXIX. This is the Appendix to 'The Judgement And Justice Of God Exemplified' in 'Scots Worthies', 3rd Edition, Glasgow, 1797.

268. Balcarres' 'Memoirs', pp. 47–8.

269. Lochiel's 'Memoirs', pp. 210–71.

270. HMC 56 Stuart Papers Vol. 1, p. 74.

271. The letter is reproduced in Proceedings of Parl., Vol. 9, July 14th AD 1690, App., p. 60.

272. 'Letters', Appendix, p. 265.

273. 'Grahame of Claverhouse', Barrington, p. 406 (App. 7).

274. Creighton's 'Memoirs', pp. 154–155. The following conversation is ascribed in the Printer's Preface to Dean Swift and the Captain:

Swift: 'Sir, I have heard much of your adventures, that they are fresh in your memory; that you can tell them with great humour, and that you have taken memorandums of them in writing'. Creighton: 'I have, Sir, but no-one can understand them but myself. Swift: 'Sir, get your manuscripts, read them to me, and tell me none but genuine stories . Hawkesworth edition of 'Works', Vol. 13, pp. 154–155. It is open to suggestion how far the memoirs were altered in the process of transcription between the two men, and how much influence the political sensibilities of the Dean bore upon the final result of this unusual collaboration.

Epilogue: The Legend

275. 'James II's Memoirs', edited Clark Vol. 2, pp. 352–3.

276. Acts Parl. Scot. Vol. 9, App., p. 62.

277. 'The Covenanters', by James K. Hewison, Vol. 2, p. 297.

278. 'Hist. Eng.', Macaulay Vol. 1, p. 442.

279. 'The Jacobite Risings In Britain', by Bruce Lenman, London, 1980, p. 24.

280. Ibid., p. 41.

281. 'History of Scotland', by John Hill Burton, 1853, Vol. 1, p. 98; as criticised on p. 23 of 'Memorials of Dundee', Napier.

Further Reading

Biographical

Most of the previous biographies are available in reference libraries and university collections and it is generally worth the effort to seek them out. In order of publication these are: *Memoir of Lord Viscount Dundee* by 'an officer of the army' (1711) – only twenty-six pages in length and also containing an account of the Massacre of Glencoe. Another interesting source is *Memoirs of Captain John Creichton . . .* edited by Dean Swift (1731) and contained in Swift's Works (Hawkesworth edition, Vol. 13, pp. 154–246). Much of this concerns the actions of Claverhouse, since Creichton claimed to have served with him since Drumclog, but, as already mentioned, it is of dubious historical accuracy. The first full-length biography was *Memorials and Letters of Dundee* by Mark Napier (Edinburgh & London, 1862) in three volumes. This contains a wealth of detail but is devoted mainly to scoring points against other historians, typically Macaulay, and against Scott, whom he accused of 'creating a plum pudding of virtue and vice and call[ing] it the character of Graham of Claverhouse'. The three volumes are rather haphazard and the index leaves a lot to be desired. *Claverhouse* by Mowbray Morris (London, 1887) is a brief sketch which gives the birthdate of 1643. *Clavers – The Despot's Champion* by Alison Southern (London & New York, 1889) is an attempt to rearrange Napier's material and is even more slavish in its admiration of its hero. *Viscount Dundee* by Louis Barbe (Edinburgh, 1903) is a brief summary. *John Grahame of Claverhouse* by Professor Charles Terry (London, 1905), with its excellent account of the battle in its 'correct' location, became the substantive biography, effectively disproving many of the previously established 'facts'. Much of the book is devoted to refuting Napier's conclusions and, in consequence, some of the best material is in footnotes. *Grahame of Claverhouse* by Michael Barrington (London, 1911) is an excellent and readable biography but was unfortunately published only in a limited deluxe edition. *Claverhouse* by Gordon Daviot (London, 1937) is, in my opinion, rather poor and introduces no new ideas, its authoress being generally better known as fiction writer Josephine Tey. Far better is *John Graham of Claverhouse* by A. & H. Tayler (London, 1939). This is an excellent and thoughtful volume, except for the gross inflation of his military reputation 'second only [to Montrose] – if indeed he was second'. In 1989, the tercentenary year of Killiecrankie, the first edition of this biography, *Bonnie Dundee,* appeared, followed by another, *For King and Conscience* by Magnus Linklater & Christian Hesketh.

Until 1990, the only volume of letters was *Letters of Viscount of Dundee* by George Smythe of Methven (Bannatyne Club, 1826), which contained twenty letters. The present author collated *Letters of John Graham of Claverhouse* for the Scottish History Society in 1990. The letters, included in a miscellany volume, number 100 and have proved immensely valuable in the revising and updating of this edition of *Bonnie Dundee*. To date, no other biographer has had such a unique advantage although undoubtedly more original letters may yet be found.

Many studies of Jacobitism include references to Claverhouse. These include: *The Jacobites* by Frank McLynn (London, 1985, pp. 5–13); *The Jacobite Risings In Britain, 1689–1746* by Bruce Lenman (London, 1980, pp. 11–50); and *The Jacobite Cause*, also by Lenman (Richard Drew in association with National Trust for Scotland, Glasgow, 1986). *The Scottish Covenanters* by Ian B. Cowan (London, 1976) has several references to Claverhouse. A useful long-term analysis is provided in Paul Hopkins' *Glencoe and the End of the Highland War* (John Donald, 1986), which contains much valuable detail on the political machinations of the late seventeenth century.

Fictionalised Accounts

Claverhouse has been used as a character in numerous novels and treated in various ways. Sir Walter Scott, whose Hanoverian head was often ruled by his Jacobite heart, felt Claverhouse had been greatly wronged, and he coined the epithet 'Bonnie Dundee', adapting the words of an older song about the town. He presented him as a hero in *Old Mortality*, first published in 1816. The most recent Penguin edition (1984) contains an informative introduction by Angus Calder. But Claverhouse also appears, as a murdered ghoul, in 'Wandering Willie's Tale' in *Redgauntlet*, one hand clasped over the awful wound made by a silver bullet. This silver bullet theme recurs in *Guy Mannering* when Bertram Dono-hoe, Laird of Ellengowan, joins Dundee at Killiecrankie and is killed by a silver button. Scott was ambivalent about Claverhouse, but when James Hogg produced his novel *The Brownie of Bodsbeck* in 1818 as a direct reply to the romantic figure Scott had created, Scott denounced it as 'a false and unfair picture of the times and the existing characters altogether. An exaggerated and unfair picture!' Hogg's Claverhouse is a devilish monster, an inhuman brute. A reprint of the novel appeared in 1976 (Scottish Academic Press, Edinburgh & London). Another Scottish novel, John Galt's *Ringan Gilhaize*, (1823), was a 'retaliation' against Scott's view of events and was it's author's favourite novel. Ringan engages in hand-to-hand combat with Claverhouse at Drum-clog but the duel is inconclusive and Claverhouse flees, crying 'Blood for Blood!' The Scottish Academic Press also re-issued this book, in 1984. Ian Maclaren, the great populariser of the kailyard school, produced a novel, *Graham of Claverhouse* in 1908 – which was swiftly reprinted – in which Dundee is shot by pistol from within his own ranks. *My Ladie Dundee* by Katherine Parker (London, 1926) is a vivid and readable, fictionalised documentary of Claverhouse's domestic life. *Phoenix And Laurel* by Jane Lane (London, 1954, re-issued in 1974) and her *A Crown For A Lie* (London, 1962) are highly readable. The first features Claverhouse as hero, the second is set in England during the Revolution of 1688.

For children up to their mid-teens, *Bonnie Dundee* by Rosemary Sutcliff (London, 1983) is an exciting and educational read and has remained in print since its first publication.

The potency of the life and career of the man and the enduring myth; the ambivalence of the evidence pursued by admirers and detractors occasionally with vehemence – suggest that there will be more books of all kinds on 'Bonnie Dundee' in the future.

Index

Index

Index